SURVIVING
YEAR ZERO

SOVANNORA IENG
WITH GREG HILL

SURVIVING YEAR ZERO

MY FOUR YEARS UNDER
THE KHMER ROUGE

The Five Mile Press

The Five Mile Press Pty Ltd
1 Centre Road, Scoresby
Victoria 3179 Australia
www.fivemile.com.au

Part of the Bonnier Publishing Group
www.bonnierpublishing.com

First published 2014

Printed in Australia at Griffin Press.
Only wood grown from sustainable regrowth forests is used in
the manufacture of paper found in this book.

Edited by Jenny Lee
Page design and typesetting by Shaun Jury
Cover design by Luke Causby, Blue Cork
Front cover image by Chhoy Pisei © Getty Images
Internal illustrations by Chhun Chandy

National Library of Australia Cataloguing-in-Publication entry
    Ieng, Sovannora, author.
    Surviving year zero / Sovannora Ieng and Greg Hill.
    ISBN: 9781760063641 (paperback)
    Subjects: Genocide survivors–Cambodia–Biography.
    Genocide–Cambodia–History–20th century.
    Cambodia–History–1975–1979.
    Other Authors/Contributors:
    Hill, Greg, author.
    959.6042092

*For all those who were a part of my life during
Year Zero, but especially my beloved mother, my
constant source of inspiration, Mrs Iv Kim Huorng.
Also for my stepmother and step-grandmother,
and for Tevy, who kept my hopes alive*

I wonder where you are now. I hope it is a good place.

Contents

Co-author's Introduction

I LAY AWAKE in bed last night, imagining. Ten years have passed since Sovannora first shared his story with me, yet its impact is still strong, threatening to devour my emotions and my spirit, as I wonder yet again how any of it could ever have happened.

Sovannora was nearly fourteen when the events described in this book began. My son Christopher is now fifteen and I wonder – what if it was him? What if Christopher saw those things happen and endured the same experiences? I had read Sovannora's story dispassionately – it is a wonderful story of survival and triumph in the face of adversity, but it took place in another country and involved other people.

But what if it was about my son?

Sovannora's book is about one person, yet it is the story of millions of people. It is a tale of the genocide that decimated Cambodia in the 1970s, and it is the story of all who have suffered in the face of intolerance, violence and brutality. It is everyone's story, but it is not mine. While many will read Sovannora's story and remember their own suffering and the violence that took the lives of their families, I can think only of my son.

My son Christopher is thoughtful and has a good heart, and I love him immensely. So it is with great emotion that I imagine him being forced to witness murder, experiencing forced relocation, torture and starvation. I see him now, imprisoned, sleeping on a hard, bug-infested floor and longing for his one meal of rice a day. I see him wondering, steeling himself as others around him are executed or tortured, or slowly starve to death. I imagine him watching another boy placed into a cage so small that he fits only because his arms and legs have been broken. Then I wonder, what if that boy in the cage *were* him and those were *his* last hours, crying and sobbing while others watched helplessly as his life-force slowly diminished and the Khmer Rouge looked on.

I feel my heart is being torn apart as I think of how Christopher would feel. The suffering, the desperation – I don't think my son could survive, even if he remained alive. Then I think of my friend – how did Sovannora survive? His experience of genocide lasted not days or even months, but four years. Even his final escape was across a minefield, where others were being blown up in front of his eyes in their mad race for freedom.

Sovannora is alive now. He went through these events and worse. I have no idea how he kept his sanity and remained a decent, caring person. But he is only one of millions who survived these atrocities with scars I cannot fathom.

As the true events told in Sovannora's story touched me again last night, they have touched the world ever since they took place. The pain does not go away. It stays with the victims and their country forever.

Yet Sovannora prevailed. His is a story of survival in an environment where survival was impossible. It is a powerful story that must be told so that we can learn from the terrible things that we, as humans, have too often done, and still do, to each other.

Sovannora's is a small but urgent voice that says: 'Stop!' We cannot go on killing and torturing, abusing and maiming. We cannot go on allowing these things to happen on any part of this planet.

Greg Hill

Introduction

I AM SOVANNORA, a refugee who escaped Cambodia in 1980. I write as a survivor of the time known as Year Zero, which extended over four calendar years. Between 1975 and 1979, the Khmer Rouge emptied the cities of Cambodia and killed two million people through starvation, overwork and execution. More than thirty years later, my country has hardly begun to recover.

Though little has been said in the international media, the Khmer Rouge trials for war crimes have been taking place since 30 March 2010. So far, the only person to stand trial is Kaing Khek Eav, better known as Duch, a relatively junior prison warden. He was convicted and sentenced to nineteen years in jail for his role in 15,000 deaths. Trials of more senior Khmer Rouge have become bogged down in legal arguments, and many perpetrators will never be held to account. Is this justice?

I can't shake the trials from my mind as I step out of my townhouse and walk the streets of Phnom Penh. My country is crying, but the international tribunal is busy, and the rest of the world seems to pay little attention. The anguish expressed in court by surviving victims has barely registered in the Western media. But I believe there are lessons for us all to learn from Cambodia's experience, stories to tell for the sake of the survivors and for those who didn't make it.

What is going on in Cambodia today? Do you know? Do you care? The people of Cambodia do care. Everyone does – we must, for the years when the Khmer Rouge held power have shaped our culture and our way of life. There are three generations of Cambodians who will never forget that time.

When I think about the trials, I cannot escape the past. Like millions of others, I witnessed the incidents that led to the trials. I watched the regime ruthlessly target teachers, managers, doctors, engineers, soldiers, students and senior government officials, dispersing them through the countryside, forcing them to work for starvation rations, spying on their conversations, persecuting them and killing them. I saw the murderous Khmer Rouge regime destroy trust between neighbours and family members. All we could think of was how to stay alive for one more week, one more day, one more hour.

I hope my story will inspire you to think about the challenges that face us all. Many in the West take affluence for granted. The perils facing poorer nations happen somewhere else; they are out of sight and out of mind. But if developed countries turn their backs, events such as those we have seen in Cambodia will happen over and over again.

I want this book to be a lesson learnt from the world's cruellest recent wars – the genocide conducted by the Nazi regime during World War Two, and the systematic brutality inflicted on Cambodia under the rule of the Khmer Rouge. My experiences have taught me the preciousness of political and spiritual freedom. This book is for all those who have fled injustice across the world, and for all who want to understand who we are and who we might become.

Chapter 1
At Peace in Phnom Penh

I WAS BORN on 1 June 1961 in Phnom Penh, the capital of Cambodia. Sandwiched between Thailand and Vietnam, Cambodia was an agricultural land of lakes and paddy fields, forests and ancient temples. There was little poverty. Food was cheap because natural resources were plentiful and the countryside was lush. The tropical climate had only two seasons, one hot and the other wet.

Phnom Penh was a large, bustling city, known as one of the most beautiful in South-east Asia. Old French colonial buildings mingled with modernist constructions in a distinctive Khmer style, which was fostered by King Norodom Sihanouk after Cambodia became independent in 1953. It was a harmonious environment to grow up in. At night, the city glowed under streetlights, and local businesses sold goods on the streets until four or five in the morning. People could travel anywhere without fear.

I was the third son in a family that eventually grew to eleven children. My family had maids and workers to help us. We treated them like our relatives, and one of our workers married one of the maids. All our neighbours were good to us regardless of whether they were poor or rich, Vietnamese, Chinese or Cham (Khmer Islamic).

My brothers and sisters and I occasionally fought, but we were all very happy because we had friends and relatives to visit and play with. The wonderful years of my childhood have left me with special memories. Every time we got our teeth checked, Mother would take us to the playground at Wat Phnom, the only one of its kind in Phnom Penh. It was somewhere that every child wanted to go, and I felt privileged to be there.

Mother was born in China. She was only two when she migrated to Cambodia with her family – her parents, an older brother and a baby sister. Her parents were unable to develop a business in Phnom Penh, and after a year they took their family back to China, but they made Mother stay in Cambodia with a family they knew.

From that day, she never knew happiness. For fourteen years, she had to work like a slave, caring for the children of that family. She was never paid or given the opportunity to go to school or play like other children. She waited for her parents to return, but they never did.

One day, my father's mother decided that Mother would make a good wife for her son because she was a hard worker and a good person. So, without telling my father, Grandmother asked her foster parents' permission for Mother to marry him.

After their marriage, Mother still worked hard. She was not used to commuting or socialising, and she had never been taught to read and write. She dedicated her time to her children – her only happiness – rather than going out with Father. I had a special place in her heart. She seemed to focus on me more than the other children, perhaps because I was always crying. Whenever I was hurting, she cared for me.

My family was not of a wealthy or even middle-class background. Father had been raised in a village, and had lost his own father when he was eight. Within a few years, he was looking after his mother, two younger sisters and a brother. He struggled hard to stay alive and support his family. Eventually, he saved up enough money to run his own business, and that's when he married my mother.

Father had established one of the pioneering private film businesses in Phnom Penh. He was a movie director and owned a number of cinemas at a time when King Norodom Sihanouk became involved in film-making and encouraged others to do the same.

I went to Santhomok Primary School, which was situated at the corner of Kampuchea Krom Boulevard and Mao Tse Tung Boulevard, near where we lived. We lived downstairs in a two-storey house on a large block that was owned by Mother's foster parents. Father also ran a bookstore from our home, and Mother's foster parents lived upstairs. On the same block, they had two more double-storey houses with two bedrooms on each level.

My mother died in 1966 when I was five while giving birth to my youngest sister, Mealea, her eighth child. When Mother died and Mealea was born, everything changed. It wasn't just that Mother had gone, but it seemed that the little sister we had all been longing to see was cursed. Mealea was taken away before we even looked at her and given to another family to be nursed.

Father gave up his film production business after Mother died, but he continued to run the bookstore. He also started to import Indian films for some of the cinemas in Cambodia. The movies he bought were not dubbed or subtitled, and Father didn't speak English or Hindi, but he was very clever. He would watch a movie again and again to work out what was going on. Then, when he was ready, he would play the movie and translate directly into Khmer through a loudspeaker. He was truly an entrepreneur. His importing business became successful, but it was quite exhausting for him to run the business alone and support his big family.

About a year after Mother's death, Father decided to remarry. His new wife could not handle the children as well as the bookstore, so Father decided to stop running his bookstore and move house. He rented another home for us on Mao Tse Tung Boulevard, about four kilometres from central Phnom Penh. It had a tarred road lined with a gutter and a cement pavement. Our new wooden house was smaller than those nearby, but it became home to a new family business selling timber, and also cement pots for storing water. While developing this new business, Father continued importing films. He also erected marquees for weddings, fund-raising events and funerals.

After the move I still attended Santhomok Primary. It was further away than before, but I was very happy. I liked our new home. We had much more space to play. I made friends with other children in the neighbourhood, but most of them did not go to school like me. Ar-Peng, who lived next door, was Chinese Vietnamese. He worked in his father's business and studied

Chinese instead of Khmer. His brothers and sister went to Chinese school.

There were sixty students in my class at school, and most of them were boys. The only boys who made friends with me at first were Sun Lee and Ung Sovannara. Sun Lee was one of the top students in the class. His family ran a tricycle business, and he rode a bicycle to school. Vannara had been in the same class as me since Grade One. His nickname was Ar-Nhar, and his father was a colonel in the Royal Army.

The other boys didn't pay much attention to me until Grade Three, when my studies improved. Then I became friends with Kong Sovichea, another top student who was a classmate. Sovichea and Sun Lee were great rivals. Sovichea was especially good at Khmer literature – in fact, he was good at everything except maths, where I was better than him. He was always happy and studied hard.

By the time I turned nine, I was very much an entrepreneur. I used Father's jars to raise many kinds of fish – Siam fish (known as fighting fish), golden fish, guppies and redtails. I raised them for fun and also for selling. I was very happy when I made money, but sometimes the jars I kept them in were sold without warning while I was at school.

As well as selling fish, I sold small fighting crickets. The crickets were black and gold – other colours too – and at night they would come and play in the light of the lanterns. Sometimes there was a real plague of them. The male crickets would fight each other. They made noises before they fought or mated, and that is how I could catch them, but they would die after about a week, so I could not ask as much for them as I did for the fish.

During school holidays, I sold newspapers and leaflets that gave the lottery results. I played with my brothers and sisters and the neighbours. My sister Mealea was living with her foster mother, and I would sometimes visit her after school and spend time playing with her. The years passed quickly and uneventfully in Phnom Penh.

But outside our peaceful, busy home, trouble was brewing.

There was war in Vietnam, Cambodia's eastern neighbour, and Cambodia was drawn into the conflict. The US government did not trust Sihanouk and began bombing the Cambodian border provinces where North Vietnamese guerrillas were based.

In 1970, Sihanouk was deposed and went into exile. Cambodia was declared a republic under the leadership of General Lon Nol and Sihanouk's cousin Sirik Matak, who were backed by the USA. Sihanouk himself became a commander in the communist Khmer Rouge, which had gained control in some of the rural provinces, and his presence massively boosted the movement's support. While I was blithely selling fish and playing in Phnom Penh, my country was sliding toward civil war.

When I turned eleven, I fell in love. I was in Grade Five, and the girl's name was Tevy. She was rich – or at least her family was. She was always dropped off and picked up by a driver wearing a soldier's uniform. I imagined her living in a large villa with many maids serving her.

I watched her walking into school all neat and smart. She was softly spoken and very pretty, with a beauty spot on her right cheek.

I tried to catch her attention, but I failed. I had nothing to impress her with – no proper clothes or school uniform, holes in my shoes and a worn, old-fashioned schoolbag.

Although I didn't tell her, thoughts of Tevy filled my mind day and night. When I imagined the future, I knew that if I was to have any chance with her – if I was to ask her for her hand in marriage one day – I would have to lift myself up from what I was.

I began to study harder at school. I knew I would have to pass primary school if I wanted to go on. The education system was tough. To enter secondary school, I needed good marks in external exams: the higher the marks, the better the school, and the more choice I would have in going to a school closer to home.

I was so busy. I developed a business for myself selling bread. Each morning, I would sell bread from 4 a.m. and then return home at 5.30 to get ready for school. School ran till 4 p.m., and then I went off to the sewage ponds behind the houses to collect larvae for my fish. On weekends, I sold timber and jars or helped my brothers build marquees for Father's business. When a new movie arrived, I would help Father at his cinema near the central market of Psa Thmei. As well as this, in preparation for the external exams at the end of Grade Six, there was extra tuition during the school holidays and on weekends.

My exam results were very good, and I was admitted to Preah Yukhunthor High School. Located at the corner of Sihanouk and Monivong Boulevards in the centre of Phnom Penh, it was the second-best high school in Cambodia. My sister Sophea attended the same school, while my brothers Sivanchan and Chandy were at other high schools. All four of us were taught in Khmer and French. My oldest sister Vanny was at the only high school in Cambodia that taught in Khmer and English. The rest of my brothers and sisters were at primary school or at home.

I still sold bread. I would buy it from a bakery and sell it from house to house around the Toulkork area, where most of the wealthy people lived.

But it was becoming increasingly difficult to make a living in Phnom Penh. In the civil war, the communist Khmer Rouge were getting closer. They had already taken much of the countryside, and we had all heard chilling reports. People were being killed. Others were leaving their homes and villages for Phnom Penh, and perhaps the KR would follow them. In the city, most people rose early, including children my age. There was work, but it paid very little, so families had to work long hours.

After a few months selling bread, and with the help of a loan from Stepmother, I was able to buy a bicycle. I was happy with my bike because I could take it to school as well as using it for selling bread every morning. I could sell more bread and do it faster than walking.

I felt good about myself as I called out, 'Bread, bread, hot and crunchy.' Women would come out of their houses, or I would sell to children and men on the streets, but when I took the bread from my breadbox after an hour of riding around, it was cold. Some customers were not happy. 'This is not hot. Why do you proclaim your bread is hot and crunchy?' some customers said. Others said my bread was cold and tough and they wouldn't buy it.

I got the idea to make a stove for my breadbox. I collected charcoal from the kitchen, placed it in a tub and put it in the centre of the breadbox, which was attached behind the seat of the bike. I was not sure how to keep the charcoal burning, though, and it would quickly go out.

'Make a vent,' one of my bread-seller mates suggested. So I created a vent in the box to keep the charcoal burning.

One day, I was calling out, 'Bread, bread, hot and crunchy!' when people began shouting at me.

'Your bread is not only hot – it is on fire,' someone called.

I kept pedalling, but someone else ran up and stopped me. 'Look!'

I turned around and looked. My breadbox was burning, and so were the bags wrapping the bread. With a little help, I put out the fire and somehow managed to continue on. I couldn't go home. I had to sell the bread first, because my money was invested in it. Fortunately, I sold most of the bread by the time I had to go to school.

During my second year at high school, I stopped selling bread in the mornings because my schoolwork became more demanding. But I did not give up my fish, not yet.

The Khmer Rouge Liberation Front had pushed forward into Cambodia from along the borders with Vietnam and Laos. By now, they had taken most of the provinces and were approaching the capital. Sihanouk spoke nightly to his people on the Khmer Rouge radio, pleading with them to join him and fight back against his cousin.

The violence that accompanied political upheaval was never welcome, but it had not significantly affected Phnom Penh yet. The Cambodian people weren't overly concerned by the Khmer

Rouge threat to the Republic. Under the Republic, poverty and corruption had increased, and the national economy had become unstable. After the problems of the previous five years, most people anticipated a change in political parties, but what they got was not what they expected at all.

One day when I was in Year Eight and sitting in class at school, a bomb whistled through the air. The class was still for a moment as we listened, then the bomb exploded in the schoolyard. 'Get down on the floor,' the teacher shouted. I could see smoke and fire. The corridor filled with students and teachers, all screaming and running.

Our teacher yelled, 'Let's get out of here. Come on! Quick, everyone!'

Thinking we were under attack, everyone began rushing from the school. I didn't waste any time. I ran from the school buildings and climbed over the tall school fence. There was a lane, and I ran across it to the nearby houses, but no-one opened their doors. All I wanted was to get away as far as I could.

There was screaming and panic all around me. I could hear teachers calling, 'Don't use the streets or the access road. It is too dangerous.' Then the streets became quiet. I jumped over fence after fence, running across people's yards, not caring how high the fences were or how sharp the wire was on top – I thought only of getting home safely.

After that, everything was quieter at night. There were no more traders selling desserts or suppers along the streets. I was not allowed to go out and find crickets or even play hide and seek with my friends. But some nights, when Father was out, I would sneak off without Stepmother knowing. While the streets were quiet, I would find crickets.

One night Father caught me. He was quick, and without saying much he grabbed me and took me home. My punishment was severe.

School was closed after the day of the bombing. I remained home until April the next year, when Phnom Penh was taken by the Khmer Rouge and my life was turned upside down.

Chapter 2
The Red Flag Rises

I WAS NEARLY fourteen when it all began on Sunday 13 April 1975, our Khmer New Year's Eve. It wasn't Friday the thirteenth, which most people believe brings bad luck, but bad luck happened anyway.

Festivities were beginning in Phnom Penh, but the mood was subdued. Khmer Rouge soldiers had surrounded the capital. They had been moving from province to province, asking people to lay down their weapons and give them allegiance, but the capital and seven provinces still belonged to the Republic. We were worried. Nothing like this had happened before. This was a time for celebrations, a time for which we had prepared for many weeks, but this was not to be a year like other years.

I could see a long way from our property on the tree-lined boulevard. I could see over many of the houses, past the trees and gardens and over the rooftops toward the edge of the colourful city and to the mountains surrounding it. I could see that Phnom Penh had swollen – Father thought it had more than a million people – and I kept asking myself what would happen if the city continued to grow.

I knew the outlying areas of Phnom Penh were unsafe and crowded. People had fled from the rural areas as their leaders gave in. There had been many deaths – Republican soldiers and officials and anyone who resisted. The President of the Republic, Lon Nol, had fled to the USA in January. He had left interim power in the hands of the parliament, which in turn gave it to the military, who passed it on to a committee.

Now I'd heard the roads were blocked and many checkpoints

13

had been established. People were coming into the city, but no-one could leave. Food prices had risen and there were shortages of electricity and water. There were now two rounds of school each day in order to accommodate all the rural children. As I thought about all this, my friends called to me.

'Come out, Nora', they yelled.

Father heard and warned me not to go out and play.

'You guys go ahead,' I shouted to my friends. 'I might join you later.'

'When I am back,' Father said to me, 'I expect you to be home.'

He looked grim as he rode away on his old blue motorbike, and I was angry: it was the eve of the New Year.

Later I heard Ar-Peng's soft voice from the steps of his family's double-storey house. I went to the cement porch nearer to him and sat on the steps. 'I can't play,' I called to him.

Ar-Peng's family spoke only a little Khmer, but they were good neighbours. I often spent time with Ar-Peng, and now he kept calling out as I sat and moped. He was excited.

'Do you know what happened this morning?' he said.

'What happened?'

'Ar-Mouy lost her purse at the market, and we have no food. Could you tell your mother my mother wants to borrow some pickled fish, if there is any?'

'What? Pickled fish?' Ar-Peng's family had never touched this type of fish before. They ate only Chinese food such as fried dishes and soup, but now they had to take what they could get.

Ar-Peng said angrily, 'Stop talking. Just ask your mum, OK?'

I ran inside. Sophea and Sokha had just returned from the market, their faces long with disappointment. They'd been gone since four that morning, and Sokha mumbled something as she sat down. She was just thirteen.

'What is it?' I asked.

'I almost punched that fish seller,' she said.

I looked in her basket and saw limes, bananas, chillies and some pork skin.

'He was mean,' Sokha cried angrily. 'First he said 200 riels.

Then a fat ugly lady said she would pay 500. So he sold it to her.'

Sophea, who was seventeen, put a hand on her shoulder. 'It wasn't only you,' she said. 'What about the lady with the chicken? She offered 550 riels, then another lady said 800, but another woman grabbed it for 900.'

'But that was our fish. He had already said our money was enough.'

'Quiet now, Sokha,' Sophea interrupted. 'The fish will not come back to us.'

She patted Sokha's head and took the basket to the kitchen.

In the kitchen, I asked Stepmother if Ar-Peng's family could have some pickled fish, and she said it was fine.

'Come and play cards,' my friends called from the street. I'd begun to run over when I heard Ar-Peng.

'Hey, Nora, what did your mother say?'

'Oh, sorry. Stepmother says OK.'

Vivath, my six-year-old brother, came out with the pickled fish.

Ar-Peng thanked me. He tried to explain that his mother would repay Stepmother later. I just shrugged my shoulders.

As the morning hours passed, I helped my family get things ready for our new god of the year to arrive. Candles were lit and incense burnt as we prepared the food and started the cooking. Then we began dressing up to go to the pagoda and visit our relatives.

Suddenly I felt the earth tremble. We stopped what we were doing. The explosion was far away. It must have been the Khmer Rouge pushing closer to the city.

Father decided not to go to the pagoda. We didn't go on to visit relatives either. We stayed at home and offered food to the new god and to our ancestors.

Since marrying my father, my stepmother had had two children, so there were now ten children in the family, but only eight of us were at home that day. Mealea was with her foster parents, and Vanny, my oldest sister, who was six years older than me, had left for Australia just weeks earlier on an exchange program sponsored by Rotary. She was fortunate to make her flight. The Australian

Embassy provided a bus that escorted her from the city to the airport. We saw her off from the embassy, because beyond there no-one's safety could be guaranteed without an escort.

14 April 1975

The morning of 14 April – the Cambodian New Year – began with a family visit to the home of Aunt Im-Lay, my father's youngest sister. Her husband was a chief officer in the Ministry of Health's pharmaceutical department. He spoke French fluently, as well as some English. A dozen family members lived in her house.

The bombs and sounds of weapons firing had stopped, and on the radio Father had heard the news that the Republic had surrendered. A new government had been installed, and peace was announced.

We played traditional games outside, then I joined my brothers and cousins to play cards. We were enjoying ourselves, laughing and shouting and arguing, when around noon we heard an explosion. The bomb was closer than the day before, and we saw smoke and fire. We all hurried home.

We had been told over the radio that we would be allowed to celebrate the New Year and that soon we would be welcoming back the exiled King Sihanouk, but all we heard now were sirens, bombs and guns. After we got home, we went up to the roof, where we saw black smoke coming from the airport. The electricity had been cut. We lit candles and ate rice porridge quietly.

Our small wooden home on the Mao Tse Tung Boulevard was close to the heart of Phnom Penh. Downstairs, there were two rooms leading off the living areas: one for Father and Stepmother, one for my sisters. My brothers and I slept on open verandas, or in a converted chicken shed, which contained two beds and a study table. Clay tiles covered the floor of the house. They had become hard and smooth like concrete. It was a busy home, with relatives of our hired workers also living with us.

Two wooden beds rested against the walls, covering the windows and darkening the house. One of the wooden beds was really a big chest where my father stored all the film rolls of the movies he had produced, and the movies he had imported from India.

There was a shed on the property that held the pots and the different timbers that we sold, and a tree that provided shade before an open area that stretched twenty metres to the gate. We had dug an L-shaped trench as a bomb shelter in front of the house. About two metres deep and one and a half metres wide, it was covered by wood, which was in turn covered with sacks of soil.

15 April 1975

I was both worried and excited. We had received a letter telling us that Vanny had arrived safely in Melbourne, to a new school and a host family who treated her like their own daughter. We had been wondering about Australia. Someone had said it was near America. Someone else said it was a continent near a country that sank into the sea. I listened respectfully.

After midday another bomb exploded and Phnom Penh began to crumble. The explosion caused raging fires. Houses burnt and people fled as sirens and the fire engine screamed along the boulevard. The quietness that had held sway all morning was gone. The suppressed tension erupted into panic.

Some of my brothers climbed onto the roof to see what was happening, but Father yelled, 'It's too dangerous!'

He left to go to another district where he was a community representative, and then my older brother Sivanchan and my cousin Hea Suor left to get a closer look at the fires. My brother Chandy and I decided to follow them out. Down the road, not very far away, we could see several houses on fire. Then we met Father. 'Hurry back to the house,' he screamed. 'Troops are everywhere and might attack tonight. Many soldiers have been killed after surrendering.'

At home the mood was fearful. My sister Sokha was trembling and asking if we were going to die. That evening the *Voice of*

America on the radio was silent. In this Cambodian New Year, I wondered if the new god was different. Perhaps he had forgotten something back in his palace.

16 April 1975

Khmer Rouge jeeps tore through the streets with sirens blaring. 'The Americans are coming to bomb the city,' they announced through loudspeakers. 'Stay calm and remain in your house.'

I ran up to the bamboo gate and peered through. Khmer Rouge soldiers were going from house to house, and people were everywhere. Passers-by reported that people who had left their homes were going missing.

Father instructed us to be prepared for the worst. I helped with the rice, then went to check the trench and helped to store mats, pillows, water, candles and other goods there.

In the house, everyone was either panicking or too busy to panic. We had to plan, but the sirens and the loudspeakers were intimidating, the marching soldiers with their guns terrifying. They were just outside our gate now. They had weapons, and they were firing.

When evening came, the streets were empty and the city became quiet. Everyone was hiding in their homes or camped in trenches. My family and I waited in the trench.

The trench was hot and stuffy, and I couldn't sleep; I couldn't even breathe properly. I peeked through a hole in the roof at one end of the trench and looked up at the sky. It was black. I prayed that American planes would not come to bomb us.

I whispered to Chandy, 'Brother, is the American plane big? How many bombs can it drop?'

'The American plane is big,' he whispered back. 'It carries many bombs. Once it hits our trench, we will be destroyed.'

I felt cold and began to shake, but I asked another question. 'What will happen to us when we are destroyed?'

'I don't know.'

We all prayed for the new god to help us and expected the

sound of American planes. I held on to my thoughts and continued to tremble until I fell asleep.

Dasy, my youngest sister, was so scared that she clung to
Stepmother. Step-grandmother tried to pull her away, but Dasy
held on tight all night.

No-one was sure what would happen now, but everyone was
praying to the new god, praying for peace.

17 April 1975

We were called out from our houses to march through the streets
and show our support for the new government. 'The war is over,'
people shouted, welcoming the military, thinking that perhaps the
King was returning. 'We will have peace again,' others yelled. Some
people were reserved, but everyone thought the new government
would be similar to what had been there in the past.

We climbed from the trench and ran to the gate. There were
thousands of people, marching and following the tanks and the
soldiers in black. Others stood along the curved road, their faces
full of happiness and hope.

The crowds were clapping their hands and shouting, 'Vive and
long live the King!' I watched a man echoing the call. 'Vive and
long live the King,' he repeated. Then a soldier pointed his gun at
him. I did not understand what was happening and I thought he
was going to shoot.

'The kingdom will not be the same as the Republic,' the soldier
said quietly.

There was a feeling of relief as the Khmer Rouge led the
marching through the streets. Tanks paved the way. The flag –
red with a yellow temple emblazoned on it – was held high and
proud. Then the marching stopped. The soldiers came up to us.

'You must go into your houses,' the black-clothed soldiers said.
'The Americans are going to bomb the city.'

Everyone ran to the house and we started moving more goods
to the trench. We were all in a panic. It was nearly lunchtime, and I
was carrying cooked rice to the trench when the soldiers returned.

'Open up!' they called through the gates. 'The city is no longer a safe place. Get out of the city now, before the American planes come with bombs. Hurry! Hurry!'

We tried to have lunch and packed quickly: bedding, clothes, dried fish and rice. We were prepared. Father had his jeep ready with the trailer attached, and we were off, the girls in the jeep, the boys standing on the side of the trailer. My thoughts were mixed. I had taken great pride in breeding my golden fish and fighting fish, and I was sad at leaving them behind, but I was excited too.

There were twelve of us: Father and Stepmother, eight brothers and sisters, Step-grandmother, and my step-cousin, Hea Suor. In all the chaos, I forgot about Mealea, who was now eight. Apparently everyone else did too.

We could hear people crying and screaming as we made our way through the city, with the Khmer Rouge firing shots into the air to direct us. The streets were already packed, and processions seemed to be travelling steadily in every direction. The traffic became so congested that we could hardly move at all. We feared for our lives as we tried to obey the soldiers, who were screaming, 'Move on, move on. Hurry! The Americans are bombing.'

Evening came, and the traffic took us alongside the railway tracks toward Phnom Penh University. Further instructions came: 'Return to your relatives on the farms or to your birth villages. Return to where you originally came from.'

Father then headed toward where his birthplace was. As he drove, he continued to squeeze beside the railway tracks, toward the grounds of the university, where Stepmother's uncle lived.

We threaded our way into the university grounds and drove up to the residential block. It was a five-storey building with a car park underneath. We arrived at about seven-thirty, parked our jeep and trailer, and looked around.

'This door,' Father said.

He knocked, but no-one answered. He knocked again.

'Who is it?'

'Is that you, Uncle Long?'

'You mean Professor Dean Kim Long?'

'Yes sir,' Father answered.

'D-5, two doors further down.'

Uncle had heard the noise and was standing outside his door with his family. We all ran to him. He was white-skinned with white hair combed to one side. He had a pipe in his mouth and wore a light-coloured silk sarong.

We stayed there three nights. The Dean and the others had wanted to leave, but the Khmer Rouge soldiers had told them to wait. Two days later, the soldiers had not returned.

Three days after we arrived, another group of Khmer Rouge came by.

'Whose jeep and trailer are underneath the building?' they demanded.

Father asked if the danger was over. Could we return to our homes?

'No,' they snapped. 'You must leave the city before the American planes come with their bombs.'

We were in shock. During the last two days we had seen everyone leaving the city, and then Khmer Rouge trucks and their families driving in. We'd thought the danger was over.

Father asked for time to pack. His request was granted, and the soldiers said they would return the next day in the afternoon. Father asked Uncle to join us.

'No, I am waiting for further instructions,' Uncle replied. 'And I will be needed here again.'

20 April 1975

The next morning, we left the university on a dirt road. It would be a long journey over rice fields and on a ferry to National Road #5, and then on to Kampong Thom, Father's home province.

My step-cousin, Hea Suor, left us that morning to find his girlfriend, whom he wanted to marry. He worked at the National Commercial Bank. It was a very good job, and it seemed that many families had wanted their daughters to marry him.

The roads were rough and littered with holes. I was standing on the back of the jeep and thinking about Hea Suor when suddenly the jeep lunged. I lost my grip and fell off in the middle of a field of dust. I was lucky to escape the wheels of the heavy trailer. But I was hurt, and I had been left behind. In all the dust, no-one even knew I had gone.

Thoughts raced through my mind as I scrambled out of everyone's way. I was desperate. I had to act quickly or I could lose my family.

I shrugged off the pain from my bruises and ran as fast as I could. Father's jeep and trailer were travelling fast on the dirt road, and I had dust in my mouth and eyes. Eventually I caught up with the trailer and scrambled back on. I had almost been killed, and no-one knew.

At about 5 p.m., we reached National Road #5, which was tarred. We were about twenty kilometres from the ferry. The road was as crowded as anything I'd ever seen. Walking beside the jeep, I almost stepped on a dead body on the road. It was a man's body, flattened like paper as if by a hundred tanks. Thousands of people must have walked on it, crushed it, and gone their way. I asked his forgiveness and hoped that he would not curse me, but curse those who killed him.

We stopped to rest for the night on the edge of the road with everyone else. At that time, I did not understand the seriousness of the situation. I was just happy to be camping out in the open air. I had been looking forward to camping for so long, ever since my older brother went camping with the school. I was tired but excited. As I rested I saw thousands of people along the road with their candles lit, looking like a swarm of fireflies. I smelt spices and rice and occasionally some pork.

21 April 1975

There was noise all around me when I woke, and I rose fresh and ready. We were instructed to move on, which we were keen to do, as the area where we had rested was now a stinking mess.

As we continued our journey along National Road #5, I imagined Tonle Sap River, where we would have a chance to cross by ferry to my father's village. When I was about ten, Father had taken me on the ferry to visit relatives. I'd had a great time standing with my brother Chandy next to the ferry's railing, watching people selling bread, boiled eggs, fruits and other snacks, and wondering how deep the river was.

The river looked no different when we arrived, only busier. A long queue awaited us as we approached, and we could see a ferry floating across the river to the other side.

'One ferry!' I exclaimed. 'Just one small ferry!'

We decided to camp nearby, waiting for our turn. As the hours passed, I set about catching crabs, snails and little fish in the ponds. I became quite good at it, which was just as well. Food had grown scarce and everyone was getting hungry.

Then there was an announcement. A man in black, escorted by a compatriot with a rifle, addressed us through a loudspeaker.

'The ferry has run out of gasoline and won't be able to cross the river again today,' he said. 'Maybe tomorrow you can cross, when the supply unit brings more gasoline.'

The crowds were increasing every minute. Then the Khmer Rouge came to talk to Father. There were five of them in black clothing with green hats and blue scarves. Two of them were carrying AK-47 folding rifles.

'Angkar will need that jeep,' they announced.

Father took off his hat and replied respectfully. 'Can we get to our village first?' he said. 'We were told that's what we had to do when we were directed along the road by the KR soldiers. We can't do this without our jeep. Besides, we have young children, sir.'

'Angkar needs that jeep,' one of the men repeated. 'Just leave it with us and you can continue your journey.'

This was the first time we had heard the word 'Angkar'. We later found out that it was the KR term for 'the organisation'.

'Angkar wants it now,' another soldier said.

Father explained we needed to cross the river in order to go to our province.

'Now,' the soldier repeated.

Father asked if they could come back and take it after we boarded the ferry. Voices were raised. Finally the soldiers left.

The land beside the river was muddy, and the wait for the ferry would be long. Each family found a small area to camp and did their best to pass the time, look after their supplies, and eat if they could.

22–23 April 1975

It rained that night, washing dirt up through my sleeping mat. The next morning, I was exhausted and felt strange. We soon discovered I had been sleeping on a grave.

I was upset and just had to get away, so after the rain eased I went exploring. I threaded my way past everyone to the nearby muddy fields. I hoped to find crabs, or perhaps fish, in the paddy fields or in the pools that had formed in the mud. Instead I found sharp, yam-like roots under the mud and cut my foot on one of them.

The cut became dirty, and later I felt sick. I slept in the rain again that night, and the next morning I woke feverish with a bitter taste in my mouth. My foot was infected. The weather was scorching during the day, and all I could do was lie in the shade inside the jeep. I was delirious when the soldiers returned.

'Give Angkar the car now,' they demanded.

'But my son? He is lying in the car,' Father pleaded.

The soldiers left but soon returned.

'You must all prepare to move,' they announced. 'There is no more gasoline: there will be no more ferry. You must move on now. Quickly! Pack quickly and move.'

We were devastated. We had now waited four days for the ferry, struggling to find food and space. We had seen many families questioned by the harsh Khmer Rouge soldiers. Occasionally, we saw families taken away, sometimes screaming, to be herded onto trucks and driven off. The trucks would return and fill again with more people, usually the city-bred families.

Again the Khmer Rouge told us to go.

It was a long walk to the next village, which was in Stepmother's province, not Father's. I don't know how Father managed it, but we kept the jeep. I lay in the jeep as our family and many others were herded along the road beside the river.

The next village was about twelve kilometres away from the ferry, and the jeep soon ran out of petrol. My father struck bargains with other travellers and more fuel was found, but my family still had to push the jeep and the cart most of the way.

I didn't know much about what was happening. All I knew was the rattle and shaking of the vehicle as I drifted in and out of sleep. My head ached. I was numb and feverish and shivering. Everything was pain.

I lost track of time for several days. Occasionally the jeep would lurch as it was pushed over a hole on the road. I would wake from a delirious sleep to see travellers moving on ahead, and others following behind.

Late one afternoon, we reached Oudong district in Kampong Speu province. I saw tall trees, mainly sugar palms, but not many houses. The few I did see were wooden places with walls made of palm leaves and thatched roofs.

We entered a village. The villagers, who were dressed in black, called out warmly to us to stop a while. They said to my father, 'Hello, Lok Bong' (meaning older brother). 'You've been pushing the jeep. You must be tired.'

It was early evening. Two Khmer Rouge on bicycles came from behind with a loudhailer and called to us, 'Settle down here in this village. This is to be your new home.' Other families near us were ordered to do the same. The rest of the long line of people moved on.

I heard so much noise that I woke with a start, but I was too weak to sit up. Forcing my eyes open, I tried to peer through the gaps in the canvas on the side of the jeep. All I could make out were fruit trees – mango, guava, jackfruit and others – as well as the tree I liked most of all, the sugar palm, standing up tall in the twilight with its green head swaying in the wind.

I stirred as I was lifted and carried to a mat under a tree. While I lay there, my family was called to register at the village. They were provided with supplies of rice and other food. They were also told that all the provinces now belonged to the Khmer Rouge, and we now lived under their rules.

'In the morning, come back here to line up and we will tell you what to do,' we were told. 'In the afternoon, build your own shelter.'

'What do they mean: "line up" and "build your own shelter"?' one of my brothers grumbled.

Morning came. My family lined up, and most of them were sent into the paddy fields to work – Stepmother and Father, my brothers Chandy, 16, and Sivanchan, 19 (we often called him Vanchan) and my sisters Sokha, 13, and Sophea, 18.

I was unconscious, with only my step-grandmother and youngest siblings to look after me in the small space we had been given for ourselves and all our possessions. Step-grandmother waited at the shelter with Dasy, aged 2, Vivath, 5, and Puthea, 10, hoping the others would come back with medicine.

When I woke, I could see at a distance the paddy-field workers removing broken bamboo and clearing the fields. Some worked in pairs collecting buffalo dung in buckets. It wasn't long before the bright sunshine of the day made my eyes weaken, and my heavy lids closed again. Once more I fell hopelessly asleep.

Chapter 3
New Rules

The bamboo house appeared one morning as I began to regain consciousness. It was really only a frame with a plastic covering for a roof, one of many such shelters grouped close to the paddy fields, which were now full of rainwater. These fields extended as far as I could see. Bright sunshine glistened on the water as the villagers toiled there.

Lying on a mat in the house one afternoon, I awoke to the sound of banging. I had been unconscious for so long that everyone thought I was going to die. I was drowsy and my head throbbed, but looking up through blurry eyes I saw Step-grandmother. The banging persisted. I couldn't think clearly and collapsed again.

I woke an hour later. This time I saw my brother Vivath and my sister Dasy sitting next to Step-grandmother. I saw them working with palm leaves as I lost consciousness once more.

The next time I stirred, Dasy was forcing a drink between my lips. I couldn't speak, and my scattered thoughts only brought pain to my head. It was a hot day, but I felt chilled. My head began shaking, and I couldn't control it no matter how much I tried. The chill turned to freezing cold, and the shaking became violent.

Fear overwhelmed me. Step-grandmother shouted to Puthea, 'Put a blanket on him!'

Puthea was only ten, but he came. I calmed a little but felt a darkness pressing down heavily on my body, a darkness that came from inside my head. I opened my eyes and saw that the roof of our house had been covered with palm leaves. I could smell them. It was a fresh smell. My family must have worked hard. But then I could think no more.

Pain increased at the back of my head. I felt dizzy. As I thought my world was coming to an end, Step-grandmother heard my jaws rattling as if they had a mind of their own.

'Sit on him,' she cried out to Puthea. 'Put something in his mouth.'

Puthea sat on me, but he was scared. He later told me my eyes were spinning and bubbles of saliva were dribbling from my mouth. Then Sokha entered through the back door. She had come home for a drink of water.

'Here,' Step-grandmother yelled. 'Help Puthea.' She rose and gave Sokha a rubber sandal. It was dirty. 'Put this in his mouth,' she commanded.

Sokha was strong and helped Puthea hold me down. She placed the thong in my mouth so that I would not bite my tongue. The saliva continued to ooze from between my lips. It covered my face as my body tensed and contracted, but Puthea and Sokha kept holding me. Eventually the violent jerking stopped, and sleep returned once more.

I woke several days later and the fever had gone. Puthea came and sat near me. He told me that everyone thought I was going to die. Father had already requested permission from the village leader to organise my funeral. He told me about my yelling in my sleep, my convulsions and fevers.

I still couldn't speak. I looked across and saw Sokha dressed in her dirty clothes for the fields. This was new. I hadn't seen her dressed like this before. Dressed for work? Work in the mud? Slowly I sat up and turned my head. I was in a new house raised on stilts, with walls and a roof and a floor made of bamboo.

Puthea fed me soup. After forcing some of it down I tried to stand and hobble outside. There was no sign of the jeep, because the KR had finally taken it.

With a huge effort, I managed to walk through the village. Everything was quiet. I saw no-one at first, then came across some people dressed in black. These were the Khmer Rouge, patrolling, guarding. Their clothing was marvellous. I admired the kroma, a handmade cotton towel that they wore around their necks, and their black sandals, which were made from old tyres. Several of them had guns. Some were teenagers not much older than me. An older man was taking notes on a clipboard.

I watched as they walked up to my house. When I hobbled back, I heard them ask Step-grandmother if she wanted to return to Phnom Penh. They were seeking volunteers, they said. Step-grandmother said she would speak with Father, and they left.

I sat down and soon fell asleep on the floor again. I woke in the evening to the sound of the chatter in the house. I saw some palm fruit had been collected. Palm fruit were like coconuts, but black with yellow marks on the top and not as firm. When they were cooked, they gave off a smell like brown sugar burning.

Some fruit was cooking now, and the smell ignited a ravenous desire in me. I craved some of that fruit. I asked Father if I could have some, but he said I shouldn't, as it might make me worse. Instead, I was given porridge.

I sat with the porridge and listened to the family talking. Father looked concerned. Step-grandmother told him the soldiers were looking for volunteers to go back to Phnom Penh, but Father firmly said, 'No.' He said we must never volunteer to return, because the situation was not safe. 'We must be careful,' he continued. 'They must not see us as rich people. They must not know what we did in the past. Tell them only that we built tents and marquees for weddings and other gatherings, and that we sold pots and wood.'

Father also said, 'No work means no food. It doesn't matter that you don't understand. These are the new rules.' He told us that some families had disappeared after their members asked questions. No-one knew where they went.

When it was nearly sunset, I managed to leave the shelter and make my way to the main dirt road about a hundred metres from the house. Across the road stood a broken Chinese shrine half-hidden between palm trees and bushes. Nearby stood a broken brick fence, and beyond it the remains of an old property and a lake.

I walked on to the lake. Tired, I sat down on a concrete step with my feet in the water and scooped some up to wash my face.

I scratched at an itch on my head, felt my scar, and fell into a contemplative mood.

The scar had been with me since I was twelve, and I recalled the day it happened. It was a day when black clouds covered Phnom Penh and the wind was gusty and threatening. I'd raced on my bicycle the short distance from school to the Neak Kro-Voan Pagoda, where my brother Sivanchan was helping to pack up a big marquee. When I arrived, one of my father's workers, Pou-Dom, was high on the wooden tent frame, removing something from the top, while Sivanchan held the other side. I joined in and was holding another part of the tent when the wooden frame snapped. I couldn't see what was happening, but I saw the tent sway. Then it came down, and the broken wooden frame hit me in the middle of my forehead. It felt and sounded like an axe whacking a coconut in half, and I ended up in the emergency room at Calimette Hospital.

I remembered the pain as if it happened yesterday, even though all that remained of the incident now was a long scar in the middle of my forehead, a scar I had grown fond of like a battle trophy.

Soon I rose and hobbled back to the dirt road. I walked toward the broken Chinese shrine I had seen, then I heard the sound of an engine, a sound I hadn't heard since the KR confiscated my father's jeep. An open-roofed military truck was approaching slowly. I stood up. Packed high in the truck was a load of yams. There were two soldiers sitting on the side of the truck.

'Here you are, Samamit,' one of them said. He waved and threw me two yams.

I felt a surge of happiness as I picked them up and took them to the house, hoping to bake or fry them.

I was getting the fire ready when Step-grandmother came in. 'What is it?' she asked. 'What are you doing with the fire? You're not well.'

I showed her the two yams and explained where they came from.

'You should not have them,' she replied. 'You are just recovering.'

I left the yams and returned to my sleeping place, disappointed.

I felt weary, and I could smell the palm fruit again as it sat under the house. I had heard that my sister was going to make it into jelly. When I asked them for a taste, everyone said no, I was not allowed to have any palm fruit. What about what I wanted? I might have been ill, I thought, but couldn't I make decisions any more?

The next day, after slipping in and out of consciousness for weeks, I woke soon after lunch feeling stronger and more determined. Again I could smell palm fruit cooking and again I craved it.

I eventually found enough energy to leave the shelter. The sun was bright and the view was clear. I sat on the riverbank, and a neighbour came and sat with me. He told me I was lucky to be alive. I told him I didn't feel lucky. I said I thought I was going to die, and the only thing I was clear about was my hunger.

That night, I woke up around midnight feeling feverish and restless, and still craving the sweetness of the palm fruit, so I collected a sack and went out, intending to find palm fruit and eat my fill before anyone woke up.

I lumbered off. Moonlight reflected off the paddy fields and the lake. It was June, and the wet season was in full swing. Crickets and other night animals were chirping and buzzing, and frogs were croaking to each other, announcing that their mating season had begun. As for me, I was dazed and perhaps delirious and I didn't care about anything except my desperate mission.

I'd noticed some palm trees around the old Chinese shrine, about two hundred metres away, so I made it my first target. As I approached, I heard the wind blowing and the branches rubbing together and creaking. Then I heard fruit fall: 'Thud!' There were bushes at the foot of the palm. I knelt and felt my way among the bushes until I found a palm fruit.

I was so excited that I held it up to the moon to get a good look at it before I put it into my bag. I looked for more fruit but found none.

Standing again, I gazed into the distance. The moonlight illuminated the horizon, and a clump of trees caught my attention.

It appeared to be a forest but it was far away and out of our area. It was past the lake and the rice fields. I knew that I wasn't supposed to go there – no-one was – but that was where I would find something to eat.

I was hobbling across when I heard the branches of the palm trees back at the shrine start to rattle. There was a rumbling sound like a ten-pin bowling ball rolling down the lane, and then the sound of two thuds on the ground. I hurried back: if I could just collect those palm fruits, that would be enough for me to return home. But I couldn't find them, no matter how hard I searched. Then I doubted myself. Did I really hear them? I wasn't sure any more, but I could definitely hear more fruit falling ahead in the forest near the lake.

That forest was calling to me. 'Forget about those two,' it said, 'come over here, there is plenty of fruit here for you to collect.'

I obeyed. As I neared, I sensed something moving above me in the tops of the trees. I looked up and saw a black shadow moving quickly, scampering through the leaves and branches.

I would have been scared to death if this had happened when I was back home in Phnom Penh, where I was the most fearful in my family. My father was always telling people how scared I was. He even told our relatives about the time he took me to the cinema to watch a Tarzan movie and I jumped from my seat and covered my eyes when I saw an elephant running toward us. 'I had to push your hands apart with my fingers before you finally opened your eyes,' he would say.

I heard the noise again and kept walking until I reached the palm forest. Edging my way deeper and deeper into the forest, I found about eight palm fruit, and then I heard something jumping from branch to branch above me. The branches shook. When I looked up, I saw nothing except maybe a shadow.

More fruit fell. I heard them falling from trees all around me and searched eagerly on my hands and knees. I was in the shadows of the moon, in the dark spaces between the bushes and the trees. They fell again and again: 'Crack! Thump!' Sometimes I couldn't find them, although they seemed to fall so near.

I realised something was playing with me, so I called out to the shape in the trees. There was no answer, but I kept talking. I explained I wished no harm, that I was recovering from sickness and all I wanted to do was eat the fruit of the palm tree.

My sack was half full, but I couldn't feel the weight. I kept staggering through the forest, stumbling over logs, falling down and then picking myself up out of the mud. I crunched into sticks that made unexpected sounds when they hit each other, and kicked something round along the ground, something like a ball but lighter than a palm fruit. The hours passed and I began to feel tired and sick. Then I heard a rooster crow. It must have been about four. I had to get home.

I staggered back in the direction of the rooster's crow. The moon was closer now but had gone behind a cloud. I could hardly see. I struggled to take another step. Suddenly my hunger was like a stake in my heart. Then I knew: this wasn't the way I had come.

'Please help me! Please! Help me I'm lost,' I called to the trees. But the shadow was gone. I stumbled further. 'Please help me and show me the way.'

I heard the cracking of branches behind me, then the rattling sound of leaves upon each other. I looked back. There it was, standing among the leafy branches, silhouetted in the dull light of the moon. It jumped down. I heard it land on the ground, then I could hear leaves rustling and cracking as it walked away from me, as if inviting me to follow.

I was exhausted. I didn't want to spend any more time in the forest tripping and searching for paths. I heard more crowing, and the rooster's calls made me panic. What if someone saw me there? Some of my strength returned, and I hurried. I couldn't see my companion any more, but fruits fell; one, then another and another. I followed the falling fruit, collecting them as I went. Eventually, as light began to cross the horizon, I staggered out of the forest and onto the dykes. I had found my way home. I returned to the shelter, sneaked in and collapsed.

Puthea called, 'Bong Ra, Bong Ra,'– 'Brother Ra, Brother Ra', which was my family name. He shook me again. 'Bong, wake up. Tell us. Where did you get this fruit?'

It was many hours later that I woke again, and much longer before I could talk coherently. I explained where I found the fruit. I told them about the shape, or was it a man, who helped me.

'You shouldn't have gone there,' Father said. 'It is forbidden. It is a dangerous place, and no-one goes there. It is a place used for executing people whom Angkar thinks are the enemy – a killing field. Besides, the Khmer Rouge people think you are sick.'

He explained why the forest was out of bounds. 'The area was set aside after the province had been taken. Many, many police, soldiers, teachers and others have gone missing – or been executed.'

Despite what Father said, I could tell he was pleasantly surprised, because I had always been easily frightened and scared of ghosts. He came closer and rubbed my shoulder affectionately but gently, for he knew how unwell I had been. Then he sat down near me for a while before he left for work.

Everyone was pleased that I had managed to find all that fruit, and puzzled that I'd been so ill but had still managed to be out all night collecting it.

Now I was hungry. Father had asked Stepmother to make cake and jelly. I asked for some of the fruit to be baked. A shiver ran down my back as I mulled over what had happened. The round thing I kicked and the sticks, were they a skull and bones?

When the food was prepared, I ate eagerly. I began to recover over the next week. One day, I went out and sat by the road again, hoping to see another military truck carrying yams. As I expected, a truck came by, but it wasn't a military vehicle, and none of the root was thrown my way.

So much had happened. Everything was different now. No more medicines, clinics or hospitals. No more friends. No more breeding fish, and no more earning an income for myself. I was tired and sad as I daydreamed of the past, and I scratched my forehead. What of my old classmates? Where were they now? We'd all had such comfortable lives. Now I wasn't even sure any of them were alive. Would any of them still be in the city?

I especially thought of the girl called Tevy who had been in the class next to mine at Santhomok Primary School. I was just a young boy, but my feelings toward her were very strong. She was kind and soft, and the more I thought of her the happier I felt. I hoped she would be safe and I prayed for her wellbeing. I hoped I would meet her again one day. The thought made me smile. Her family had been wealthy, but now we were all equal and I would stand a better chance if…

But so much had changed, and everybody was different. First, I had to become well and be with my family. They didn't talk much together any more, and I could see how unhappy my brothers and sisters were.

I felt strong thinking what I'd been through. Was it a ghost looking after me at the forest of palms? Now I felt I had a spiritual power that made me ready to do things, as though the spirits of the dead were with me.

Two weeks later, a message came to my family as well as to many others.

'You have to go,' the Khmer Rouge announced. 'Your family is one of those chosen by Angkar. Pack up, now. Get ready and we will come back tomorrow. You will have to move on.'

Father feared the worst. We had been there for about two months. We had just finished the shelter, which still smelt fresh from the palm leaves. Now we packed in a daze.

Father warned that when we arrived in a new place we must not say anything, especially about the nice things we used to have in Phnom Penh. When I thought about it, I realised that even now my family had more possessions than any of the other families in the village. 'Only take what is necessary,' he said, 'and valuable things that will be useful in the future.'

In the morning, a man with a loudspeaker called all the families who had been chosen. 'Come out from your shelters,' he said. 'Line up along the road.'

The road became dusty with so many feet. Our belongings strapped to bamboo sticks, we stood in line together with the other families. It seemed as if almost everyone was being moved on. We were told that trucks would soon arrive. We waited. The dust settled. The sun became hotter, and the remaining workers in the fields glistened in the distance like shining beacons.

Several hours later, another announcement came. 'Angkar has told us to move you by boat. Move now. This way.'

They showed us which way to go, keeping us in line like schoolchildren.

'This way! Come now,' the command from the loudspeaker repeated.

Some families had brought pots and pans. One boy was carrying a hen. Some had their belongings on their shoulders, but no-one had vehicles any more.

Two of my brothers carried a stick threaded through a basket. My sisters carried rice and clothes on their heads. My stepbrother and stepsister walked beside Stepmother and Step-grandmother, who carried goods on their heads wrapped in sarongs. We walked, with hundreds of others, without knowing where we were going or why. We were all one class now, and it was the lowest class. Our tattered black clothes and few belongings testified to this.

Chapter 4
The Wat Chrey Commune

AFTER TWO DAYS marching, processions of relocating families eventually reached Sala Leg Pram district in Kampong Chhang province and rested beside the river. This was the Tonle Sap River, the great river that runs all the way from the ancient city of Angkor Wat in Siem Reap province to the capital city of Phnom Penh.

The crowds waited for a barge to transport them to Battambang province. Three days later, the Khmer Rouge changed their mind. We were among the many families who were herded onto a barge and carried upstream to the west, to Kompong Chhang Provincial Town. We all left the barge at Kampong Chhang port and walked or travelled in ox-carts to the train station, a few hours away. The waiting train had about fourteen carriages, many of them already full of people. Hundreds of us newcomers crushed into the crowded carriages to wait for the rest of the day before the train steamed away from the provincial town.

Along its journey, the train became shorter as carriages were left behind in remote districts of Kampong Chhang and Pursat provinces. The population was being spread throughout the country. We'd been told that everyone had a responsibility not to shirk from any task and to share resources with the whole community. This equality and sense of duty were not to be questioned.

My family had boarded the sixth carriage on the train, which now had twelve carriages, and I was sleeping. I slept through the rocking motion of the train but woke when I heard its whistle blow sharp and loud.

'Where are we now and what time is it?' someone said.

'Probably reached Mong Russey district of Battambang province,' a man answered.

It was dark, but I saw houses with fluorescent lights on. It made me feel excited and hopeful that we would move to a better lifestyle in this new province. I was hoping to get back to my lifestyle as it used to be: maybe I would soon be breeding golden fish and chickens back in Phnom Penh again.

It had been a long journey. Weary and hungry, we were herded from the carriage onto ox-carts as the sun rose. The Khmer Rouge then led us deep into the darkness to the Wat Chrey commune along Mong Russey River, about half a kilometre from Mong Russey railway station.

We were carried along a bumpy dirt road in ox-carts, with some old people marching along behind. The ox-cart was not as comfortable as riding in Father's jeep. I had no cushion and was sitting flat on the wooden floor.

The Khmer Rouge shuffled us from place to place without explanation. We were all quiet when we reached the Wat Chrey commune in Battambang as administrators gathered information and recorded people's names and the families they belonged to. The commune had seven villages: Sahakor One, Sahakor Two, and so on to Sahakor Seven. Other communes had eight or nine Sahakors. Sahakor has a similar meaning to 'village', but it's a place where families live cooperatively, not individually. We were resettled in Sahakor Seven.

On the night we arrived at Sahakor Seven, a number of families, including mine, were instructed to sleep in a big hall. We swept and cleaned the area to make room for sleeping. The village leaders had told all the adults to attend a meeting the next morning, so Father got up early, but my brother and I slept on. We were woken around 7.30 a.m. by a loud bell ringing near where I was sleeping, and I saw people coming toward the hall and then gathering around outside. The KR instructed us to pack our stuff quickly, so we did. I saw a number of ox-carts with food supplies in them. Then a man on a bike arrived wearing a black uniform and smoking a homemade cigarette. He stopped in front of the crowd and then ordered his men, who were also dressed in black, to divide the food among us according to a list he had been given.

After we received the food supplies, Father told us to move our belongings to a house near the hall. Father knew a family that was related to one of the village's deputy leaders. The family was originally from Phnom Penh as well, but they had arrived a couple of months earlier. We were to stay in the house while we built our own place, in a line with all the others.

We marched in a line too.

There were thirty to forty families in each village. About a third of them were families who had been in the village when the Republic was overthrown. These families had embraced the Khmer Rouge and were now leaders in the village. They organised allowances of salt and sugar, collected data and asked questions. Accompanying them as bodyguards were young soldiers with ammunition strapped to their bodies and guns in their hands.

It was easy to tell who the leaders were. Like the Khmer Rouge soldiers, they wore black with kromas around their necks, and the Khmer Rouge black or green cap. Most of their children had left to join the KR army. Some had returned and some had not.

I wondered what happened to the other families who used to live in the village.

Sahakor Seven had a dining hall, where they held the village meetings when the bell rang. The hall where we spent the first night had a blackboard and tables, and doubled as a classroom. Outside the hall and surrounding it were the original village houses, now occupied mostly by the KR. They were built on stilts, and livestock and oxen were kept underneath. There were no fences between. I liked this, and I liked the fact that there were fruit trees.

Behind the village were rice fields, separated by dykes. Beyond these were other communes, other fields and villages reaching all the way to Tonle Sap Lake. Some of the rows of paddy fields ran beside the road, which followed the Mong Russey River.

About a week after we had all settled down in Sahakor Seven, the first meeting for everyone was called, to be held at the nearby Wat Chrey temple. Khmer Rouge soldiers and administrators were waiting there as the families marched in and sat on the ground.

Shouts of 'Vive Angkar! Vive Angkar! Vive Angkar!' came from the front of the hall as the meeting began.

I looked up. The children in the first two rows were wearing black, and they were excited and attentive.

Several Khmer Rouge were standing at the front, facing everyone.

'Now we live under Angkar's rules,' they yelled, and the people at the front clapped.

'Angkar saves our lives from Americans and the American puppet government,' a man in the front row shouted. The applause grew louder.

I still wasn't sure what 'Angkar' meant. The word literally meant 'organisation' but listening to the applause and the cheering of the KR group, it sounded as if they were talking about a person, a powerful leader who was giving direct orders.

The clapping continued, faster.

'We will be united. Angkar will not let you die. Everyone will live equally.'

The first to clap were those at the front – the original villagers who had survived the takeover – but everyone else joined in. It was like a fever, a way of thinking that was contagious.

'We start from scratch,' one of the KR at the front announced. 'America has bombed and destroyed our crops and infrastructure, but in five years time we will have created a powerful community of rice producers under Angkar's guidance.'

The mood of the meeting was welcoming. Everyone was encouraged to learn to share and to follow the rules. The main rule was this: 'We now live as a group; one Sahakor, sharing food and eating meals together. No more individual kitchens. We share all food. When anyone finds food in the field or in their own garden, they must hand it to the kitchen to be cooked for all to share. This applies to everyone in Sahakor Seven. If anyone dares to disobey the rules by not sharing – then you will be classed as the enemy.'

From today, we were told, meals would be provided in the hall when the bell was rung. If people had anything to say about the food, about what they wanted to eat, they could bring their requests to the meetings and the group would decide.

That night I struggled to see the moon through the cover of the trees, but it was large and bright. I guessed another month had passed since I had gone looking for the palm fruit.

The next day, in stifling heat, Sahakor Seven was called to another meeting. As I waited for the meeting to begin, a man in black, riding on a bicycle, came directly to the hall. He walked in and everyone clapped their hands and shouted 'Vive Angkar! Vive Angkar!'

'In our managerial system,' the man said, 'we divide everything into three groups. The first group will consist of parents and couples, and children up to six years of age. Second will be the teenagers' group, those aged between fourteen and twenty-five who are not married. The third group will be for children between six and thirteen. Children will resume school as soon as possible, but the school will only be for children under thirteen or fourteen years of age.' I was still fourteen, so I knew I would be in the school group.

He went on: 'Listen to your names when we call them out, and those we don't call must register their name with our Samamit sitting at the table, the man in black,' he said, pointing to the table behind him. 'You will also be divided into groups of ten families, and each group will be headed by a leader who has lived here before. Now, everyone to work.'

Our family was grouped under the man who owned the house where we stayed. Father was pleased. He got along well with that man and thought it was a good omen.

When schooling began the next day, I was very excited. I went to look for a class without asking my younger brother and sister to come along. But it wasn't what I expected. The teachers were young women, really just older teenagers. One was tall, the other short. They wore the Khmer Rouge black uniform: a long-sleeved shirt and long skirt with a blue-black kroma. They were from another village but had been trained and indoctrinated to carry out their tasks and be Angkar's teachers. They didn't seem to know as much as me, but it didn't matter. What they were teaching was what they had learnt at camp, and it was all about Angkar's vision.

'Everyone must work for Angkar,' they said. 'Nobody is allowed to work at home.'

They explained about splitting into classes and how we were to address each other.

'You must address one another as "Samamit",' they said. 'Samamit' meant 'comrade'. The teacher said, 'When we speak to Mr Na or Miss Thoern, for example, from now on we call them "Samamit Na" or "Samamit Thoern". This will be the way we speak to everyone now.'

We were told that our system of government was now under Marxist rule like Russia or China. We all had to address each other in this manner. The teachers were not to be called Sir, Madam or teacher. They must also be called Samamit followed by their given name.

We were told Angkar would provide books and paper and pens and pencils – but later. For now we had to run home and collect what we could find. Some of the families had books and pens, so they sent them along for the children to share, but this didn't create a good feeling among the KR children. The family we stayed with were kind. They provided some pens and other resources for us.

On the second day, the teachers spoke about belonging.

'Today we'll explain how important it is to live under Angkar,' one of them said. 'Angkar saves us from America, eliminates capitalism, gives us a better life. Now, we ourselves are devoted to Angkar. Therefore, as your parents have been informed, we will share in unity. There will be no-one richer or poorer any more.'

This teacher looked around while the other teacher stood beside the chalkboard. The first teacher selected a girl from the front.

'What's your name?' she asked. 'How many brothers and sisters do you have? How many grandparents?'

The girl told the class about her parents and how many brothers and sisters she had.

The teacher listened, then she said, 'Let me draw a picture.'

I could tell she was sketching the answer because she could not write well. On the chalkboard, she drew a picture of the girl and her siblings going to school holding hands with their parents.

Then she asked all of us to pay close attention.

'Who are they?' the teacher asked as she pointed to the children. 'Who do they belong to?'

The children at the front, the village children in black Khmer Rouge clothes and kromas and shoes, anxiously raised their hands to answer.

'Who do they belong to?' the teacher repeated. She did not pick those at the front, although I heard them answer softly: 'Angkar!'

Then another child put his hand up. 'They belong to Mamma and Papa,' he answered.

The teacher turned and wrote Angkar at the top of the picture, and erased the hands in the diagram so that the parents were no longer holding their children's hands.

'Who do they belong to now?' she shouted.

'Angkar, Angkar,' a child in black at the front answered impatiently.

'Angkar, Angkar,' all the children at the front yelled.

'That's right! Now we're liberated,' the teacher continued. 'We all belong to Angkar.'

The village children led in clapping their hands quickly and enthusiastically. The teacher went on, 'We are all now the children of Angkar. Our parents' obligation is to give birth to us. But because they themselves also belong to Angkar, they work for Angkar and we belong to Angkar. Then everyone is belonging to Angkar and equal.'

The children in the front row started singing a revolutionary song, but we could not follow because it was new to us. The teacher said the song was called 'Love our Angkar and be faithful!' and that it must be sung every morning before class.

The parents' meetings were different. They were taught many rules. Their group leaders also taught them how to dye their clothes black. This had to be done within a month. The true black dye the Khmer Rouge used would be available later. Meanwhile the parents would have to use dye frequently, or our clothes would fade to grey.

On my third day at school, we were taught basic grammar. 'Today, we begin with the first letter of the alphabet – the letter Kor...'

The lesson was too elementary for me, as I had already been to high school in Phnom Penh. As well as being more advanced in my learning, I was much older than the other children. Although I was in the children's group, I was almost fourteen. I looked like a teenager and I was ready for the teenage group.

I didn't attend school for the next two days. I stayed home, where everything was very quiet, and sat with my sister Dasy, my brother Vivath and Step-grandmother. On the second day, the Khmer Rouge came by and saw me. They were big, dressed in black and brimming with authority.

'Why are you here?' one of them said.

'To drink water,' I answered.

'You better go back.'

I went back to school. I went back to class and learnt all over again that two and two equals four. I quickly lost interest. My teacher noticed I was bored and said she would take me to another group.

I didn't know there was another group. I left Sokha and Puthea in the class and followed her through the village, then into the rice fields, where she passed me across to a man.

She addressed the man. 'He should join your group,' she said.

I was nervous and I was sulking. I had no idea what to expect. The children's group was no good and I had no reason to think this would be better. But Father had taught me, as he had said to all of us, 'We don't know what they are capable of. We must keep our thoughts to ourselves.'

The man nodded. 'Oh! Another one,' he said. Dressed in black, he looked about seventeen. His name was Samamit Von and he didn't ask my name. The teenagers in the group chatted and laughed about their leader's stories of struggling in battle, of shooting and killing the American puppet soldiers. Later I heard more – he spoke very proudly and described himself as a great soldier, a hero. Although the village leader had placed him in charge of the boys who were assigned to work in the fields, I learnt that this man behaved like a boastful child.

He gathered us under a mango tree. 'Let's go to help our parents in the rice fields,' he said. 'Just pick up sticks and twigs, roots and other rubbish to clean the fields up and get them ready for replanting.'

We followed him on the paths that ran along the dykes between the rice fields. On the way, I saw village children herding cattle on the outskirts of the village. Some were riding the cattle and some were holding ropes and walking them, carrying their lunches with them in bags and singing the revolutionary song, expressing their gratitude to Angkar for saving them from hunger and poverty, and from American bombs.

There was so much to see. It was like being in another world, watching the boys with their cattle. This special scene impressed me. I'd always liked animals and I imagined how wonderful it would be if I could be one of them – a herd-boy riding the cattle and having lunch under a tree.

I was daydreaming about being a cattle boy when Samamit Von came and tapped me on the shoulder. He smiled and said, 'Keep up with your work.' Then he walked through the paddy field, splashing water and mud over his head as he went. There was a group of girls in the water, while his colleagues were sitting on the dyke eating something. He was going to say hello to them.

Suddenly, there was a loud scream from a teenage girl. 'What animal is this?' she yelled.

She raced from the water, trembling, and jumped onto a dyke

not far from me. She was scared and lifted up her skirt, screaming for help. There were two black leeches attached to her leg. The KR village people laughed. A man came to help her and tried to knock them off with a twig, but they stayed attached.

Samamit Von came over. He picked them off her leg, then he stamped on them. He smiled. 'This is just a leech,' he said. 'It sucks blood from humans but it is nothing. We have been working in this field for generations and we can still defeat them. Otherwise, how would we be able to defeat the Americans at war?'

The incident happened so fast. It looked funny when the girls realised there were leeches in the paddy fields and immediately became cautious. One of them left the water and went to the dyke, and the rest followed.

The teenage girl leaders came over to encourage the girls to get back and finish their work. They asked what they preferred – not to work in the fields and die of hunger, or to have food but be bitten by the leeches. Some of the leaders were younger than the girls in their groups, and several of them huddled together, whispering. They seemed to have doubts about the girls.

This was my first day at work. I spent the morning in the paddy fields, outside in the heat and far from the village. After the lunch break at the village hall, my group was instructed to help with cleaning the hall and stretching materials for making baskets. I was now called Samamit Ra, not Sovannora.

Days passed, and I continued to work in the fields. At night, I would go home to my family. It took only weeks for our new home to be built. Raised on stilts and made of bamboo, it was about one and a half metres high from the bamboo floor to the roof. It had a kitchen at the back, but there the roof was very low and we had to bend down. This area was only used for boiling water or heating food. After a month, when the temporary rules changed to permanent ones, nobody was allowed to cook at home because the food was held in common among all the inhabitants of Sahakor Seven. To cook our own food would mean not sharing: we would be the enemy.

So much was happening. It was all exciting. But soon I realised the village children who had been in the commune before the Khmer Rouge came were no longer attending classes. It also became apparent that as newcomers from the city, we were seen as outsiders with the status of servants. The village children prepared lunch and herded cattle. Some of the village parents tended to the oxen. Most of these parents and children wore black, and I wanted to be like them.

But some of the villagers were excited about meeting people from Phnom Penh. It gave them the opportunity to see and hear about things they had never experienced. They were always interested to see things such as a nice watch, a diamond ring or gold bracelet, silk clothes, or leather wallets and shoes. Many had only heard about these things and had never seen them in real life. Because of this, and because he was a good businessman, Father made many friends. Some of the Khmer Rouge villagers would come to him to request a specific item, and Father always managed to get it for them. We used these items as collateral in trading for palm sugar, rice and salt.

One day in July, Father asked me whether I wanted to look after cattle. He knew a man and his wife who had no children to look after their cow and bull. They were KR village people. I said yes immediately, without considering if I knew how to do it.

The next morning, I made lunch and went to fetch the cattle. The man who owned them said the cattle must be washed after herding, and I had to light a fire to keep the mosquitoes away. Untying the animals, I was excited. I wanted to hurry, to follow the other boys and their cattle as they walked along the dykes. I was looking forward to being out in the fields with the others, combining work with play, but I had no idea how to look after cattle.

As soon as I untied the ropes from where the man had fastened them, the cattle started dragging me off to the field. They just kept dragging me out of the village as though they knew their way, and once they reached the outskirts of the village, they walked straight onto the dyke.

I couldn't control them to make them walk in the middle of the dyke. One of them slipped down over the edge, breaking the dyke wall, then stumbled into a corner of the rice field.

I pulled and pulled but it just kept walking along the edge of the rice field while I stood on the dyke. Some people laughed, but others became angry when they saw how the rice plants were being damaged by my ox. Some insulted me, calling out, 'Ching Chong! Move your oxen out of the rice field immediately before we report you to the Samamit leader!' Most of the boys just kept riding on their cattle or leading them along. The boys were roaring with laughter.

'I don't know how to do this!' I screamed at the ox and the boys.

A boy who knew the owner of the oxen called out to me: 'Swap them. Put the male to the front and the female at the back.'

I didn't understand. Another boy jumped off his bull and handed me his rope.

'Here, let me help you!' he said.

He took the rope from me and pulled my ox back up on the dyke.

'Your white ox, the female, is very shy,' he said. 'She wants to follow, but you were keeping her in front. She kept turning around, looking for the bull. Put the brown one, the bull, at the front, and he will lead. Then you follow behind him with the female behind you. You have to put the bull's rope on his back. You flip the rope on his back to the left or to the right, then the bull will respond to your instructions.'

I thanked him for his help, and he told me his name was Thoeun. He was friendly, and we talked. He told me he was an orphan. His parents were killed during the war, and now he lived with his uncle, who was one of the village KR people.

After his lesson, my cattle walked better and responded to my pulling. I was happy again. I was successful. The next time they stopped to feed, I smiled as I stood in the sun. I smiled as I stroked the cattle and I felt good about myself, though right now all I could manage was to walk the oxen with one at the front and the other behind me. I didn't dare ride on my oxen like the other children.

About dusk, I took the cattle home proudly and tied them up where they belonged. The owner's wife came out and greeted me.

'Have you washed them?' she said. 'You must wash them.'

She said her husband was at the river, waiting to show me, so I untied the oxen and led them there.

'You collect grass to wash them with,' the man said. 'Roll it up like a sponge.' He showed me how. 'It must be a shallow part of the river. Here.'

I led the animals down into the water.

'You brush like this,' the man continued.

The washing went well, although I didn't know why it needed to be done every day, but the next day when I went back for the cattle the lady gave me some sugar palm to eat with my rice. The washing must have been important, I thought.

When I was walking the cattle, I didn't want to talk to the other boys. They kept teasing and laughing at me, often calling me 'Ching Chong'. But Thoeun, who helped me on my first day, asked me if I wanted to join him. Of course, I said yes.

I watched him riding one of his two oxen. 'How do you do that?' I asked.

'I'll show you.'

He took me to an abandoned village some distance away, further than I'd been before. I looked around and saw bullet holes and burnt-down houses. We stopped at a ladder beside the ruins.

'The cow won't allow you to ride her,' Thoeun explained. 'She's sensitive. But the bull will. Watch me.'

He showed me by getting onto the bull, then helping me to do the same. I stayed on while the bull ate grass.

Thoeun was kind. We continued to talk, but I didn't say too much in response to his questions. I asked him about the slingshot he used to kill birds and reptiles, though. He also showed me how to catch rats with a bamboo trap. The trap had a stick with a spring attached to a bait. When the rat touched the stick, it released the spring and snared the rat.

While we were talking, some of the other boys came over with their cattle. They all had animals to cook – frogs, fish, crabs, snails and a snake they'd caught. A fire was started, and they prepared their food.

One of the boys dressed in black didn't join in. 'Soon you won't be able to eat like this,' he warned. 'There will be new rules now our new boys' leader has arrived.'

I ate my lunch with them, but they did not share their food. Then I waited. I knew they all thought they were better than me. Most of them were from the old village families and many of them were dressed in black. I knew I wouldn't get along with them, so when they left, I stayed well behind them.

Then I saw a crab crawling along next to the dyke. It looked huge. I didn't know what to do, but I pulled to make the bull stop, knelt down, reached over and grabbed it.

It grabbed me.

'Ouch,' I squealed.

It held on and wouldn't let go, but I let go of the cattle ropes. I stood there dancing wildly as I shook my hand around. Then I realised what I had done: the cattle had wandered into the fields and were eating the rice.

'Oh no!' I raced after the cattle and the crab fell off. I sloshed among the growing rice, as there were no people in the fields. I pushed and pulled and finally led the animals back onto the dyke. 'Whoa!' I thought. I was lucky.

It was late afternoon when I arrived home, exhausted. I had led the oxen slowly, allowing them to eat too much. Then I watered them, but did not wash them with the grass-sponge.

The next morning, I took them out again. When I reached the dirt road, I was so anxious to ride on the back of my bull that I climbed up a termite hill to get on.

Finally I was a herd boy. I sat there thinking how nice it was riding on the bull when he suddenly dragged himself over to a hedge around the old pagoda. I shook the rope on his head to lead him away from the bushes, but he would not respond. He scraped himself against a row of thorny bushes. 'Ow. That hurt,' I screamed, but he continued to scrape against the bushes. He pressed harder and harder against the thorns. My leg was bleeding through my trousers. I began to panic and fell off, landing heavily on the ground.

The oxen ropes fell from my hands and the animals ran. I was very cross with the bull, and the bull knew it. He ran faster, with the cow following behind. He kept running and glancing back at me. Finally I caught the cow but not the bull. He just kept running off the dirt road toward another village until I was too tired to chase any more. I gave up. With the cow and my cuts and my bruises, I limped back home.

As I dragged the cow along, a KR soldier with an AK-47 came riding up on his bike, pulling my bull behind him. He asked me whether the bull was mine and complained that it had gone where it shouldn't and had been eating the rice in the fields. 'Be careful with your bull, because if it goes to the wrong place, like the military camp, it will be slaughtered,' he added.

As I continued toward home, some of the boys came up and teased me.

'Why are you laughing?' I asked quietly.

'The bull, and probably the cow too, haven't been washed properly,' they said. 'They had bugs on them. The animals were scraping against the brambles to get the bugs off.'

Hurt from falling off the bull and tired after chasing it, I did not bother to let the cattle graze. I tied them up at the owner's house, then fed them with some old hay and went to rest. Later, I took the oxen to the river for a wash, keeping my distance from the other boys.

I led the animals to the water and jumped on top of the bull. This would make it easier, I thought, until I dropped the other rope and the cow started swimming away. The water was deep, and the cow moved quickly. I jumped off the bull, swam as fast as I could and grabbed the cow's rope.

I couldn't stand, so I had to swim to shore, dragging both animals with me. But they liked to swim. As I swam, the bull, which was a much better swimmer than me, came up from behind. It came closer and closer. I tried to swim faster, but it reached me and I had nowhere to go but down. I was trapped between its legs, and its huge hooves kicked and squashed me.

Swallowing water, I swam for my life. I surfaced further down-stream, across the other side of the river, and collapsed. After I caught my breath I looked around. But where were my oxen? I couldn't see them. The light was dull because it was early evening and they could be anywhere.

After resting for a few minutes, I swam back across the river. Finally I found the cattle – back at the house. Their owner had tied them up for me because he thought I was coming close behind them. He did not know they had almost drowned me and then walked home by themselves.

In the junior boys' group, we spoke about our concerns and problems at meetings after dinner, from 7.30 till 10.30 every night. At the next meeting, I had bruises and scratches all over my body from being trampled in the river, and I found it hard to walk. One of the other teenagers spoke out about me.

'Samamit Ra is not able to look after the cattle,' he said. 'He doesn't know enough.'

The KR spoke among themselves. Later, they discussed the matter with the village leader and the owner of the cattle, and I was given another chance to prove myself.

I was relieved to not have to work in the fields with Samamit Von. He was always bullying and teasing, mocking my family and accusing us of being rich.

A month later, someone reported a boy for cooking and eating food he had found.

'This is illegal. You should be sharing,' the leader said. 'You don't want to be seen as the enemy.'

The boy was reprimanded and sent to other duties. It could have been worse.

Anti-American and anti-Republic talk dominated our meetings. There was much clapping and learning about the Khmer Rouge way of life.

'You now live under Angkar rule,' we were told. 'Angkar will guide you and teach you. You must obey Angkar's rules.'

We didn't talk much, because we didn't have much time. The system kept us busy from when we rose at five o'clock until long after it became dark at six. There was no time for mixing with other families. Among ourselves, my family kept talking about our house in Phnom Penh, and the younger children asked when we would be returning home. There was sadness and uncertainty, but Father always looked fit and strong and in control.

Stepmother had known much hardship before she met Father. She had been raised along a river and was familiar with cleaning rice and smashing the husks, tasks which others found difficult. The Khmer Rouge saw that she knew what to do. People without farming backgrounds were considered to be pro-capitalist, pro-American and dangerous. With Stepmother's help, Father quickly transformed himself into a farmer. We all did.

I was walking through the village one morning and looked in on the children's class. There was no-one there. There was no more school. The children were now assisting their parents in the paddy fields. Everything took second place to growing rice – just rice. But supplies were running short, and only four spoonfuls of cooked rice were allocated to each person per meal.

It was now September, and we had been living on three or four spoons of rice for over a month, with almost nothing else to eat. There was no more breakfast. People continued to work in the rice fields in the morning, and in the evening we worked in the village on tasks such as making buckets or hoe handles from bamboo. We were still forbidden to find food and take it home to cook. If we were found out, we would be considered enemies of Angkar.

But this rule didn't seem to apply to the original people of the village. Some of the new arrivals started to criticise the management of Angkar quietly in their own homes. It was unfair that they could only eat communal meals, they said, when they could see most of the KR village people cooking in their homes at night.

The village people were allowed to do that, because most of

them had given over their own food and resources before the Khmer Rouge started the new system. Still, we knew that all of us must live under Angkar's rule now, and no-one was allowed to cook and eat separately from the hall. But the village people still ate quietly in their homes and treated us like servants.

We newcomers did not dare raise this issue in the meetings. We knew it would only mean the same instructions would be repeated: 'Living equally means we must all bring our goods to store in the sahakor's storeroom at the hall kitchen.' And we knew that the women from the village were in charge of the kitchen. They saved most of the food for their own people and took it home at night.

Father told us that there was one man who wouldn't accept the unfairness and raised his concern at the meeting. Someone said the man had been a lawyer during the Lon Nol regime. A couple of days later, he was escorted from the village by a KR spy, who told him that Angkar had assigned him to a special mission in the city. Later, his dead body was discovered among the large bamboo bushes.

Father had heard he was executed by a boy leader, but he did not believe that rumour. Father knew that boy leader's family, and his parents were very kind and helpful. As a matter of fact, Father had obtained most of our food from that boy's parents.

Father continued to exchange his valuable things with other village people so he could get food for the family. He sold his Omega watch, once worth US$300, for ten cans of sticky rice. The food he got was for my younger brothers and sisters, because my older brothers and sister were with me in the teenage group at our own camp, but when Father got something to eat, he sent us a secret message through my younger brother or sister.

I became hungrier and hungrier. One day when I was out with the oxen, I caught a fish and a crab and swallowed them raw while were still moving.

At a group meeting soon after this, the leader made an announcement. No-one knew how, but he'd discovered that one of the boys had caught an eel, made a fire, cooked it and eaten it himself. The boy was told he could no longer look after cattle. He was tortured and put in a cage for three days without food. Upon his release he was skinny, pale and almost dead.

I knew I wasn't allowed to cook, but from time to time I caught crabs, snails or small fish. Sometimes I would eat them, raw of course. If any were left over, I would throw them away before returning to the village. I didn't know how to make a fire but found the uncooked animals quite acceptable. Shrimp was very nice. So were the fish. Crabs were OK but their skins were a bit too hard to chew. One day I caught a gecko and managed to find the burning embers of someone else's fire to cook it with.

The appointed chefs, mainly women, were thought to be very fortunate. Animals found in the rice fields were always given to the chefs, and never seen in the meals that were served to us. When questioned, they would say, 'It's already in the soup. It's been chopped into very small pieces.' The new arrivals didn't believe this. It was now early October, and everyone was getting hungrier.

The hunger became worse and worse each day, even for us. Though Father tried his best to continue supplying food, nothing he did helped much. And anything we got to eat from Father we had to eat in the dark like thieves, making no noise even when we were chewing the food in our mouths. The amount of food was also very small. If I dropped a grain of rice down on the floor, I would pick it up and eat it. The big wok in the kitchen where they cooked the rice was polished smooth without us having to clean it, as every grain of rice would be picked up to eat.

One evening when I took the cattle back to the house, the owner called out to me, 'You are back! Good! Tie them to the tree. I will make their fire, because last night the fire went out in the middle of the night and the cattle were unsettled. You probably did not make the fire properly. Did you use the dried oxen manure, not the wet one? And the dry hay? That will make a good smoke for the oxen to keep the mosquitoes away.'

I told him I did, but I knew I didn't. I hadn't been able to focus on my work because of my hunger, and right now I was thinking about how I was going to cook a gecko I had caught. The man told me to go home, but I said I wanted to help. 'I want to watch you and learn more from you,' I said.

He nodded and asked me to get the dry hay, then he left the fire to have his meal. I went under the house – high on stilts – to fetch the hay. When I looked up through the cracks in the floor, the inside of the house was dark. His wife had lit a candle made from tree resin, and I could hear them eating quietly. I stayed there a while, hoping his wife would call me to join them. I waited, but no-one called.

The fire was burning freshly and I could tolerate my hunger no longer, so I went back over to the fire and put my gecko in. But the fire had not produced any hot embers yet. The gecko was just burning with the hay's smoke, and sometimes it caught in the fire.

Suddenly I heard the man shout from the house, 'What is that smell? Something is burning, Samamit Ra!'

I replied, 'I can't smell anything, except the cow's tail has just touched the fire. I've moved her now and tied her a bit further away.'

'OK, that is a good idea, because the cow doesn't like the flames.'

Soon I heard his wife packing up the dishes. I felt so relieved. 'Pou! I am going home now,' I shouted.

I could think of nothing else but what I was going to do with my gecko. I could not think or wait any more. I took it out and started to eat: sometimes it smelt and tasted of smoke, and some parts were totally raw, but I craved food so much that I didn't care. I just kept on chewing and swallowing.

Everything was becoming tougher in the village. Leaders demanded that everyone work hard all day, and some of us even had to work at night. But the food supply was limited, and we became hungrier each day.

Each family had someone who rummaged for food. Around the village, we were still able to find lizards, small frogs, grasshoppers and some fruits and vegetables and leaves, and even chilli. People also picked and ate water lilies, which grew in the wild as well as around our homes. We ate them because there wasn't enough food: we were always hungry, whether we were in the children's camp, the teenagers' camp, the women's camp or anywhere. Everyone searched for food, even though we had been told not to and warned not to eat it ourselves. If we ever got caught not sharing what we'd found, the consequences were torture, sometimes death.

The leaders were given more land to manage now. The monsoon rains had come, and people had to walk further to reach the rice fields. The new fields had to be prepared. The soil, already partially submerged in water, had to be levelled, and cow mulch added as fertiliser. Rice with husks was thrown into these fields. A month later, it would be thirty centimetres or a foot high, growing in clumps. This rice would then be pulled out and replanted.

I appreciated the freedom I had with the cattle. I had to eat some animals raw, but now I was used to this. I was careful. I knew the danger but felt I was somehow invincible.

One day I wanted to take my animals and explore the west side of Sahakor Seven, so I crossed the river with the cattle. I knew nothing about the other side. All I had seen across the river was trees and bushes, but I'd heard the noises of children at play. I imagined they had been told my side was for the newcomers from the cities.

The swim across was not easy, at least not for the oxen. I rode on the bull again. His head was just out the water and the current was very fast, but we made it. Once on the other side, I pushed my way up the slope and led the cattle along a dirt road. There was a lot of green grass along the road, and the oxen enjoyed themselves. I wanted to search for food. I looked up and saw guava fruit, and nearby I found a barn with a pile of hay.

I tied the cattle near the hay so I could have time to find something to eat. I was scared but excited. This was an opportunity for me to eat as much I could. I searched carefully around the area; perhaps I would find a fruit tree or a lizard. There was corn growing and I gathered some cobs, but then I realised I had no way to carry them back, so I hid some under the hay. I found fresh coconuts on the ground in their green shells; I gathered these and ate them all. After that, I fell asleep on the hay. When I woke, it was time to take my oxen back home. The return trip went smoothly.

The next day I returned to the same place. I picked more corn and used my kroma to wrap up the cobs and tie them around my waist, then I covered my waist with my shirt. Later, as afternoon came, I walked near a village. I found a guava tree with some ripe fruit. I climbed up to get them, but then two small boys came walking toward the tree. They looked about eight and ten years old. I remained quiet, and initially they did not see me.

Then I was spotted and one of them called, 'Hey, Samamit, what are you doing?'

The other boy turned and shouted. I climbed down, without the fruit.

Three other children ran up. One of them, a boy about thirteen, was shouting to the others to bring guns.

'They are his oxen,' one boy yelled.

'Let's get them and take them to our leader,' another screamed.

They chased me as I ran. I hurried to my oxen, quickly untied them and pulled them out from the barn, but the children caught up and grabbed the ropes from my hands. The boys were all over me. 'We must arrest this man,' they shouted. 'His cow is eating our hay.'

Nervous and scared, I couldn't think. I had to escape, so I punched the oldest boy hard with my right hand, knocking him to the ground. The others screamed and moved away. I grabbed the oxen, went into the river and crossed back to the other side. I took the oxen home immediately and tied them up. I heard the owner's wife call goodnight. Then I ran to the dining hall, where the parents had just finished, and hid under one of the tables.

About seven o'clock, two large black-clothed men rode up on motorbikes and came to see the village leader. The leader's house was not far from the hall, and I could hear the conversation.

'A boy has been hurt,' I heard the men say. 'We need to teach the offender a lesson.'

I was shaking under the table. I heard them start looking for the oxen. Luckily it was dark and they could not see the cattle clearly. The village leader said he would help them to find the boy who hurt the boy in their village. After further conversation with the village leader, the men went away.

I stayed under the table and fell asleep. Then I heard the bell ring for an emergency meeting.

I went straight to the meeting and sat behind some of the other boys.

The group leader spoke. 'Which boy went across the river, let their cow eat our Samamit army's hay, and hurt their little boy? It is a serious offence for us to hurt our respected cadre. If I find out who did this, that person will be sent to our Samamit's army for punishment.'

They never found out it was me.

A few days later, the owner of my cattle reported to the group leader that he wasn't happy: I wasn't looking after the cattle properly. He said he would take care of the oxen himself now that all the rice fields had been ploughed.

I was fourteen and a good size for my age, so I was sent to join the teenage group. The teenagers no longer lived with their parents but had a camp of their own, directly behind the dining hall, near the rice fields. I packed my things, and Step-grandmother gave me a hammock before I left.

Now I had to understand the adult system. I felt sad and nervous. Something didn't feel right about this move. I had been hoping to avoid joining the teenagers, and it seemed unfair that I was the youngest. There were about forty-five children in the group including my brother Chandy and my sister Sophea, but she was in the girl's camp, not far from ours.

I was pleased to be with Chandy, but I did not see my oldest brother, Sivanchan. Chandy told me that Sivanchan was in the elite group camping past the rice fields. His group started earlier in the day than we did and worked harder. We met him the next morning in the fields. Both my brothers looked skinnier, and they didn't talk much to me.

I was placed in Sub-Group Number Three, which consisted of one leader, two deputies and ten teenagers. The groups operated like military units. Sub-Group Three rose at five every morning. There was no breakfast. Several minutes later, we would hear a whistle and line up, then march into the fields to start working when the sun rose at 5.30. The teenage girls followed closely behind. Each morning, we would hear a bell, then see the women walking along the dyke, always in a straight line, followed by the men. But the teenage boys were always first into the fields.

We worked very hard for our leader, an arrogant, lazy young man who was mostly concerned with showing off his clothes and seducing the Khmer Rouge girls. At 11 a.m., we would come back to camp for a lunch that was supplied for us, then we would return to the fields to work again from one until five.

In the twilight, we would line up again to march back to camp behind our leader. Muddy from climbing back up onto the dykes from the fields, we would wash and prepare for dinner. Dinner was followed by a three-hour evening meeting, beginning at seven. This was followed by guard duty throughout the night, if it was our turn. The disciplined lifestyle was very different from what I had been used to.

There was no time for thoughts of parents or families any more. I would only see mine for five minutes every other evening or wave to them as I passed them in the fields. There wasn't time to think. I felt settled enough, but my only concern was staying alive.

Chapter 5
Spy Boys

ONE EVENING, AFTER several days with the teenage boys, I went out to speak with Father so he would know where I was. When I returned, another boy approached me.

'I'm Thon,' he said. He pushed me firmly on the shoulder, his way of showing friendship. 'I saw you go out,' he continued. 'Don't you know the rules?'

I had been wary of Thon because he seemed to think he was smarter then me, but now we hit it off. I told him about my family and what my father had done in Phnom Penh. We tied our hammocks next to each other, and over the next few weeks we worked together, keen and proud, always finishing our tasks quickly.

Almost two weeks passed, then one morning when it was time to go to the fields, Thon and I were approached by the leader of the teenagers and another man we didn't know. I wondered what I had done. Had they discovered that I had taken cattle across the river and punched the boy?

'Sit down,' the leader said. 'No rice fields today, Samamit Ra and Samamit Thon. Angkar wants you to become Chlopp Phom.'

'Chlopp?' I hadn't heard the word used that way.

He explained that it meant I'd be a spy. 'We have six boys spying for our village, but we need two more. We want to promote you. We have been watching you boys work willingly and proactively for Angkar.'

We followed the leaders to meet with the other spy boys. They were aged between twelve and fourteen, all Khmer Rouge dressed in black. Now I was in the Boys' Special Unit, it would be no more rice fields for me. Soon I too would be wearing black.

I was assigned to work with a boy named Samamit Tha. Not much happened at first – just instructions about how to spy on newcomers, especially my own people. I told my parents I was spying and warned them that they would be spied on as well, as spy boys' families were kept under close surveillance. Father was not happy to hear what I would be doing, but I knew he had no right to stop me – we were all the children of Angkar now. He just warned me to be careful and not to report exactly what I heard.

During my third day with the spy boys, I was told to rest well into the afternoon. Our leader, Von, called us up in the evening.

'Crawl under every newcomer's house, especially the houses with lights on,' he said. 'Listen to what they complain about. Make sure you don't let them know you're there, but listen.'

Samamit Tha was unwell that night, so I had to go out alone. The houses were all on stilts about a metre and a half from the ground. I crawled from one house to another all night, just listening.

Around dawn, I went to Samamit Tha's house to check up on him, hoping he would be able to join me. I saw him eating with his family, and he looked OK.

'Hi, Samamit Tha,' I called. 'How are you getting on?'

He was surprised. His father called back, 'Tha is still not well. He will be away from work for a while. He still has malaria.'

I came back a little later and hid under their house. I heard his mother say she did not want him to sneak under people's houses. She preferred him to work in the fields or help his parents in the village.

His father wasn't so sure. 'There are many new arrivals who still favour the Americans. We need to remove these enemies. But … perhaps Tha is still too young to do this work.'

I realised that this spying work would be different from anything I had done before. Some people might not understand Angkar, I reasoned, and this should be brought to the attention of the village leaders so they could be sorted out. I knew that. It was my responsibility to be a servant of Angkar, and I knew I would do my work well. Still, I wondered about the people who were starving or struggling to get enough food. Some were my neighbours and even cousins, who had been sent to the commune at the same time as my family.

I stayed awake until about 8.30 p.m., when people were going to the evening meeting. Then I returned to my unit and rested in my hammock, realising it was the first time in a long, long while that I'd had the opportunity to do nothing. As I drifted to sleep I thought. I thought about my relatives and my classmates. And I thought about Tevy. I wanted to see her again, and the hope of this gave me strength to fight hard to stay alive.

'Samamit Ra! Are you in here?'

'Baat!' I replied. 'Yes!'

It was so dark that I could not see who was calling me, and I was confused, because I had fallen asleep.

'Why are you still here?' Samamit Den and Samamit Khom, two of the village boys, had come back from the meeting. They criticised and teased me.

I was back at work around midnight, sitting under a house. The floor of the house was made of bamboo, the walls of clay and hay. Voices carried easily through these materials, and I was amazed at what I could hear. I moved on to other houses, hearing many conversations and learning which families did the most talking. Most families talked a lot after they returned home from meetings; others didn't talk much at all. Some families whispered, and I thought they must have known I was there.

Reporting back after each night spying, I heard what the other boys had to say.

'This household is suspicious,' one boy said. 'They talk a lot and they whisper. They talk about what they think and they are not happy. They don't like village life and complain about wanting their life to return to what it used to be.'

The boys became excited as they spoke about what they'd heard. They seemed to know which families were doing the wrong thing and speaking dangerous words. They named families that didn't like Angkar, and families that had secrets. Von listened carefully. I hadn't known that a household was suspicious just because they whispered. I reported to Samamit Von that I heard many people complain about how America was weak and not able to save them from the war.

As a chlopp, I was enthusiastic and happy and had no reason to question anything I was told. Being a chlopp meant being well fed and supplied with extra shoes, a torch and a hammock; we were looked up to by the other boys and given more freedom. While the other teenage boys worked in the fields all day or walked their cattle, we rested, and no-one gave us any trouble.

But I was wary of the proud, unfriendly boys in the Boys' Special Unit. They teased me and never spoke directly to me. As time passed, I noticed that many of the KR boys would patrol for a while, then sneak off and sleep. Samamit Thon and I continued to perform our duties as requested, but we never met. Our areas for spying were well apart.

In my spying, I heard many complaints about insufficient food and poor health. In some houses I could hear children crying, even dying from having not enough food; or sobbing mothers trying to persuade children to wait until morning to eat. One mother was telling her children that Father had disappeared and wouldn't be back because he had disobeyed Angkar: he caught crabs, shrimps and snails in the fields, and the KR accused him of bringing them home for his family to eat. The mother begged her children to be quiet and to try to sleep, but the children whispered back to her that they could not sleep because their hunger was too great.

Some families were wondering when the promised food supplies would arrive. I knew the food had come, but the KR did not share it with the newcomers. In other houses, brothers and sisters and parents fought each other for food. Some found food in the fields and did not share with their own families. Others threatened to report another family member to the KR village leader. I could sense that trust had gradually been broken, all because of hunger, and I reported everything I heard. One night, I went out alone as usual. One house I visited, which was about a metre above the ground and located further away from the others, was the home of a woman whose husband had died two months earlier. I sat, because there wasn't enough room to stand under her house. Then I heard a sound like a splash. There was a horrible smell, and it grew worse as I sat there.

I crawled across and my hand reached into mud, but it wasn't just mud. I pulled my hand up toward my nose and stifled a yell. I wondered if they'd heard me. My hand smelt so bad it was as if they must have dumped their sewage there. I heard drops of something falling to the ground nearby. My hair became wet, and I felt something trickle down my neck. They knew I was there, they must! I listened. There was movement above, shuffling. Were they trying to pour it through the holes in the floor, trying to pour it onto me? I slipped as I tried to get away. I was covered with all kinds of putrid-smelling stuff. I crawled out and made my way to the river. I washed again and again, wringing the water out of my clothes to get rid of the smell before I went back to my unit and to bed.

I awoke late the next morning with a bad headache.

'Get up,' Samamit Tha said.

'I can't. I'm sick. And my stomach is aching.'

He reached across and felt my forehead. 'You're burning.'

'I'm not, I'm just sick.'

Then I had to get out of bed because I had diarrhoea too. After I returned and lay down again, Von came back to the camp.

'Your clothes,' he grumbled. 'They smell!'

He held my wet shirt on a stick. I had left it nearby after trying to clean it the night before.

He leaned across. 'You smell too,' he said.

I had to rest that day. I was fed well, but I was very weak. Then my condition worsened. I became dizzy and lost my appetite. I had a troubled night's sleep while the others did their spying, and when I woke I couldn't eat.

There was no sanitation. We just went into the fields, behind any bush, behind any tree. On the second day I was ill, my leg started to swell. I used my fingers and pressed them into my skin. They went in deep, but when I released the pressure, the skin didn't bounce back. I washed my face and looked in a mirror. It was pale and swollen.

There was no-one at the camp to look after me, so I lay down and closed my eyes. Late in the afternoon, I heard footsteps. There was a tap on my shoulder. I struggled to open my eyes. When I did, I saw Samamit Von sitting beside me. He was thinking.

'We no longer require your service,' he finally said.

'What?'

'Not for now. We will send you to the clinic.'

He got up and walked off. I closed my eyes again. Some time later, two of the boys came and put me onto a stretcher and carried me to the clinic.

The clinic was a room with a wooden table and a wooden bed, but no mattress or pillow. It was occupied by a chubby, tall young Khmer Rouge woman. She couldn't have been more than twenty.

'Let me have a look,' she said, but she couldn't tell what disease I had and sent me back to camp.

As I lay there day after day, I continued to lose weight and strength, and I realised my parents probably didn't even know where I was. The nurse visited, but there was nothing she could do. She didn't check my pulse, and she didn't even have a thermometer. The only medicines she had were herbal remedies made from bark and plants.

Chandy was in the same camp, and he eventually told Father what was happening. When Chandy was on his way back, a leader caught him and rebuked him for leaving the camp.

Father didn't come to see me. I knew he couldn't. I no longer belonged to him. My life was now in Angkar's care and I was the responsibility of my group leader.

Chandy helped me and tried to feed me whenever he could, but soon I could not hear, see or feel. I felt alone, as if nothing was around me. I felt I was leaving this world peacefully ... and yet hopefully, for images came. My mind dragged me to fond memories. I saw myself at Santhomok Primary School. Again I thought of Tevy, the girl I was so fond of. My strong feelings for her had once made energy and joy flow through my veins.

In the jumble of memories, my mind flashed to when we first spoke. It was in Grade Six. We all attended extra tuition near the market behind my house. One day, when I had missed a few classes because I was feeling unwell, I was walking through the market. There was Tevy with her friends on a break from tuition. I was infatuated and crazy in love but too scared to approach her. Then I turned a corner and we connected. We hit. We stared at each other. I couldn't speak, but she smiled.

'Why don't you go to class any more?' she asked.

My stomach churned. I began to shake, joy and nervousness jostling inside me.

'I ... I haven't been well for a few days now,' I mumbled, turning my eyes away. 'I caught a bad cough.'

'Oh no! But are you getting better now?' she asked quickly and confidently.

I just smiled and walked on. I must have seemed so rude. I was happy, for Tevy had noticed me, but I never forgave myself for not speaking more with her.

It was pleasant to think of these things while my body was numb and weak. Then I thought of the mother I had lost. I thought of Father and Step-grandmother and my brothers and sisters. I hadn't thought of any of them while I was sick until now.

A while later, I woke from my trance and looked up into the sky. Everything was dark, even though it was morning. Focusing on my body, I saw my legs and hands were swollen. 'It is a lack of nutrition,' I heard someone say.

I passed out again. Later, I tried to leave my hammock to relieve myself, but I tripped and fell. It was a painful fall, and I hit the floor like a plastic bag filled with water. I felt too weak to stand, but managed to pull myself up and lean on something. With a stick, I made my way from the camp to the field for a pee. It took me thirty minutes to hobble ten metres from the tent, and the return trip was longer.

I collapsed on my hammock and wondered about death. I decided I wasn't ready for it. I didn't know what it was or what it would mean. Suddenly I was thinking of my mother again. A smile crept over my face. I wondered what she was doing now, and I thanked her for the love that she had given us when she was alive.

These thoughts nourished me. Tears rolled down my cheeks, and I found myself crying with gratitude for her hard work and dedicated commitment to her seven children. She never said she was tired or complained about all the trouble we gave her.

Her memory taught me that to live is to have hope, as she lived and had hope for her children.

The next morning I awoke to noise and excitement. Samamit Von, my group leader, was screaming and ordering the boys about. Some he told to go and get the pork from the dining hall, others he assigned to work in the fields.

I sat up on my hammock, and he glanced across. I looked away, up at the sky. I thought it was probably a bright day, but I wasn't sure. In my head there was mostly darkness.

I collapsed back down. Samamit Von took a step closer, looked at me and mocked me. 'Bad luck today. There is good food.'

I saw Samamit Von's mouth still moving but heard nothing more. I knew I wouldn't be getting any food. Why would they waste it on me when I wasn't working?

I blacked out. I woke hours later to the smell of more cooking: it was supper now. I could tell the time by the meals as I lay there, day after day. All I ate when it was my group's turn was a small portion of porridge.

The days passed and I woke less often. Each day I would pass out, and my body felt weaker and weaker. My feet, my hands, my face and my whole body were swollen and I didn't feel hungry at all. I felt as if I was dying, and from time to time I would think about death. What would it feel like to die? And what would happen next?

Two days later, I could not move at all. I screamed very loudly for help. No-one heard me, but I kept on calling. My chest tightened. It seemed I couldn't breathe, and my head felt dark and heavy. I blacked out, and I think my heart stopped beating. I felt I had gone – at peace now – without saying a word to anyone.

I saw myself somewhere else. Like in a dream, but different, I saw myself running from my friends into a wooden house on stilts, surrounded by an open terrace. I had a feeling it was a house belonging to my family. The floor was made of pine planks next to each other, with small gaps between. I could smell the coconut oil that the floor was polished with. As I ran onto the floor it was slippery and shiny, reflecting the sunset outside. I tripped over at the far side of the house, leading out to the balcony, and knelt there with my hands outstretched on the wooden panels. Looking up to the sky, I took a deep breath and realised how beautiful it was. Some birds flew away, and I felt great, but when I rose from the floor, I immediately felt hungry.

Looking behind, I saw my grandmother, Father's mother. She was rocking gently on a chair, looking down and knitting. Next to her was a table with a plate of Cambodian biscuits. As I leaned over with my hand outstretched to take a biscuit, someone tapped me on the back. I turned around and saw Mother.

Grandmother and Mother were both dead. I was only eight when Grandmother died in 1968, two years after Mother. But here they were. Mother said only two words – 'Not ready.'

The moment she spoke, I was back in the real world. I was being carried, staring out through slits in whatever it was I was being carried in. 'Thump.' I was dropped onto the ground and I could smell freshly dug soil, but there was no feeling in my body, no pain.

Opening my eyes more fully, I saw I was wrapped up. But where was I? Was it a hammock? I *was* in a hammock – my hammock. It was tied up with a bamboo rod attached at both ends.

I was about to be buried. All I could do was close my eyes again. Was I really that sick?

Then the hammock opened.

Through slanted eyes I glanced across and saw the nurse. She had opened the hammock and was placing my belongings there with me. I strained. I tried to move but I was wrapped tight. I tried to speak but I couldn't even groan. I opened my eyes a little further. I must have moved my eyebrows, the furrows on my forehead.

She fell back with her mouth wide open. I wriggled and managed to move some more.

'He is still alive!' she screamed. 'He is still alive!'

The boys opened the hammock wider and stared at me.

'Are you all right?' Beside them was a hole – my grave.

I managed to sit up.

'This is not possible!' one of the boys said.

The three of them laughed and spoke about how incredible it was. They discussed how it couldn't be that I returned from the dead. They had checked my pulse and my breathing, and I was gone. That was at lunchtime. Now six hours had passed and it was dusk.

'Were you dead or pretending?' one of the boys asked me.

'You checked him first,' another said. 'You lifted up his hands and they dropped down and you said that confirmed he was dead. I said to do a double check.'

'Anyway, we thought you were dead,' the first boy said.

I couldn't muster the energy to respond. But I was not happy to realise I was back in the same world. Just a moment ago, I had seen my mother and my grandmother. And now? Was there a biscuit in my right hand, or was I dreaming?

I did not want to move, did not want to be back in this world, but I checked my hand, then lay down again, still inside my hammock near my grave. Then I thought of my mother saying 'Not ready!' and kept it in my heart that she wanted me to live on.

'Now, what are we going to do with him since he's alive?' one boy said.

The KR boys looked agitated. 'Mealtime has already started,' another replied. 'We must go back.'

'Go,' said the nurse. 'I'll look after him.'

The boys went and she leaned over.

The setting sun made her kind face shine. I looked at her and smiled, and tears ran down my cheeks.

'Can you get up and walk with me back to the camp?' She grabbed my arms to help me up.

I didn't know what to say, but I was feeling famished and thinking of the biscuit I had seen in my vision. I wondered if I was still in a dream, but I tried hard to focus. I knew I had to stand up. I concentrated. I lost the feeling of hunger, then the biscuit and Mother faded from my mind.

I stood. The nurse helped me back to camp and gave me some of her food before leaving to speak with her superiors. I ate everything she gave me, and when I finished I felt alive again.

At that moment, the nurse returned.

'You must leave,' she said.

Her sudden announcement surprised me.

'You are too sick. You will not survive here. No medicine I have can cure you, and no-one will waste food on you. You must go somewhere else and find help, or you will die.'

She told me she was sending me to Mong Russey Hospital, which was located at the pagoda in the town of Mong Russey. I didn't have much choice but to go. Finally I said, 'OK, tomorrow morning I will leave.'

The nurse said, 'Rest well before the others return. You will need energy for tomorrow. I will not be able to accompany you, but I will give you a letter.'

I slept until morning without noticing the others return. I rose early and dragged myself to my father's house. He was sitting on the front steps, about to roll a cigarette. He didn't know I'd been so sick. He didn't know I had passed out and been given up for dead.

'Uh! You look so skinny,' he said.

'I came to tell you that I'm being sent to Mong Russey Hospital this morning.'

Father pulled out some leaves, put tobacco in them and rolled a cigarette. Then he started to smoke.

'Good luck,' he said. 'You take care, because I can't help you.'

I saw grief in his eyes and it looked as if he was about to cry, but he said nothing more. He couldn't open up and say anything that would jeopardise his family and his life.

Chapter 6
The Shrine

IN THE HALL, the teenagers lined up ready for work. The group leader as always went around, checking everyone.

When he came to me, he said, 'All right, you are assigned to go for treatment at the district hospital. You'd better get yourself ready. It is a long walk, and we have no-one to go with you. Here, let me see your letter from the nurse.'

He soured his face as he glanced briefly at the letter, then handed it back, took his gear and marched off to the rice fields. Though very weak, I felt a lightness as I packed my things. I felt no less sick, but somehow I could go on, as if I was now tapping into some special store of strength.

I grabbed my possessions and a bamboo stick, then walked slowly along the dyke, where I used to carry hundreds of bundles of rice plants. I had a kroma wrapped around my head to protect me from the sun. A pack sat awkwardly on my back.

I walked slowly toward the horizon. Everything was green. I could hear distant noises and songs coming from where the women and boys were pulling and replanting the rice. I focused on my walk. I didn't want to fall, and I kept looking straight ahead.

The district hospital was supposed to be near the river, but the river meandered, so I took a shortcut. I could feel the energy pulsing through my body from the excitement of leaving the village, but I knew I was still extremely weak. The shorter my walk, the better it would be for me.

Walking soon became very, very difficult. I walked for about five hours along dykes beside the quiet paddy fields, where I saw team after team of workers. Finally, just before midday, I reached the edge of Mong Russey District Town. I calculated the distance I had come. It was only about five kilometres, but it had taken me more than an hour to walk each one.

The district hospital was located in a pagoda known as Wat Mong Russey, which was surrounded by trees. I approached slowly, gazing at all the people dressed in black with scarves around their necks. Most were wearing caps. Some were wheeling bikes out and others were wheeling bikes in. At the gate, two soldiers stood guard. Through the entrance, I saw more trees and many shrines. There were so many people, mostly in black, and everyone seemed busy. It was hot now, and as I came through the gates, I saw many sick people, including children, sitting on the terrace of the pagoda or under trees or in the shade of the shrines.

Soldiers were everywhere carrying AK-47s, but there were no monks. It shocked me to think they had been expelled from such a sacred place. I remembered what the Khmer Rouge leaders had taught us in the village. 'You are no longer required to have a religion. Angkar is all you need.' I became nervous. I felt too weak to think and I didn't know what to do. Was there really a hospital here?

I kept gazing around. Many houses sat near the hall of the pagoda – wooden houses on stilts with brick veneer roofs. Around the hall was a large outdoor area, very flat and smooth; no grass, just dirt. Out of this dirt grew the trees that provided shadows and shade, and there were more palm trees situated along the fence.

I saw the back entrance. Many people were entering here too. Most were dragging the sick behind them on stretchers. I stood and watched. I couldn't think clearly and I was very hot.

'What is your problem?'

It was one of the soldiers, carrying an AK-47. I walked up to him and handed him the letter. I was tired and thirsty and didn't say anything. All the time I'd been walking from the village, I'd only drunk a little water from the rice fields.

The soldier glanced at the note, then across to one of his comrades before turning back to me.

'All right,' he said. He pointed to where I should go, but he didn't tell me where to stay or where I should put my things. I felt lost. This was a big place with more people than I had seen in a long time.

I walked to where he pointed. It was a dining hall raised about a metre above the ground, with two staircases leading to the veranda. As I approached, I could see a number of sick people in the open room at the top of the stairs, some lying in hammocks and some on the floor.

These patients just stayed where they lay or sat. They were completely helpless, and no-one was assisting them.

There were not many steps, but the sun was getting hotter, and suddenly I felt so exhausted that I could not climb the steps. I sat down, then crawled on my hands and knees to pull myself to the top.

'Samamit Ra?' I turned around on the veranda of the old dining hall, the hot sun now in my eyes. 'Samamit Ra, is that you?'

It was a soft voice, but I recognised it immediately: lying in a hammock was Samamit Kosal from the teenage camp back at Sahakor Seven. He had come to our camp from another village and left again soon after. Like me, he was from the city, and I was happy to see him.

'How long have you been here?' I asked.

'A month, nearly a month. No medicine at my village,' he replied. 'Had to come here. They give us medicine once in a while, but I'm not getting any better.'

'What do we do here?' I asked.

'Basically ... almost nothing. Sometimes you get food and —'

'But what about medicine?' I knew I needed medicine to get better.

'There is no real medicine. Only the same stuff we got in the village, made from the trees and the plants. I've heard they have requested good medicines from the provincial headquarters, but none have arrived.'

'So what time do you have lunch, and how many meals per day do they provide?'

'Only two now – the instructions of Angkar. Around ten, then around four or four-thirty.'

Kosal turned to me. 'Did you have anything to eat before you left the village?'

'I was told to come here to have my first meal, but it seems I'm too late,' I answered. 'So the morning meal has been served already, right?'

I had crawled nearer to him now. He leaned over, pushed me in the ribs and laughed.

'There is food sometimes. I told you. Don't worry.'

The forced smile on his thin face made me worry more than ever.

'Have you eaten yet today?' I asked.

'No. Today we are all still waiting.'

Around us, quietly and slowly, many patients were being moved on ox-carts or carried on hand stretchers. Some were tied up in hammocks, just as I had been.

'But it's nearly one o'clock!' I said.

'That's right!' Kosal rose from his hammock. 'I bet you are starving! Here, have this.'

He handed me a bottle, and I took a sip. It was honey and water. I had not tasted honey since long before the Khmer New Year. Kosal quickly put the bottle away again.

There was suddenly a lot of noise coming from the front entrance. People were crying and groaning, shouting and screaming. I could hear movement, much movement – the marching of many feet.

I raised myself up on one arm and tried to focus. It was a group of children marching. They were boys and girls of all ages, even my size. They came to a stop at the gate in front of one of the big shrines, which had a fence around it. Some were crying, and others were busy talking about the meal that they had been promised when they were persuaded to leave their villages. The fence had a gate, and I saw two Khmer soldiers, a man and a woman, guarding it. The man had a belt of ammunition across his chest and carried a rifle. The woman wore a cream uniform and a scarf around her head. She was sitting in front of a table with an open notebook in front of her.

'What's going on?' I whispered.

Kosal explained that they were children who had been collected from the villages – children whose parents had died either of starvation or from execution after being accused of being an enemy of Angkar. 'They are orphans,' he said.

'Really?'

'Yes.'

'Where are they going?'

'They will be taken to the orphanage centre.'

I didn't know anything about this orphanage centre.

He said, 'I heard it is somewhere in Battambang. Once they get there, they will belong to Angkar, and will be known as Angkar's Revolutionary Children.'

A stirring then took hold of me. I slowly got up and began to walk carefully toward them.

'What are you doing?' Kosal called. 'You can't go – your parents are alive.' But I took no notice of him.

I felt bad about leaving Kosal without saying goodbye, but I had to get away from that hospital. I stumbled down the steps, then hurried toward the children, who were lining up in a long queue. Now I was sneaking along from tree to tree. When I was nearly there, I stopped, watching, waiting.

The Khmer soldiers arranged the children from smallest to largest, and I was as tall as the tallest. Suddenly I felt nervous. It seemed that none of the KR had noticed me, but I did not want to make it obvious that I was planning to join the children's line, so I pretended to be resting under a tree.

There were soldiers nearby, and many of the children were crying. Some stopped and sat, while others stood around in small groups. Some were looking for their brothers and sisters. Some were calling for their parents.

The queue of children led all the way to the gate of the big shrine. As I watched, two KR ladies took a notebook and handed it to the lady in the cream dress sitting at the table. While they were busy talking, I sneaked behind the line and joined the queue. The girl who was last in line turned around and stared at me. 'What are you doing back here? You should go to the front of the boys' group,' she said.

There were two lines in fact, one of boys and the other of girls, so I squeezed in between the lines quickly while the KR soldiers were busy chatting among themselves. The children in the queues were packed together tightly, but I kept moving until I ended up in the front row.

A nurse was there, dressed like the Khmer Rouge nurse who had taken care of my group back at Sahakor Seven. She was organising the children and reporting to a male colleague. She was pretty, and she had an intelligent look about her. In her hands were a clipboard and a pen, and she was standing up next to the table.

What would I say? My name was not on their list, and I wasn't an orphan. My whole body trembled. As I approached the nurse, she spoke without looking at me or checking her list. Just at that moment, she was interrupted.

She pushed me across to the man standing next to her. He had not been paying attention because he was flirting with her female colleague.

'So what is your name?' he demanded, but not so serious.

'Samamit Ra!' I said.

'Your village's name?'

I told him.

'What happened to your parents?'

'They have died.'

At that moment, I thought of my mother and how much I was missing her. Tears started flowing from my tired eyes. I stared straight at him, and I thought he saw the sad look on my face. At least he could see I was tired and hungry, my lips were parched, and I struggled to stand without looking as if I was about to fall over.

Each moment was an ordeal for me. I had been so sick, and

now I was hungry and thirsty. It was only some sort of miraculous energy that kept me going. Then I realised the soldier wasn't really listening to me; he only looked at my miserable face and let me go, in a hurry to continue flirting.

The colleague he'd been speaking with was now talking to a young girl, and he went across without saying any more to me. The woman with the clipboard turned back. I feared she would see me and not recognise me, so I took my chance and hurried through the gate toward the crowd of children inside the shrine. I did not bother to look back, but looked for a place to hide. Around the side of the shrine, I found a small door and crawled in.

I knocked against bodies, and I heard soft groans. Settling on a space near the door, I let my eyes adjust. My companions were children, all children. Some were girls caring for sick younger brothers or sisters. Some were coughing, some whining for their parents, and some crying for food. They were all ages and they looked ill, worried, scared, dirty and lost.

I sat down in horror and clasped my legs, hiding my face between my knees. I prayed to Mother that the KR would not find me in this room. I prayed too that Kosal would not report me to the KR for leaving the patients' designated area.

There was so much sadness around me, and the children were helpless. What must they be feeling, so small, and without their parents to comfort them? But I knew I had to look out for myself. There was nothing I could do except keep crouching there. My fear of being found out was stronger than my hunger, exhaustion and illness. Eventually, I fell asleep.

I woke with a scream. I had been dreaming that I was arrested and taken back to the village. None of the children took any notice. They must have been used to people waking from bad dreams.

I looked at them and wondered where all this would end. I wondered if I was safe now. I felt hungry and extremely tired and thirsty, and I needed to go to the toilet.

I crawled to the doorway of our small room and peeped out, looking for water, and somewhere to go to the toilet. But I couldn't see. Everything was dark now except for candles shining from some of the shrines inside the pagoda, and it was raining, soft drops landing gently in the dust.

Later, it stopped raining and I moved toward the doorway again.

'Ouch! Ouch!' a small child yelled. I had stepped on her. Her older brother was mad at me. 'I'm so sorry, sorry, sorry!' I said.

I left that room and walked toward the gate. It was a dark night, and I could not see well. About ten steps out of the shrine, I had a pee on the fence. On my way back, I looked around for water, but all I saw were children lying everywhere; some were asleep, some in pain, some waiting for their first meal, most of them probably wet.

There was simply no food. Some of the children had been crying for hours, begging for food, and some cried until no more sounds came from their mouths. I could hear some girls begging the KR guards to bring food for their younger brothers or sisters, who were dying of starvation. But no food came.

The rain started showering down again. I wondered what it meant. Was the god of heaven crying, feeling sorry for these children, because nothing could be done for them?

I went back into the shrine and thought about my own situation. How was I still alive? In my condition, I should have dropped dead by now. Instead, I felt as though I'd been disconnected from the world for hours in some strange drama. I couldn't believe how I had kept going all day, travelling from the village to here, being so ill and having no food except a honey drink from Kosal. Wasn't this some kind of miracle?

I got up, leaving my backpack in the room, and went to ask the children outside the shrine whether anyone knew where the well was. When I asked, a boy snapped angrily, 'Don't know and go away!'

But then I heard another voice. 'It is over there near the rice field,' a girl said. 'It is far away. Now it is too dark, so I can't go for my water. Tomorrow you can bring me some back, OK?' I barely saw her, and kept walking among the crowd lying on the floor.

I stepped on someone. 'Ouch! I'm so sorry,' I said, but there was no answer.

Then a girl's voice said, 'You want water?'

'Yes,' I answered. 'Please.'

'Over here.'

I didn't know where she was.

'Over here, not there!' She reached out with her water bottle and I drank almost all of it. Her hand reached back toward me, and she shouted, 'Leave some for my younger brother!'

'Sorry. I was so thirsty. I will bring some back for you tomorrow. Thank you for the water.'

The water helped. I hurried back to the small, dark room where I had left my belongings. My bag had been opened while I was out. 'What!' I yelled. 'Who opened my bag?'

No-one said a thing. I checked my backpack again. I hadn't lost anything, not even my hammock. I realised they'd just been looking for food.

Then from outside came noises. The soldiers shouted, and it was raining again. I waited, holding my pack and praying I wouldn't get caught. If the KR soldiers checked their list, they would know I shouldn't be there. And if they found my father, my whole family might suffer.

I felt more and more tired and ill again. My mind was spinning and I felt an overall sickness, a weakness that made me think I would soon fade away.

There was more shouting outside. It was clearly difficult organising the children the way the leaders wanted. Then I could hear people walking around, but there were fewer voices now. Some of the children crawled over to the door and looked out, but soon everything was quiet again.

I looked around again. I estimated there were fifty children there with me. They were all skinny, and in the light of the lanterns that shone through the holes in the walls, they looked miserable.

As time passed, my hunger, which had begun to settle, slowly returned. I couldn't tell the time, and it seemed the darkness would be there forever. I could hear frogs calling and crickets chirping from the paddy fields that lined the shrines at the back of the pagoda. What was going to happen to me, to all of us? Would we be fed tonight? It was getting later and later, and the children in this big shrine were dying of hunger. We had no purpose, except we all hoped for the cry that would announce the arrival of food.

The door opened. Two KR girls stood there. Looking. Staring.

'When are we going to get any food?' I asked one of them as the other turned away. 'Do you know?'

'No.'

She held a clipboard, and I could tell she was thinking. I was grateful that she couldn't see me in the near-darkness. Then she turned from her pad and her lantern and looked at me.

'There is no food,' she said. She looked directly at where I was, and I was scared she was trying to recognise me. 'There is no food supply at all in the pagoda. We will be given food when we arrive at the orphanage camp later tonight. You are all very lucky that the food will be prepared for all of you and you will become the children of Angkar.'

Her words inspired me and all the other children. We suddenly had hope and some energy to fight back against our weakness and hunger, so that we might remain alive that night.

'What time are they coming to get us?' a voice shouted from outside.

'Normally it's about this time,' she shouted back. 'We all just have to wait.'

The KR girls left, and I tried to nap. It wasn't easy. My gut was hurting as I listened to the children. Many spoke nonsense, or sobbed softly. Several of the older girls put their hands over their younger sisters' mouths. 'Don't say anything,' they whispered. 'Calm down.' The whispering around me was like a forest of trees speaking to each other as they swayed in the breeze. But I was the one who was swaying. I fell in and out of a painful sleep that was more like losing consciousness.

Suddenly, we heard a truck. There was shouting and screaming from the children outside. 'Let's go, let's go, let's go, let's go,' men's voices demanded.

Another voice shouted, and it was a voice of pain. 'What about our meal for today, Samamit?' Everything froze for a moment.

The Khmer Rouge whispered to the children, 'Just keep moving. They will provide you with a meal at the orphanage centre. The quicker we get there, the quicker you'll get your meal.'

The children became excited. I looked for my bag while the children shuffled all around me and over me, trying to get to the door. Everything would be OK now, I told myself. But when I finally tried to stand, I fell down again. I had no energy left. I knew I had to move now or lose my chance. I struggled hard to crawl out slowly behind the other children and get to the truck. Fortunately, it was night. The weather was cooler after the rain, and the swelling of my limbs was not at its worst.

When I got to the truck, all muddied and wet from crawling, I was so exhausted that I had to rest. I lay on the ground behind the truck with the smallest and most helpless of the children. The truck was already crowded.

Two men approached. 'Hurry and you might get there on time for our meal,' one of them said.

The truck was painted in green military colours and had an open back. Its tailgate rose about a metre from the ground. Children were still pushing to get in, climbing up hurriedly by themselves or being helped by the men.

Soon almost all the children were on. I waited for a chance to climb up, but then one of the two men closed the tailgate. Struggling with all my might, I managed to stand and hobble closer. The KR guard saw me almost standing straight and must have realised I was an older boy.

'Get on quickly,' he said. 'The truck is going to leave soon.'

He went to the front of the truck, jumped in and started the engine, but his colleague walked to the side with papers in his hand and spoke with another official.

As I heard the engine, I began to panic. With the tailgate up, the back of the truck was now much higher for me to climb. I badly wanted to call out for help, but I was too weak. Why didn't the KR driver help me?

I knew the truck must be full. I could only pick out the back of the vehicle from the dim light of its flashing indicators. I realised at that moment that there was no point waiting for help – this was my only chance to stay alive.

I reached for the tailgate and found the loop-chain hanging down at the back of the truck. With my bag over my shoulder, I grabbed the chain with both hands and strained. Using all my remaining reserves of strength and willpower, I tried to pull my body up onto the back of the vehicle.

I screamed loudly through my tears. My legs were so numb they seemed paralysed, yet they trembled to the sound of the truck's engine, shaking itself, ready to go. No-one heard me screaming. It was just a noise in my head.

My tears became a river inside my heart. Why had life been so unfair and brought all this injustice to me? What had I done so wrong that I needed to suffer like this? My heart was sobbing. I blamed myself for not dying yesterday and sparing myself what was happening to me now.

Just when I had managed to climb about a third of the way up, the truck started lunging forward. None of the children in the truck offered to help me. I had little to celebrate, but they were screaming with joy as the truck left the pagoda.

The jolt of the truck moving nearly flung me off, but luckily my right wrist was stuck in the loop of the chain. The driver changed into second gear, and the truck began running steadily. I kept holding on to the chain with all my strength. My arms were battered and bruised until they became numb to the pain. Eventually, I managed to reach over the top edge of the tailgate and roll into the truck, landing on a number of children.

'Ouch!' voices said. One said, 'Go away!' I could only whisper that I was sorry and squeeze into a corner, exhausted but relieved that I had made it.

Chapter 7
Orphans

IT WAS DARK, and we drove on and on. The floor of the truck shook every few seconds as we drove over potholes or swerved to avoid objects in the dark. My whole body ached. Whenever the truck shook, I shuddered. I was so weak and skinny now. I thought of my family. It was Chandy's birthday soon, and I hadn't said goodbye to him.

Finally, the truck stopped. The tailgate was unlocked and dropped down.

'OK, we are here. Get off now.'

The children all jumped down off the truck and rushed to follow a KR soldier, who was leading them with his torch.

'Let's go and get food,' they shouted.

They spoke about how hungry they were and talked of the food they would get because they lived under Angkar's roof. I too had jumped, but I fell. I stayed there unmoving, as the children jumped over me then disappeared into the darkness.

Finally, I managed to get up and stagger after them, craving food as much as they did. There was a path through the trees. I followed it, but soon I couldn't hear the voices any more. I lost the track and collapsed onto the twigs and dirt.

Then I saw torchlight in the distance. I rose and started walking again through bushes and branches and prickles and thorns. As I kept going, the vegetation became thicker and it became more difficult to move forward. Eventually I could go no further. I turned around and made my way back to the path.

I began to sob. 'Why has this happened to me? Why does God

continue to curse me?' I called out to Mother, 'Why can't I be with you? Why can't we all be together?'

I kept walking slowly and found the path the others had taken.

Listening to the frogs and the bats flapping from tree to tree, I became unafraid. My mind and my stomach were aching for food, and my only thought was that someone else would eat my meal before I got there. I dragged myself on until I heard footsteps. I waited on the path. A lady was wheeling an old bicycle and carrying a flashlight. She saw me.

'Oh, Samamit, why are you still here?' she asked.

'I'm lost. I am unwell. I … I don't walk fast,' I replied. 'Bong Srey' – a polite way to address an older sister – 'where are we now? And have you seen the children passing through here?'

'You are in Battambang province, in the district of Anlong Vil,' she replied. 'I heard the children as I came out from my post. I guess they have already arrived at the camp. It's all right. You don't need to worry. I will take you there. Come.' She took my pack. 'Can you walk?'

She led me toward the camp. As we drew near, I heard crying and sobbing, arguing and fighting. I think the arguing was over spaces to sleep. I did not hear any clinking of plates and spoons or any talk about food.

The camp was a village school that had been closed down and converted into an orphanage. It sat on a concrete base about half a metre from the ground and had four entry points and an open veranda all around. It was a brick veneer building, about twenty metres long and six metres wide, with a zinc alloy roof.

I saw a KR leader with a torch busily organising places for children to sleep. There were many more children than my truck had carried. Everyone was fighting for a space, and he turned and looked at me.

He said, 'Go find some space to rest for tonight, and tomorrow morning I will come and reorganise things for all of you.'

'Is there any food left?' I asked.

'No, tomorrow morning that will be provided.'

'We were told we would get food when we arrived. We haven't eaten since this morning!'

'We were told only to greet you and settle you in this camp, nothing about food. Anyway, we will bring food tomorrow morning.' He looked at his watch. 'It is now nearly midnight. Go and find a place to rest.'

Children were everywhere. Every piece of ground on the path, in the school hall and beside it was taken up with small bodies sitting or standing. Being the last to arrive, I had to go to a far corner of the hall, where I found a broken bed with no mattress. As soon as I lay down, my eyes closed by themselves and I slept.

In the morning, I was woken by a loud voice. Two soldiers were standing at the far end of the hall. One carried a rifle that looked like an AK-47, and the other had a book in his hand. 'Get up. Get up,' he said.

It was only about 6 a.m., and the sun was just coming up. I had slept so well, as if I was back in my own bed at home in Phnom Penh.

'OK,' the soldier said. 'As we are living under Angkar's guidance, there are rules that need to be followed and respected. Therefore we need to arrange you all into groups, just like in your own villages before you came here. All right?'

I could hardly hear him when he spoke because I was so far away, and there was a lot of noise from children crying or demanding food. 'If you don't form your groups now and don't keep your noise down,' he yelled, 'then there will be no food for you today.'

Suddenly everyone was silent.

'OK.' The man started to make groups as he walked around. 'One, two, three, four, five,' and so on, all the way to thirty. 'Now, one, two, three' – he pointed – 'You three, take care of this group.'

He formed another group, and another, each with a leader and two deputies. When he started grouping at the far end of the hall, I lost interest and began dozing again.

'Is there anyone who is not in a group?' he finally asked.

'There is another person here,' someone called, pointing to me.

There were five groups with thirty members and three leaders in each. I was the only one left over. When I opened my eyes again, the KR man was standing there trying to examine me.

'Samamit! What is your name?' he said.

I tried to stand up but fell back down. I told him my name. He came and grabbed me. 'You are the one who is left. I want you to take charge over these five groups and report to me when I return.'

'Oh no,' I said. 'Sorry, Samamit Bong! I am not well and how can I do this job to look after these children?'

There were so many children. I stared at the children. Some were quite big, much larger than me.

'OK, Samamit! You look after these children, and you will report to me. That is an order from Angkar.'

He was making me the leader. He looked at my eyes, my face, as if he saw something there. Did he know I could read and write? Maybe he liked the way I spoke to him, respectfully calling him 'Bong'? Or perhaps he remembered I had been the one asking him questions last night.

'What's wrong with you?' he demanded.

'My body swells during the day, and then it shrinks down at night. During the day, when that happens, I am very tired and very slow; it seems like I have no energy in my body. So I don't think I can chase after these people.'

He approached me, checking my eyes, asking me to open my mouth.

'That's OK,' he said, 'no problem. Just wait a minute.'

I could see him thinking.

'OK, pack your things and follow me.'

As we walked through the hall, all I could smell was faeces and urine. I followed him outside to a field of green grass. Across the field were banana trees and what looked like an orange farm. The man led me into a small room beside the hall. He gave me a package, and a bottle of water with vitamin C. He asked me to drink.

'Later on we will provide food for you. OK? Then I will bring you some medicine. In the meantime, your job is to keep the children from going to other places. Make sure they behave, and make each group cleans up their own area. Get them to report to you. You report to me. If there is anything wrong, let me know, and I will take action.'

As he walked out, the bodyguard with the gun followed, carrying the first man's bag, which had a red cross on it. So he must be a doctor or nurse, I thought. But I didn't care. I was feeling better after having a drink. I had just been given a responsibility I couldn't even think about, but I had been set aside for privileges, and this was my room.

I rested for a few minutes on a bed with a mattress and tried to think about what I must do. The room had two windows, one facing the hall and the other looking out to the field. The walls were a light cream colour. There was no table or toilet, and the light switches were broken.

After resting for a while, I got up and left the room through another door, which led into a corridor. On my right was the hall. On my left, other rooms branched off on the way to a dead end. All these rooms were padlocked.

Using the wall to support myself, I walked out to the hall. 'Come,' I said. 'All group leaders come here. And everyone else line up on the terrace in your groups.'

The three group leaders were all older boys who would know this system and how it worked.

'Now we try to live as a family,' I said to the leaders. 'Each of you let me know what's happening. Try to clean up your area. Um, tell your group not to go away from here, especially not to go to other villages, because that is the instruction I was given.'

I sat on the terrace and wrote down the names of the children and their groups in a book I had been given. I told them to go and clean up, then I went back into my room and closed the door.

Soon there was a knock. It was a girl about twelve.

'Oh,' she said, 'my sister is dying. Please come and have a look.'

'Which group are you in?' I asked.

'I don't know.'

'All right, let's go and look.'

I really didn't want to move. I wanted to rest on my new bed, but I went with her and found she was in Group Five. I called for her leaders, but they were all gone. Meanwhile she was crying.

'Here, let me see,' I said.

The sister was younger, maybe seven. I felt her head and she was hot.

'She is not dying,' I said. 'She's just hot, OK? I'll get a towel and some water and put it on her.'

'Oh. Thank you.'

'There is nothing I can do now as I have no medicine. Wait for a while, and maybe a nurse will come.'

I told her to take her sister's clothes off and use the wet towel to cool her body. The sick girl's body was as hot as the embers in a fire. She was tiny and very skinny. I told her to stay with her big sister and explained that I wasn't well either and had to go back to rest.

I went back to my room, but straight away there was another knock on the door.

'There's a boy fighting outside,' someone yelled.

'I can't do anything,' I said. 'Look, I'm too tired. You tell your leaders. You have a group leader. You find your leader and let me know.'

I was trying to close my eyes, but people kept knocking on the door. I didn't respond. Then in mid-morning the children started screaming, 'Some food is coming! Angkar is coming and he has food.'

It was the man I met last night. He knocked on my door as he walked in.

'No need to get up! I was told you tried to help one of the little children,' he said.

I begged him to come with me to see the girl and told him about her condition. He took a wet towel and placed it on her forehead. He produced medicine from his bag and gave it to her.

'Don't forget to give her more medicine before noon and at night time,' he instructed.

'Yes, Samamit Bong!'

He walked out and called everyone together. 'My colleague will soon get here with the food,' he said, 'so you should all line up properly.'

A short time later, I opened my door to a knock, and there was another Khmer Rouge man waiting.

'This is yours,' he said.

He came into my room with a pan and a wok and a lot of food, enough for many meals. Meanwhile, outside on the terrace, I saw all the children lining up with plates or bowls, if they had them. Khmer Rouge people were going around with a container of thick porridge, really more like rice, and pouring it into the children's bowls. I came out and watched: each bowl seemed to be full.

'You are in charge?' It was the lady supervising the distribution of the food.

'Yes,' I said.

'Samamit, is that enough?' she asked. 'Have we left you enough food?'

I went back to my room and examined my meal. The porridge was more solid than what the other children had been given. And there was fresh fish, and pickled cucumber in a plastic jar. I started eating immediately. I ate and ate, but I couldn't eat it all.

I kept the leftovers in my room. The children were watching me and knew exactly what I had. When you are so hungry, your mind cannot think of anything except food, and the children were all still hungry; they hadn't had the luxury of a nutritious meal like mine.

After the meal, two boys began trying to curry favour with me. One of them, a group leader, offered to be of assistance in any way he could.

'Would you like me to wash your clothes?' he asked. 'Do you have anything else you would like me to do?'

I was flattered, because I had never been served like that before.

But I knew that what they really wanted was my food. 'OK,' I said, 'go and finish my meal. Eat it, then clean everything up.'

I couldn't believe how fast they ate that food. After they cleaned up, they came back and began acting as my helpers. They guarded me in my room and checked if there was anything I wanted or problems I needed them to deal with.

Then the doctor came back with a plastic bag of various tablets. The labels were in French, and I could read them – vitamin C, vitamin B, iron.

'Take these vitamins three times a day,' he said, 'and you will be fine in a couple of days.'

'Really, Samamit Bong?' I was excited. I couldn't believe how well things were turning out.

'Don't call me Samamit Bong, just Samamit. Remember, we are now a classless society. So, how are the children?' he asked.

'They are doing OK, but I am still feeling so tired.'

'I know. Just relax, it will get better.'

He spoke to me kindly, and I found out his name was Sarim. It was a fine day, so I walked with him, and he showed me around the area. The school was built on the edge of a farm called Orange Farm because of the orange trees that grew there. Beside the farm and immediately in front of the school – about fifty metres away past the long grass – was a banana plantation. I could see the bananas, thickly bunched, and I wondered how many of the children must have wandered across to them.

'The plantation belongs to the military village,' Sarim said.

We watched some children playing, then I saw the houses at the edge of the village that must have belonged to the Khmer Rouge military. Around to the south, at the back of the school, was a wire fence that marked the boundary of the Khmer Rouge camp. The camp entrance was a kilometre away on the main road, where the truck had delivered us the night before.

'Remember, don't let the children go to the military villages or families nearby. If they are caught, they might be punished or killed. I won't take responsibility for this.'

I told him I couldn't take any responsibility either. 'I will instruct them. I will inform them as you have told me, but I don't think I can do anything if they keep going.'

'I understand, but they must learn to obey the rules. Otherwise, there will be punishment. Now, this afternoon I will bring spades and hoes and baskets so the children have something to do. And I will bring you some clothes.'

He left again with his bodyguard. Time passed quickly. I walked around with my two helpers following. It was overcast but still warm. One of the boys, whose name was Banh, had a slingshot in his hand. Banh was dark-skinned and didn't speak much, but he was excellent with the slingshot.

I went with him to the banana trees, which grew to about three metres and sat in rows that had been raised above the surrounding soil. Between each row was a canal like a small stream. There was plenty of fruit on the trees, but none of it was ripe. Then we saw a shiny lizard wandering near the bananas. Banh took a piece of clay he'd shaped into a ball like a marble, and with one shot he struck and killed the lizard.

I warned him that we couldn't get our own food and eat privately. It had to be shared.

'Yes, I know,' he said, 'but I will keep it for you.'

'You'll have to be careful.'

He nodded.

'Well, how are you going to cook it?'

'Don't worry, I know the place.'

The children were becoming restless again, even though they had eaten just a couple of hours earlier. I found it hard to believe they were still so hungry, but I was too, even though I had eaten better than them. It was because there wasn't enough nutrition in the food. It was basically rice and water with some pickle, but our bodies were eager for more.

Thirty minutes later, there was a knock at my door. It was Banh.

'What is it?'

He walked in. He didn't say anything but reached into his pocket and pulled out about five freshly baked lizards wrapped in banana leaves. From his other pocket he produced some salt. The lizards smelt irresistible. As I stood there with Banh, it was as if I could taste and feel the flesh in my mouth.

'How did you do this?' I asked.

'Near a village. There was a place where they make palm sugar. There were some embers left in the fire, and I cooked it after I saw the last man leave for his home.'

'So the hut making sugar was far away from the village?' I had to make sure. I didn't want there to be any chance of him being seen.

Banh nodded his head and asked me to try the food now while it was still warm.

'But where did you get this salt?'

'Salt was nearby.'

He looked at me with no fear. I was worried he might be caught and punished or killed, but my hunger said I needed to eat meat, so I ate the lizards. It was like eating a delicious steak, juicy and tasty.

As I was eating, the other boy, Banh's friend, knocked and came in.

'OK, you can have half,' I said.

After eating, I told the boys I was going to rest and I wanted them to look out for me.

When I woke up, they told me, 'The Khmer Rouge have left spades. They didn't want to disturb you, but they said to tell you that each group must have one.'

The days passed quickly, and my health improved. I had put on weight and could now walk and speak better. But it wasn't easy to control the children or explain what they needed to do.

Then one of the children had a nightmare in which she saw her parents being killed by the Khmer Rouge. She screamed in her sleep, calling out for her mother, saying the soldiers were there, killing her family. I came out from my room and went to her. I held her and tried to wake her up, but she died in my arms. She was about thirteen.

Another girl was lying beside her. She told me the dead girl was her sister. After being taken from her village, where her aunt and uncle still lived, she hadn't wanted to talk to anyone or eat anything. She had refused to take any food or medicine, except sometimes she would drink some water.

I was shocked. I blamed myself for being selfish and not paying enough attention to these children. I held her tight in my arms. 'I am sorry. I am so sorry,' I said, bursting into tears.

The children nearby stared. Others came and surrounded me. I realised it was her suffering that had killed her, not my neglect.

By early December 1975, I had regained a lot of energy. I felt stronger but hungrier than ever. The children were hungry too, and every night, two or three of them would cry out with nightmares, screaming for their parents or a brother or sister.

A Khmer Rouge woman always brought the food to us, and one day I asked her why the children had so little to eat.

She replied, 'At least the children have some rice. In some villages, people are starving to death.'

'Why?' I muttered to myself, but she heard.

'They haven't been able to organise everything. It's not working.' She spoke quietly, as if she too was talking to herself. Later, I realised what she was saying: the Khmer Rouge were failing in their strategy to build a new society by simply producing more rice.

But I didn't ask many questions. It was a regime where I felt we had no right to question or make requests. I tried to make do with what we were given, until one night.

Around 7 p.m., a couple of hours after our evening meal, I heard soldiers calling from outside.

'Samamit! Who is in charge of this camp? Come out!'

I came out and saw two soldiers carrying guns. They were from a neighbouring village and had a boy with them. He was tied up tight and looked as though he had been dragged all the way into camp. I looked at the boy. He was eleven or twelve, and his face was white and angry, determined and defiant. I could see no pain or fear in him at all.

Everything else was quiet and peaceful. I could smell the scent of the orange trees drifting on the breeze. But the soldiers were shouting at me.

'Samamit, you must watch this boy very carefully,' they said, shining their torches into his face, then mine. 'Otherwise we will shoot him. He does belong to your camp, doesn't he?'

I didn't know him. I couldn't tell which group he belonged to or even if he came from this camp. They were still yelling, telling me to watch him, because if he went to their military camp again, they would shoot him.

'What did he do in your camp, Samamit?' I asked.

I knew I shouldn't have asked this question, but it was too late.

'He came and stole our sugar and salt, and sometimes we lost our food without knowing who stole it. This is the first time we caught someone, so we assume he stole our food.'

'All right. I will try to do something about this. I promise he will not go into your camp again.'

I took him from the soldiers, but I could tell they were still unhappy. They glared at me, and I felt they thought I was to blame. I felt they were deciding if I asked too many questions.

The boy remained quiet, showing no concern. His face was still full of anger and hatred, and I was in shock. I didn't know what to say or do. I didn't know what to think.

I looked at him. He was kneeling and his hands were tied together behind his back. His arms were skinny, thin and flexible enough to be tied together so that they touched. They were tied so tight that his wrists were touching also. I could not believe they would tie him like this, like he was the enemy.

I begged them to leave him and I said I would train him and encourage him to stay put at our camp.

They pushed him to the ground, then raised their voices. In a fierce tone, they said, 'If you do not look after him, if you do not train and educate him, we will kill him.'

'Yes, Samamit,' I responded humbly. 'I will educate him and I will make sure he will not do that again.'

Please go, I thought. I thanked them and said I would find out which group he belonged to, but I could tell they were still not happy.

In their minds, they would see me as one of them. I was the supervisor. I was working with the Khmer Rouge. But I had failed and shown them I didn't know how to manage my own children in the orphanage. Above all, they wanted to prove they were the masters here.

Again I wondered what I should do. I went to the boy and lifted him up. I heard the soldiers walk away, taking their torches with them and leaving us in the dark. I took the boy – I didn't know his name – and walked with him toward the door of the hall. There was silence between us. Only the natural light of the stars illuminated the stony field around the hall. I looked back and saw the soldiers disappear in the distance.

At the entrance to the hall, I untied the boy. Even in the dull light, I could see how his hands had swollen. There was a mark around his upper arms. They were bruised and red, because he had been dragged by the rope.

'I hope you understand,' I told him. 'You must not to go there again.'

He didn't respond, but began to swear about the two soldiers. 'If I had a gun I would shoot them,' he added, 'I would kill them.'

'No,' I said.

He turned to me.

'Do you want to eat some bananas?' he asked calmly.

'What?' I replied. 'After all this? Where would you get bananas from? After all they said to you, you're not scared?'

'No, I'm not going to worry. I will bring them tonight to you. I have some ripe bananas.'

'No, I don't need your bananas. All I want is that you don't go to any military camps or villages again, because when you get caught, either you will be killed or I will be blamed. So please stay in this camp. That's all I want.'

'No, no, no,' he said. He ran into the hall and disappeared.

I thought maybe he had just gone back to his own group. I returned to my room. I had to find that boy, and if he didn't belong to a group, then I would place him in one.

The next day, when I was resting in my room during the afternoon, I smelt something cooking. The odour came through the open window, and I couldn't believe how beautiful it was.

When I left my room, a large group of boys and girls ran up to me.

'Look, look, they have something to eat!' one of them yelled. 'We don't have anything. Can you help us? It's not fair. It's not fair. We want to eat too.'

'Where?' I asked.

The children pointed across the grass, where a group of boys had clustered around a fire. They had a pan, and I could tell they were hiding something under it and in their shirts.

I walked over, followed by a crowd of children.

'Give it to me,' I said.

'No, no,' one boy answered. 'It's mine. It's mine. We found it.'

'OK, let me have a look. What is it?'

I grabbed the boy's hand and saw meat, grilled on one side only. Still it smelt delicious.

I made the boy turn his hand so I could see the other side of the meat, the uncooked side. It was the most unusual colour. It was blue and violet, like nothing I had ever seen.

'What is it?' I repeated.

'We don't know.'

'We found it,' another boy added.

'We think it's pork,' a third one said. 'Another boy found it in the bush in the middle of the orange farm, near the banana trees. It was on the ground. Look over there – another group is cooking some of it too.'

I glanced across and saw another group preparing a fire.

'All of you have to stop immediately,' I yelled. 'If Samamit Bong finds out, we will all get into serious trouble. Maybe we will not be fed any more. So you'd better stop. OK, let me have another look at this.'

I took the meat out of his hand. It was blue like it had been bruised.

'My God,' I said.

As I took it from his hand and turned it over again I lifted it to my nose. It was rotten, just an awful smell.

'It's mine, mine,' the boy said.

'OK, I have to use my authority now. I want all of you to give me that meat.'

I raised my voice so fiercely that they knew I meant what I said. Other boys and girls pointed out those who had the meat, and I collected it all.

'I want my team to follow me,' I announced. 'All the leaders come here.'

When the leaders joined me, I grabbed one of the boys who had been cooking and made him lead us to where the meat was found. When we got to the place, which was deep in the orange farm, there was a mass grave.

Many people had been slaughtered here, and body parts were showing above the ground. They had been cut with saws. It looked as if some of the people had been tortured before they died. Some of the bodies were rotten, but others weren't. I was sure this depended on whether there were souls protecting the bodies.

One of the boys asked me why the meat could be preserved and why it smelt delicious when it was cooked.

'Some of these people were tortured and salted around their body where they had been slaughtered,' I explained.

I was shocked to see this area of massacred bodies. It was so close to our camp. And I was shocked to realise how desperately the children were in need of food.

I told the boys to cover the area. We kicked and pushed and dug with sticks and rocks until we covered the bodies. Some of the boys jumped on the soil to compact it, then we placed clumps of grass over the area. I tried to disguise the track to the place and did everything else I could to make it hard for anyone to return there.

I was sad as we walked back. Who were the people who had been killed? Did they have families who were trying to survive somewhere? I also thought about my family: I hadn't seen them for weeks now, and I wondered when I would see them again.

That night, around nine or ten, there was a scream.

Then I heard shouting: 'Thief, thief, thief!' Someone was running. A girl ran up to me at my door.

'Help me! Help me!' she said. 'It's a thief. He stole my things.'

Another girl came up and said, 'Someone took my blanket! A thief stole my blanket!'

I ran out of my room, followed by the boys who were sleeping outside my window, but we couldn't see anything.

Then the next night we found a boy with many blankets wrapped around him. It was the boy who had been brought in by the Khmer Rouge soldiers.

I was very angry. 'Wake up,' I said. 'Tell me your name.'

The boy said, 'I am Ar-Gor.'

Gor means 'mute', and the boy started using his hands to speak with me.

'But you can talk,' I said.

'No – I only talk to girls that I like.'

This boy may have had his reasons, but I was upset with him.

'Why did you steal other people's blankets?'

'I was feeling cold.'

'Why didn't you ask me? If you felt cold, why didn't you come to me?'

He didn't reply.

'All right,' I said, 'you'd better give back the blankets.'

I held up my lamp and looked around. 'Whoever needs to get your blanket back, come and take a blanket,' I said.

The children came one by one and took back their blankets.

About twelve of them came. Then there were no blankets left. Children were still looking for blankets that had gone missing, and there was nothing for Ar-Gor.

'You come to my room now,' I said. I took him there and gave him my blanket. 'Here is my blanket. Now, you'd better stop stealing blankets. It's not right.'

He stared at me. 'No-one has ever been kind to me before,' he said. 'I recognise you now – you were the person who released me from the evil Khmer Rouge.'

I sat near him and we talked. He cried as he explained how he had seen his parents begging for their lives before they were killed. 'So from that day I hate the people that wear black,' he said. 'I hate the Khmer Rouge.'

He stayed that night on the blanket in a corner of my room, and in the morning he said he had more blankets to give back.

'Where from?'

'Just follow me.'

I did follow, with Banh and another boy called Sok, all the way into the orange farm, where many dead bodies lay rotting. We saw where Ar-Gor had been storing bananas, using the blankets to help them ripen.

'Ar-Gor, you come back with us,' I said. 'I will look after you.'

'No, I will stay here. I don't want to go back. I don't want to be given food by the Khmer Rouge. I don't like them.'

'OK.' I thought about it. 'As long as you're happy, all right.'

I left him with three blankets and took the rest back to the camp, along with some ripe bananas. I wondered if I had done the right thing, leaving him with no proper food, no proper place to stay.

It had been an extraordinary day. When we returned to the camp, the boys reported to me that Sarim, the medical man, had been looking for me.

'We told him that you went into the bush,' a boy said.

When I went to my room, I found he had left me some more vitamins. He never asked me where I had been that day.

One day in mid-December, the Khmer Rouge came and told me they would be examining the children. They would have medicines and could help with any problems. I was organising the children when I found Ar-Gor lying on a bed in the hall. He looked as if he was in pain.

'Ar-Gor, why are you here? What's the matter?' I asked.

'I can't walk. I hurt my leg.'

'What's wrong with your leg?'

'I got bitten by a snake in the bush.'

'Really?'

'I stepped on it.'

I pulled away his blanket and saw two marks on his leg. His leg was pale and infected and beginning to swell.

'How long ago did this happen?' I asked.

'About … three days ago.'

'So what did you do?'

'I didn't do anything. I had no medicine.'

'Well, you'd better come outside and line up for treatment.'

'No, I don't want to come out. I don't like them and I don't need their help.'

'But now you do, because if you don't clean your wound and you don't take some medicine you will get very sick and eventually die.'

'No, I would rather die. I don't want their help.'

I saw how stubborn he was, and how ideological his thinking, so I went out to the nurses myself.

'There's another one,' I said. 'There's a boy inside lying on his bed and he's been bitten by a snake.'

The female nurse came inside with me. Ar-Gor was almost asleep. The nurse pulled away the blanket and saw the wound, but as she did Ar-Gor woke up. He went wild. He kicked out and hit the nurse in the stomach and on her arm.

'Let go of my leg. Don't touch my feet,' he shouted. 'You are a dirty killer.'

The other children in the hall watched and didn't dare move.

The nurse was very angry. 'Don't ever give anything to this boy,' she shouted back. 'Let him beg for help.'

She hurried out of the hall, and I turned back to Ar-Gor. He was suffering and I felt pity.

'I will get some water,' I said.

I went to get some special water boiled with tamarind leaves that was used to clean wounds.

'Can I clean this?' I asked him.

'That's OK,' he answered.

When I helped him clean up, I saw that there were larvae in the wound: it was not only infected, but flies had laid their eggs there. I squeezed the water on to the wound, and Ar-Gor screamed, but soon the larvae came out. Ar-Gor was still screaming, but he tried to keep still so I could finish the cleaning.

He seemed delirious, and that night he groaned in his sleep. The next day I found more larvae in his wound. His leg was swollen and had turned blue. It looked terrible.

'You must let the nurse clean this and give you medicine,' I said. 'You have to. I can see your skin is decaying. The wound is opening up. The nurse can treat this properly.'

He sat up. 'I'm fine, I'm fine,' he said, trying to sound better. 'I don't need a nurse. I'm happy with how I am.'

I sent one of the boys for a nurse and while I was thinking of how I would keep him there, he rose from his bed and tried to stand up.

'I have to go,' he said. He stumbled, but again tried to stand.

'No, you can't go. You can't even walk properly.'

'I'm fine, I'm fine.' He hopped along, then hurried out of the hall. I followed and stood watching as he made his way quickly to the orange farm.

A couple of days passed, and nothing changed: we all coped as well as we could. I was realising that many of the children had been shattered by what had happened to them and their families.

At night, they would lie awake and talk by moonlight or in total darkness. I heard them telling stories about their past and about what had happened to their families. They were troubled, and not sleeping was one way of coping – it kept the nightmares away. They would try to stay awake and talk so that they wouldn't sleep and remember. When they slept, they would have bad dreams and scream and cry.

Still, I was better off than I had been at Sahakor Seven. There was enough food, there was little work we had to do, and there were no daily meetings and none at night. We had no idea of our purpose, but I didn't care. I was too busy doing what I had to do each day. I felt much better and I'd gained some weight. When I looked at my reflection in the water, I could see the skin on my face had tightened, and I appeared fresher and healthier than before.

One morning we had a visitor. It was another Khmer Rouge man dressed all in black. He walked and talked as though he owned everything.

He came to the door of my room. 'Good morning, Samamit,' he said. 'Angkar has plans. Angkar would like some of you to be ready as the Angkar children.' He paused. I just looked at him and waited. 'Therefore we will send some people to another place. You have been chosen to go along with the children. We will be leaving in three days.'

I didn't feel sad or surprised. I had recovered from my terrible sickness, and I felt I could do anything.

The day before we had to go, I was out walking with the doctor, Sarim. We talked about the wellbeing of the children, and I mentioned Ar-Gor. I told him that Ar-Gor had disappeared into the orange farm two days earlier and not come out.

When I returned, Banh ran up to me.

'They've got Ar-Gor,' he called. 'He's in the hall.'

The children had caught Ar-Gor sneaking into the hall at night, and he was now sitting on a stool, waiting to be treated. I went up to him and saw he had a kroma tied around his leg. The nurse, a young woman, was speaking to him and preparing to remove the kroma.

Ar-Gor was wriggling and looking very nervous. Two older boys were holding him and another nurse, a man, was watching.

'I thought it was lunchtime,' Ar-Gor yelled. 'I'm here for a meal.'

'No,' said the nurse. 'The meals have been distributed. Now it's time for treatment.'

Eventually Ar-Gor let the nurse remove the kroma. I hadn't seen him for a few days and I was curious, so I moved closer to look. The nurse untied the kroma and I saw his leg was badly swollen – all of his right leg was now green.

He didn't say anything as the nurse prepared warm water with tamarind leaves.

'Put your leg here,' she said, placing a bucket in front of him.

He put his leg in the bucket. As soon as his leg rested in the water the maggots began to come out.

'Ahhh! Ouchh!' he screamed. But he didn't cry, though he bit on his lip and screwed up his face.

I returned to my room and began packing. Ar-Gor's treatment continued, but I was told that he fainted with the pain. It didn't look good.

A little later, while I was napping, there was a knock on my door. 'Come in,' I called.

It was the nurse.

'It is too late to save Ar-Gor's leg,' she said. 'He left it too long. Now the infection has reached to his bone. In order to save his life, they would have to operate and cut off his leg. It will be Samamit Sarim's decision.'

The nurse left. Soon after, there was another knock.

It was Ar-Gor! 'I want to go with you tomorrow to the new place,' he said.

I replied, 'Ar-Gor, the decision to leave here was not mine. It came from Angkar. I don't know what will happen to us, but I was told that we will be taken to be Angkar's children. I don't know. Tomorrow I will ask. OK?'

'You must take me along because I have no relatives,' he said. 'Only you have been kind to me.'

Tears filled his eyes. His leg was swollen, and blood flowed from his wound when he tried to stand up and walk. I wondered if he would be able to keep his leg. I even wondered if the infection might kill him.

I let him stay in my room and rest. There was no need to explain to him that he would not be allowed to come with us in his condition.

Chapter 8
Village of Bones

THE NEXT MORNING, the truck arrived before our first meal.

I wanted to eat before we travelled. I had given all of the food in my room to Ar-Gor, because I thought we would be fed before we left.

We lined up, climbed onto the truck and left about eight o'clock. Banh and Sok were with me. The promise of lunch receded as the truck drove through the nearby village and kept going through others until we came to Battambang Provincial Town. We drove east through the town and over a bridge across the Sangkae River, then followed the winding river road. After about an hour's driving, we stopped at Wat Sla Ket pagoda.

My thoughts returned to Wat Chrey, the hospital I had walked to from Sakahor Seven. A soldier spoke. 'All right, you're here. Come down.'

Every shrine and building was full of people. We were led to the basement of the temple hall, where every corner was filled with orphans from other provinces. The basement had a window that allowed light in, and we waited near the light to be called for our meal. Much later, we heard a bell. Everyone began to leave their places, so we followed.

We soon found ourselves in a dining hall. Others were sitting in an organised fashion and we joined them, waiting for our food. The meal was distributed – dried fish with two large spoonfuls of rice and some soup. It wasn't enough.

'There will be a meeting,' we were told after the meal. 'You are all to go to the top hall of the pagoda this afternoon. Return to your places until you hear the bell.'

We went back to the basement. The children from our orphanage all followed me, waiting for me to instruct and reassure them. I tried to convince them that I was no longer their leader.

The bell rang for a meeting at the top of the hall in the main pagoda, by a big Buddha statue.

'Welcome to the Angkar's Children Orphanage Centre of Battambang province,' a KR lady said. 'I am to introduce you to certain rules. You are not allowed to leave this camp, and you're not to talk to people from the village. You must stay here until you get notice from a senior official or other word from Angkar.'

She explained more rules, then I raised my hand. I said, 'All of us here are children of Angkar, so we should be treated equally.'

I was nervous, but I didn't stop. I looked up at the Buddha's face in the hall and felt something inside me telling me I had to speak up.

'But this didn't happen,' I continued. 'Some of the children had only two spoons of rice, but I saw those giving out the food. They took more.'

I paused for a moment, but no-one said anything. I felt butterflies in my stomach, but I kept going.

'We were wondering why, and the meals you have – you have enough to eat and more, but you haven't shared this with other children who are still hungry. I believe the children here are all children of Angkar. Therefore, why should we be treated differently?'

When the children heard me, they began to make noises of agreement. I looked from face to face among the Khmer Rouge, and I could tell some of the women were angry. But they didn't know what to say, because indeed we had been told we'd been accepted as Angkar's children.

The KR spoke among themselves while we all waited, the children now quiet and still. Moments later, one of the KR women stepped forward. She glared at me, and I wondered what discipline was about to come my way.

'We will talk privately,' she said, 'but we will talk later.'

They asked me not to raise any more questions and went on

with the rules for the centre. They wanted to ensure discipline and insisted any issues must be reported to the group leaders before informing the centre's leader.

We returned to our place in the basement. I was worried, but the children were very nice to me and I felt honoured to have their respect. We did not dare leave the basement except to go to the toilet.

The next day, one of the Khmer Rouge leaders came to the basement and walked slowly over to our corner. He was big, and I saw another man behind him near the doorway.

'You,' he said to me. 'Come here.'

I rose and walked toward him.

'You are invited to join the management group. Come.'

He turned, and I saw he expected me to follow him immediately. He had spoken loudly, and all the children had stopped their chatter. They were concerned, but none of them could do anything. None of them dared raise any questions about why I was being removed from their group.

Banh and some of the other children followed as we left the basement. We made our way to another building and went in through the kitchen.

'Stop.'

A man stood in the doorway and leaned past me. He held one hand up and shooed away the children with the other.

'Back to the basement,' he said.

I reached over and held on to Banh. The man hesitated, then let him in.

'This is where the monks used to have their meals,' he said. 'You will stay here with us now and we will decide your duties later.'

The room was very dark. Another man was sitting on the floor, repairing his worn clothing.

There was nowhere for me to tie up my hammock. I was given an empty rice sack for myself and one for Banh. They were for us to use as mattresses on the hard clay floor.

So now I was a member of the management team for this orphanage, an orphanage so large I didn't know how many children it held. There were so many groups spread out around the pagoda's premises, each like a small village.

According to Angkar's rules, playing caused bad behaviour, so children were forbidden from playing. Singing revolutionary songs and dancing, however, were permissible. Children were allowed to have showers once a day. It wasn't compulsory, and many of them only washed their faces.

The Khmer Rouge had given Banh and me black uniforms to show we were with them now. We were told our tasks would include managing the new arrivals, and carrying water from the river to the tanks used for bathing and kitchen supplies. We were also instructed to guard the children so that they did not wander off to the villages, try to go back home, or swim and have fun in the river.

When evening came that first night, it was time to sleep on my sack of rice. I had never slept this way before. It was comfortable enough until I began to itch. I couldn't sleep. Banh stayed close to me, and he was wriggling too.

After the sun rose next morning, I lay in bed thinking about lice. Head-lice jumped easily from one head to another, and often I saw children finding them in each other's hair. But the lice also jumped from the head to blankets. And they liked fat. Around the kitchen, where there was the smell of food or fat, they crawled onto cloth or linen and stayed there, awaiting further prey.

My hair was short – I always cut it short because I didn't like long hair – and head-lice were rarely a problem for me. But I had to check. I also wanted to check for another insect, a small bug, a bloodsucker that lived mostly on mats or on wooden beds. It looked like a louse with six legs, but had a larger body and smaller head.

I was thinking about these creatures as I lay in bed and squirmed. Quickly I got up and took my rice sack out to the sunlight. As soon as I started looking, I found hundreds of lice hiding along the edge of the sack. There were too many of them to squash with my fingers, so I emptied my sack into the river and washed it, then dried it in the sun.

These head-lice had no mercy. Back in our room, I kept searching for them. 'Look, Banh,' I whispered. 'There are many head-lice on my shirt. Why don't you check yours?'

I pointed to the lice on my shirt. Then Banh found them on his shirt as well. He began crushing them one by one with his thumbs until the noise of crushing them irritated me. There were just so many of them.

When I was at the first orphanage, I didn't need to concern myself with sanitation or cleanliness. I left that to the Khmer Rouge. But here I realised I needed to think differently.

As part of the Khmer Rouge children's leadership group, I had to take turns in guarding the perimeters to prevent children from straying. We also had to stop the villagers coming to steal food or equipment from our kitchen, and this involved guarding the pagoda at night.

One night when it was my turn to be a guard, I was woken for duty at about two o'clock in the morning. I was to be one of two guards, one at the front and one at the rear of the pagoda. I was supposed to guard the front for an hour and then wake another to take my place.

It was a beautiful moonlit night, and I was enjoying the quiet as I looked across to the other side of the river. I began to think about the past. I remembered my old classmates and wondered where they were now. I thought of Father and Stepmother and my brothers and sisters. Were they all right? How could I get a message to them? I was thinking of them as I walked when I suddenly saw a bright light.

The moon was just setting and the sky was dark, but the light was real and growing larger. It was coming from far across to the side. It was flying through the sky from the east. It flew over the pagoda, and then directly into the top hall. Suddenly the whole hall was lit up.

I was frightened. I shook my head to make sure I was not dreaming, but the light was still there. I ran to my room, woke Banh and dragged him to the door.

'Look at the light!' I yelled.

He was still half asleep and mumbling.

'Look,' I repeated.

He rubbed his eyes and tried to open them. As he did, the light began to diminish. I had been holding him up, but I dropped him when the light faded. He fell to the ground and this roused him properly.

'Wha … wha … what?' he said, shaking himself.

'I saw a light. It was a bright, strong light like a comet,' I answered. 'It flew into the pagoda hall, up there.'

'Really.'

'Yes. Will you come with me?'

He nodded and ran with me up to the hall. We got there quickly, but there was nothing.

'I don't know, ' I said. 'I don't know what to say, but there was a light.'

I walked around to the back of the pagoda to find the other guard. Perhaps he had seen the light? But I couldn't find him. I kept looking until I found him in bed in his sleeping place.

I went outside again with Banh and sat on the steps of the hall. The night was very quiet and calm.

'I really don't know what it was, but it was a strong light, and it flew.'

It was dark now that the moon had set, and the end of my time on duty, so I woke another boy to take my place on guard.

When I awoke next morning, I wondered what had happened. I busied myself with our routine, and it was as if nothing had gone on at all the night before, so I kept quiet about it. I carried out my tasks and wondered again where all this was leading. Why had I been moved in with these Khmer Rouge people? Was it because they wanted to keep an eye on me? Or did they have the idea that I would be a good worker for Angkar?

Later that morning, a cyclist came into camp. Children gathered around but kept their distance. The leaders strolled over to him. All dressed in black with his kroma and cap, he brought orders from another place. He met with the leaders for a short time, then rode away again.

The leaders called us all together.

'Angkar demands some children fulfil duties in other places,' one of the Khmer Rouge men announced. 'The rice is ready now in some places. It is ready for harvesting in Svay Duon Keo commune, Mong Russey district. We need children to go and help the parents. Also, if anybody would like to return to their own village to visit your relatives, you can go.'

When I heard Mong Russey district mentioned, I immediately began thinking of my family. I wondered if they were making it through the year, or starving while I was surviving comfortably over here.

I did not want to lose the opportunity, so I raised my hand. 'I would like to go to my village to find out if my relatives are all right,' I said.

I asked Banh if he wanted to come with me, but he said no. He had hopes of going home to his own village, which was next to the old orphanage camp.

We left in mid-January 1976. The morning bell rang and we were ready. Angkar had given all of us a set of black clothes, a kroma and a cap, but we had no shoes. I was thinking about how we all looked when Banh came up and grabbed me. He was emotional and began talking.

'Bong bros!' (Big brother!) 'I don't talk much,' he said, 'but I've been with you for months. It's been good, but now we have to go and look for our families.'

I held him tight for a moment.

'I like you, Bong,' he said. 'I will miss you.'

'Look, you just take care of yourself,' I answered. 'I will come back.'

I grabbed my belongings, jumped on the truck and waved goodbye, feeling positive about what lay ahead.

The truck rolled away and I settled into my thoughts. Then I noticed a Khmer Rouge lady sitting with us. 'Samamit Bong, where are we going?' I asked.

'To Svay Duon Keo near the border of Pursat province,' she replied.

I must have looked puzzled because she added, 'It's a bit past the Mong Russey district. Where is your family?'

'In Mong Russey, at the Wat Chrey commune,' I replied.

'Oh,' she said, 'but we will not stop at Mong Russey. We need to go and help with the harvesting in one of the Svay Duon Keo villages, so we will be going straight through your district. Where we are going is just a bit further down to the south-west.'

As the trip continued, my home and my family were like an obsession in my mind. It was a long journey, and the truck arrived around noon.

'Hurry, hurry,' the KR called as they waved us off. It was a friendly 'hurry'. The leaders greeted us as if they handled children every minute of every day. They hurried us to a long hut made of bamboo and thatch.

'You must stay here. It is your place to sleep,' one of the leaders said. 'You are all welcome. Put your things down, then come and line up. There is a meeting before lunch.'

It was a warm, sunny day and the meeting was outdoors. Most of the leaders stood at the front, and others stood among us. A tall man, older than the others, was standing on a box.

He said, 'You are known as the children of Angkar – the first of a new generation of the Khmer Rouge children.'

He stopped, waiting for this to be absorbed. Clapping began from the children closest to him, along with shouts of 'Vive! Long Live Angkar Padevat!' ('Padevat' meant 'revolution'.)

The village was located in an isolated area, and only a few damaged houses remained. I looked away from the village, and in the distance I saw golden rice fields ready for harvest stretching for a mile or more. Among the fields were some elderly Khmer Rouge dressed in black. Ox-carts were everywhere. They were carrying bundles of harvested rice to where we were for processing.

My attention returned to the man speaking.

'It is harvest time,' he continued as the clapping stopped. 'We will go and harvest the crops tomorrow and I hope we will not disappoint our Angkar. We must harvest all these rice fields before the new year. We will have to work in rotation to collect all rice crops on time, which is when the rice is ready to fall off. We expect all of you to perform as best you can, along with your Samamit brothers and sisters. You will be divided into groups for the work. So you must all be prepared, and prove to Angkar that we are the real children of Padevat.'

After lunch, all the adults went to work at the rice processing area in the paddy fields, but we were told to relax and be ready for a show that night. As the afternoon passed, I noticed there were many Khmer Rouge children turning up from other provinces. They were all dressed in black. Their sleeping hall was not far from mine, and I could see them gathering together, practising their dancing. Their dancing props included wooden guns, harvesting knives, baskets, hoes, sticks and water containers. I had no idea what they were rehearsing.

Other children were practising revolutionary songs with a woman leading them. It all sounded very promising, but I did not listen for long. I also decided not to take a nap in preparation for the next day's work. I was curious. While others rested and waited, I wandered around the village.

I decided this place was not an ordinary village when I realised there were no trees with edible fruit. The only trees I saw were cotton-fruit trees, whose fruits are used for filling pillows or cushions. These trees were usually planted around ponds away from the villages to provide shade for the farmers' cattle. I had a feeling that this village had been chosen for city people. Had they been punished or tortured here, away from the Khmer Rouge village?

I could not estimate how many people had lived here. There were now lots of temporary huts and halls built by the Khmer Rouge, so it was more like a camp set up specifically for collecting these rice crops. But I wondered what had happened to the people who lived here before we were fetched to do the harvesting.

As I wondered, I walked. I was on a dyke, but there was no water in the field beside me. On the other side of the field were trees, and behind them were many small houses that looked as if they had collapsed or been destroyed. Some had no roofs and some had no walls. I walked over to have a look. Three houses were standing strong among the rest, but their frames were all that was left. It was like being in a ghost town. I was glad I wasn't wandering there at night.

I looked more closely. All the ruined houses had been temporary dwellings, and they were situated around the cotton-fruit trees, not close to the rice fields, where the new halls and huts were. They must have been built for people deployed from the city to work on rice production; that would be why the houses were made of bamboo and thatch, materials that did not last.

This ghost village was mysterious and barren, and almost totally destroyed. Then I got closer to the old huts and saw human bones. First I saw them inside the huts, then draped on stairs and on the ground outside. The more I walked from place to place, the more bones I saw.

There were some full skeletons lying down next to each other. I saw two people who seemed as if they might have been holding hands. The bones were scattered at first, and then I saw some of them made trails. I followed a trail of bones across the dry dirt and gravel and clumps of grass and old logs to the other side of the village. The trail comprised skeletons of people, or bones of their body parts. Some were large, others the bones of children.

Soon I found graves. Most of the bones were here, lying in or near the graves. There wasn't a hint of flesh anywhere as I walked past the uncovered graves. Then I saw movement. There were people living here. I couldn't believe it. People were living here as if it was their village.

I saw shelters of thatch and twigs that couldn't even be called huts. Looking into one of these, I saw two children. They were alive inside this pretend hut. I was shocked. The children were so bony, so skinny. Their knees and joints were swollen to about the same size as their heads. They heard me and opened their eyes, but there was no crying. They stared as if they had no memory, no thoughts.

'Where are your parents?' I asked.

I saw movement on the faces, but they didn't open their mouths. They couldn't speak. They looked totally lost in their minds, and in their eyes I saw so much suffering. I didn't bother to ask again. I just stared for a moment, then kept walking.

Another shelter had a bone tied to the roof. It looked like a rib. I kept finding shelters. More people. Adults and children, barely alive.

As I walked on, I heard footsteps. I turned around and saw a Khmer Rouge lady hurrying up to me.

'Samamit,' she said, 'what are you doing here? You are supposed to line up.'

'Really?' I said with a puzzled look.

'We have been waiting for everyone.'

'All right. Sorry, I didn't know.'

I ran back to the front of the main hut. She was right, all the children were lining up: about a hundred or more stood there.

'There is cleaning needed,' another woman announced. 'We need to clean the houses and collect the bones.'

She explained that people in the village had died in and around their houses. We had to collect the bones and bury them properly in a grave. It wasn't a job I thought I would like, but I was led away to join other children given the same task.

Then I saw an old friend among them. I couldn't believe it. It was my classmate from primary school, Kong Sovichea. We had studied together until Grade Six, but I lost contact with him after that, because he attended a different high school.

We recognised each other immediately. He ran right up to me

and held me close as if he had missed me dearly, then we stared each other in the face.

'How are your parents?' he asked. When I told him they were alive as far as I knew, his eyes began to fill with tears. I held him tight and asked him to control his emotions as we walked to the old houses.

I told him what had been happening and how I had joined the orphans when I was sick. 'What happened to your parents?' I asked him.

He told me his whole family was dead, except for one brother. He didn't live far from this village now, and he had been gathered by the Khmer Rouge and assigned to help with the harvest.

He was very happy to see me. We spoke about other classmates while we were collecting bones in our basket. He had met some old school friends during his journey to this province, but they were separated once more. I told him that this was the first time I had met anyone I had known before.

He began crying again – because of the political situation, the turmoil, the killing and the sadness of losing his whole family. He must have seen them die. He would have found it difficult to forget this when he heard that my parents might be still alive. I tried to encourage him to stop talking and thinking for a while and to start working.

'We are here to replace the other people who have died,' he said.

We collected the bones from around the houses and started cleaning up. We had buried many of the bones by the time the whistle blew hours later. All the other children of Angkar returned to the camp, but our group was lined up. Before we could return to our camp to wash and eat our meals, the KR woman in charge said, 'Tonight there will be a show for our entertainment, so don't be late for dinner after washing up.'

After dinner, we lined up again, all dressed in black as instructed. I was not as excited as the other children; I had been hoping to see Kong Sovichea, but he was not in my line. Then we marched in. Upon reaching the place for the show – just an open, flat area of land – we were told to sit down in a large circle. Two fires were burning inside the circle to provide light for the show. I could see the show well where I sat, but it was dark behind me, so I couldn't look around for my old classmate. He was nowhere to be found.

The show began. A girl about ten sang a song called 'Children of Angkar', describing how grateful the children were after being released from the capitalists, from hunger and from sickness. Other songs followed, about twenty in all, mostly with action or movements to complement the lyrics. A group of boys and girls came out and mimed harvesting, while others pretended to rebuild a new road and railways, and another group performed a short play attacking the 'American puppets'.

I had never seen a show like this before. I found it very interesting, and I learnt some of the songs. The show finished around 10 p.m.

I slept well that night because of the pleasure I'd had that evening and because the breeze was bringing the smell of ripening rice. Early the next morning I woke feeling I had dreamed of Mother. As I rose, I felt she was with me; her love was here, supporting and sustaining me. Outside, under a beautiful night where the moon was still visible in the sky, I saw rice fields everywhere.

Then I heard footsteps.

It sounded like many feet, moving quickly through the nearby village. I walked across. As I reached the dyke between our camp and the village, the footsteps left the village and raced into the rice fields. I stood still. What was it? I could hear a group of adults working hard processing rice, but these frightening sounds came from the opposite direction.

Then the howling began.

I stayed still. My legs began to shiver, then my whole body. The howling came from the rice fields, then closer, from the village again. It was a pack of wild dogs coming to look for the flesh of the people who had died. They would be here a while, because many of the graves were not yet covered with soil. I did not feel scared, but did not want to break any rules that might put my life in jeopardy either, so I returned to bed and went back to sleep.

'This morning we will start at rice field number four,' the leader announced.

I waited under a cloudy sky as we were divided into two groups and told where to go for harvesting. We were each given a sickle. Some children hung their sickles over their shoulders and some stuck them on their waists behind their backs. I found mine too pointy and sharp, so I just carried it in my hand.

Soon we were marching along dykes into the paddy fields, as I had done months earlier in Sahakor Seven. Some of the children sang as we marched. It was a song they'd been taught for harvesting, and we arrived in high spirits.

This was my first time harvesting, and I learnt by watching other children. I learnt to tie up the rice, pack the bunches together and carry them to where we had to put them on carts. It was much heavier work than when I had gathered the young rice plants in the past. The weather was fine, and everybody was so happy collecting the plants. It made me happy to forget the past, and I anticipated we would not starve again during the coming year.

About twenty minutes later, a group of children arrived with our food supplies, and I could see steam rising from the rice in their baskets. The leader of our group blew a whistle, and we all stopped and came over to the dyke. We were each given a plate of rice with a portion of pickled dried fish. I was very hungry. I ate quickly and finished before the whistle blew again for us to return to the fields.

Later, after hours of work, we heard another whistle. We lined up again and walked back to camp for lunch. After we had eaten and rested, the whistle blew once more. I got up and walked back to the fields with the others. I began to sing along with the other children, but I did not dare to sing loudly because I was afraid I would sing the wrong words.

One night after food was distributed and eaten, we were called together for a meeting outside the hall. We were all well fed and attentive. The meeting began with brief announcements, but it was more like a rousing gathering to lift our spirits. It was almost like going to church or the pagoda. The Khmer Rouge propaganda song was sung, followed by their devotional song. All we did was sing, in fact, and then we watched some of the children dance.

They danced when they wanted to. Those children knew their rights. They would not listen to any adult Samamit, nor would any adult Samamit dare try to stop them. There was an atmosphere here that I hadn't known before.

I sat there watching and listening, and slowly I was drawn in by the singing. The children were enthusiastic, and they had all been trained. I tried to learn the words and actions to imitate the style of the singing children, but then they sang songs I didn't recognise at all.

All the dancing, the singing in groups – it was so revolutionary. This really was the new system for Cambodia, and we were the dedicated children of Angkar.

I looked around and finally saw Kong Sovichea. He was sitting by himself, so I went and sat next to him. He wasn't smiling like the rest of us and he wasn't interested at all.

'I just want to stay alive,' he said, 'and hopefully go back to my village in a couple of days. I have a sick cousin there. I want to find out if he is still alive.'

'I also have to go back to my village to find out if my family is still alive,' I said.

When I said this, he lowered his head. I saw that there were tears in his eyes.

'I can never go back to my family,' he said. 'There is no second chance for me.'

He explained that his family were not killed but had starved to death, while he and his brother survived. I sat there with him in silence for a while, watching some of the children dance. When this finished, a leader spoke again. It was a motivational talk to strengthen our thinking about the Khmer Rouge regime and to show us how important it was to obey.

The village was in a remote area and isolated by a swamp downstream from Tonle Sap Lake. Wild dogs inhabited the region, and at night we could hear them howling.

As the days passed, we harvested the rice closer and closer to the swamp. Then one morning, a group of us found a hole under a large termite hill. It was too large to be a snake hole and we rightly guessed it was a wild dog's den. We dug around it, and one of the boys reached in. In it we found three reddish-brown pups.

During the harvest season, many things were happening in the fields. The rats were busy eating the mature rice, and the snakes increased in number to feed on the rats. One day I saw a snake. It noticed I was there and moved straight toward me. I whacked it with my sickle and sliced it in half. I couldn't believe I did this.

I didn't need the snake. We had plenty of food to eat now, plenty of rice and meat and vegetables. Our meals were sufficient but I thought about how much of a treasure the snake would have been in other circumstances.

It took us only two weeks to finish the harvesting in this area, then the leaders gathered us together.

'Do you want to return to your own villages?' they asked.

I thought of my family. I'd had plenty of food to eat, but I wondered if they had enough. I wondered if they wanted to see me as much as I wanted to see them.

'Angkar is very happy,' a leader told us. 'The country is developing well and we have so much rice now. So you are welcome to return to your own villages.'

I asked if Kong Sovichea could come with me, but he wasn't allowed to. He had to go to his own village or return to the children's camp, because he was truly an orphan. He was not happy with this, and he was upset as we said goodbye.

That was the last time I saw Kong Sovichea. There had been fifty of us at school together during those early years, but he was the only one I had seen since the Khmer Rouge overtook Phnom Penh. I wondered about the future: would I find more people from my past in years to come?

Chapter 9
Home Again

THE TRUCK TOOK me to Mong Russey district, where I was dropped off at the pagoda and given permission to walk to my village. I was now a real child of Angkar, yet I still secretly longed for the past. I would have given anything to return to my family home, family meals and a normal life free of fear.

I took the short cut by walking along the dyke behind all the Sahakor villages. Looking ahead, I could see people marching along the dykes. They were singing and they all looked well fed.

I reached the village at about eleven that morning and looked for my house, but everything had changed in the six months since I left. I nodded hello to a few people then found my old house, but that was different too. There was an older woman there, and it wasn't Step-grandmother.

I asked if my family was here. 'No,' she said. 'They are there.' She pointed toward the back of the village.

I saw Stepmother first. She was walking past a hut and between two trees with my stepbrother and sister, who looked older and bigger. They saw me, and Stepmother smiled. Dasy and Vivath ran to me and held my hands.

'Bong Ra, Bong Ra,' they said, 'where have you been?'

'Far away,' I answered. 'Where is Father?'

Stepmother came over. When she first joined our family after marrying Father, we were very close. Since then, she'd had her own children, and our relationship had changed. Still, she was pleased to see me.

'He was asked to go to the lake,' she said.

It was February, and the lake water would be getting shallow.

It was the season for fishing. Father enjoyed his fishing, and I felt happy for him.

'Where is Grandma?'

'She is dead,' Dasy shouted. 'When you are not here.'

Stepmother took my hand. 'She was sick. Luckily, we were able to bury her properly at Wat Chrey Pagoda.'

She led me to the house. 'Everyone is OK,' she said. 'Sophea, Sokha, Sivanchan and Chandy were at the teenagers' camp. They have just returned. We were talking about you and wondering what had happened. They will be pleased to see you back.'

So I was home again and there were people I knew around me – people I had a history with.

Our new family home had an open space inside with four small windows. At the back was a door leading to a small terrace that served as a kitchen and held a large water jar.

Stepmother began preparing a lunch for me. Then I heard the bell: 'Bong, bong, bong, bong.' Stepmother grabbed her plate and bowl and walked off. I hurried after her.

Many people saw me and came and talked.

'You look well!' they said. 'How are you? Where have you been?'

The village leader saw me and called me aside. He had been good to Father, and he did not ask me much. Perhaps he already knew my story.

'You will need to move to the teenage boys' group,' he said, then he shouted to the lady in charge of the kitchen to provide another meal for me. There was plenty of food, and I was even allowed to take some back to the house.

Puthea arrived. He had come from the river, where he had caught a fish. We sat and had our own meal together. It was great to be home again, though it was not the same as when we lived in Phnom Penh.

The first bell rang at five o'clock next morning, and I packed and went to the teenage camp. Everyone had gone to work except the cooks and Samamit Von, the deputy leader of the boys. I could tell that he wasn't feeling well from the look on his face and the way he was hunched over.

'Oh, you're back,' he groaned. 'Welcome.'

'Good morning, Samamit Bong,' I replied.

He said, 'Now, what do we do with you? Which group were you in before?' He looked at me, probably wondering at how I had changed.

'I was with Group A.'

'OK, Group A? Remember Thon? Now he has been promoted to deputy leader of that group.'

Thon and I had worked closely together before, and I was keen to see him again. Meanwhile I was sent out to join a group in the fields. There was no more rice to harvest, but now we were digging canals and building dykes for irrigation. Around noon, we came back for lunch.

Thon was there, waiting. He looked at me and smiled, then walked past me. He didn't seem to be the same person. I felt the presence of evil, but I put it from my mind.

In the afternoon, I joined the teenage boys' group and saw my brother Sivanchan again.

'Welcome,' he said. 'It's good to see you. You look better, brother.' He hugged me and held me very tight. I could tell he was glad to see me back alive.

When he let go, I looked at him. He seemed taller, but he wasn't: it was just that he had lost so much weight. I saw he was crying, and we hugged once more. Then we lined up again to go back to the rice fields.

I had been given a hoe, and we went to work. It was the same old routine. We came back to camp about 5.30 p.m., cleaned up and ate again, then the bell rang.

I followed the boys to a special meeting in the dining hall. It wasn't just for my group but for all the boys and girls, including the younger children.

Samamit Kon, the commander of the teenage camp, stood up. He was solidly built and had a moustache, and was almost as old as Father. During the meeting, I was welcomed back and asked to speak.

Everyone was quiet as I walked to the front.

'When I got to the hospital, Angkar selected me to be in the orphanage group and sent me to the provincial town. I was very well looked after there with medicine. Under Angkar's care and supervision, we children were able to survive, and then obey and follow the direction of Angkar.'

They all clapped.

'During this time we had the opportunity to do some singing training,' I added.

'Go on,' some of the children called. 'Show us.'

I felt Mother was watching, and this gave me courage. I started to sing the songs I had heard. I sang the song about how being a republican child is like living as a dog compared to living as one of Angkar's children. I sang another song about how living as Angkar's children means living freely and with power. I displayed the movements that accompanied the words and everyone watched me. Some of the Khmer Rouge children knew these songs, and they joined me as I sang.

As the days passed, I spent some of my time in the children's group, teaching them and telling them about what I'd seen. The rest of my time was spent with the teenage boys. As the weeks went by, food supplies were slowly reduced. By March, we only got two meals a day, though the evening meal was so generous that we took some away with us for breakfast. It had come from the communal kitchen, so we were allowed to eat it at home.

As the food stores diminished, people became unfriendly, especially Thon. I had questions about things that I dared not speak of, and I was lonely.

When I returned to the village, some families had left for Vietnam. Others just weren't there any more. No-one dared say a family had been executed or killed. We simply said they disappeared. I also noticed many teenagers were missing, especially those who used to be in my old Group A. There were only four teenage boys' groups now instead of five.

I was very lucky my family were all still alive, though not

together. Father was still fishing on the lake. Sivanchan was assigned to the senior Teenagers' Elite Force – a special group that worked at the district or provincial level, closely monitored by the Khmer Rouge and guarded by their guns. They worked on the biggest irrigation sites – building dams.

Now that harvesting had finished, we worked on irrigation. I was digging canals and building dykes. The dykes were in parallel pairs and sat two metres wide at the base, and one metre wide on top. They were a triangular or pyramidal shape with the top part cut off.

At that time, we didn't know where the water was going to come from, but our assignment involved building these dykes every day. A metre was the quota for each of us. With our leaders there were thirteen in our group: this meant thirteen metres of dyke.

Sometimes, team members were lazy. This was discussed in the many meetings that occurred in the evening.

'I don't care,' the leader of all the teenage boys finally said, 'as long as each group completes their quota each day.'

Our group decided each of our members would construct the same amount of dyke. We would dig the soil, call our group leader to check, and then the camp leader would come and measure. Then we would return to camp. The village leaders noted the eager workers and told their superiors.

Messages came from Angkar: 'We have to go and help other Sahakors. Some of them are short on people. We must help them with canals and dykes, because many people starved last year.'

One day, when work was over, my group met under a tamarind tree. The meeting finished quickly enough, but when we were about to go back to camp I felt very, very strange. Suddenly I realised everything was different. Everything was dark, nothing was the same.

'Today there is no moon?' I asked one of my friends.

'Yes there is. There. See?'

But I couldn't see. I opened my eyes wider, straining to make out anything. It was very dark, darker than usual – it had to be. I stood up, but the ground seemed further away.

'I can't see,' I said to my friend, and I stumbled on to him.

I stood still as he held me. I strained my eyes as much as I could. All I could manage now was to see about a metre. Beyond that, it was only dark shapes.

I began to panic. Was it something I'd eaten?

I sat. Others of my group were nearby and must have been watching me. 'Why did you have to open your eyes so big?' one of them asked.

But where was he? Why couldn't I see his face?

I didn't answer but stood again. I tried to walk but struggled and fell into a hole and hurt myself. One of the boys saw me and pulled me up.

'Oh, you have chicken blindness,' he said. 'You cannot see at night.'

'So I'm blind?' I squealed.

'No, in the daylight you will see again. It's only at night you cannot see. I had it last year.'

I held his shoulder and walked to the camp. I felt helpless, and my eyes were sore because I kept opening them too wide and straining their tiny muscles.

'Thank you, Samamit, for bringing me back here,' I told the boy who took me back to the camp.

'I am Sri,' he said. 'Don't you remember me? I started here when you did, when you first arrived here.'

'Sri! So it was you. Are you in my group as well?'

'Yeah!'

I had thought I was well, but now this. I could not explain at first, but then I worked it out. Our meals were barely sufficient – only rice with a piece of dried fish or fried wild morning glory, a flowering weed that grew near or on the water. We didn't have enough vegetables and our nutrition was poor. This is why I contracted 'chicken blindness'.

The next day, as the morning light came up, I could see again. I was so pleased. But that evening I was blind again. Chandy was in a different group and we hardly saw each other, but the next morning I saw him and told him.

The following day after work there was no meeting, but we had to help another village. I saw one of my friends with a hoe, so I grabbed one too. As I walked across to the area where we would line up, I heard music. We had electricity now, but it wasn't often turned on and I didn't understand how it was generated. This was the first time it was used to play a gramophone.

It was communist music and it was loud and it was beautiful. It was a cold but pleasant afternoon and as I lined up I sensed that everyone else was inspired too. I hadn't heard music for so long. I felt a joy deep inside me and forgot about my eye problems.

We marched off to the fields and worked, but it was different. Mothers and fathers and children from our villages and other villages were all working together, trying to clean up the canal. I could hear them; I could hear their joy as I listened to the buzzing of the insects, felt the sweat dripping down my back, and smelt the dusty soil all around me.

We packed the baskets with earth and passed them along the rows. We dug and dug and dug. And we built a dyke, a huge dyke about three metres wide at the top and six at the base. As the evening grew dark, my sight again failed me, but I coped. I could see about a metre ahead and I was OK as long as I didn't have to move anywhere quickly or walk far.

Around eight or eight-thirty that night, food was brought to us. It was quite late after we finished eating, but we went back to work. Around eleven, a whistle blew. We packed up and lined up for the march back to our own camps.

'Bong Dy,' I called to Chandy.

I knew he was nearby because I had heard his voice. There was no answer.

'Bong Dy.'

This time I heard him answer: 'Ar-Ra, I have it too.'

'What?'

'I have chicken blindness.'

I made my way to him. He was talking with some other boys

and explained to me that he'd had it for almost a week, a few days longer than I'd had it.

I heard everyone rushing around us and I asked Chandy how we would get back.

'Here, hold on to my shirt,' he said. His friends led him, and I followed. He said, 'There are others, you know. Lots of boys have chicken blindness.'

At camp the next day, Samamit Thon teased me, not for the first time.

'Stop pretending to be weak,' he said. 'There's nothing wrong with you.'

One day I found a new friend from another group. His name was Sothy and he was very quiet, but kind.

'Eat this, it will help you,' he said.

'What is this?'

'I only have half. It is the liver of a rat. It will really help you.'

'Why?'

'It has helped me. One of my brothers gave it to me. It does cure.'

I took it, ate it raw, and the next night I could see. It was a miracle, I thought. It was wonderful being able to see again at night, and I was so happy.

About a week later, the blindness came back.

I felt terrible, and my eyes hurt more than last time. Would I ever be really cured? Whatever was in the liver was clearly not enough. I had no idea what the nutrients were that had helped me, but I guessed it was something missing from my normal diet. Still, I had to go on. Angkar had work that needed to be done, and no-one was special. We all had to do our share, or we wouldn't eat.

Samamit Von, the deputy leader of the Teenage Boys' Camp, didn't like me. He didn't like me before and he didn't like me now I'd come back. He kept pushing me, like Thon, and said I was lazy. I tried to avoid these two and kept closer to the other deputy leaders or to Samamit Kon, the camp leader.

One day, when I returned from working in the fields, someone told me my father had returned from fishing at the lake. He had been there for many weeks. I asked for permission and rushed to him.

'I have chicken blindness disease,' I said. 'Do you have any rat liver?'

No-one said they were happy to see you any more.

'Oh, it's you,' he replied. 'No.'

Father was fat and looked so well. We talked for a minute, but he was tired.

'But I'll try to get some,' he added. 'I still have some dried fish, I will try to exchange it for some.'

Father couldn't help, though, and as each day passed I became more anxious. What if I had chicken blindness for the rest of my life, and Von and Thon teased and mocked me almost every night? I had to get a cure. So I decided I had to catch a rat. Then I remembered I knew where to find a rat-trap. Thoeun had taught me how to use one when I was in the village before, herding the cow and the bull.

I worked harder the next day so I could finish early and sneak away. I'd seen a broken trap abandoned in the bamboo at the back of the village. It was covered in dirt and spider webs. Its string and stick were broken, but the rest of the trap was fine. I took it to the river and cleaned it carefully. It hadn't been used for months, but I knew that if there was any smell of dead rats on the trap, it wouldn't work.

When the trap was prepared, I returned to the back of the village near the bamboo, and looked for what was called the rat trace – the droppings and other evidence that told me rats had been there. Eventually, I found a rat path that led to a hole near the rice fields. I hid the trap in the bamboo, near where I had found it. The rule about not being allowed to cook or eat your own food remained, but there had been no reminder for months.

My sleep that night was full of restless dreams. About four in the morning, I rose to check my trap. It wasn't far from the camp, and I had memorised the way. With the help of a stick to guide me, I found the trap quickly.

It held a big rat, which was still struggling. I pulled it out and released the string from the bamboo's spring. Blood poured out from the rat's mouth. I struggled to hold it in the darkness then smashed it hard against the ground until it died.

Then I didn't know what to do. I was scared. I used my fingernail to break its neck and then I skinned it. After throwing away the organs I didn't want, I was left with the liver and the rest of the rat. I wrapped banana leaves around it and hid it, intending to return after work the next day to cook it.

After work I fetched the rat's remains and wrapped them in a shirt, which I tied around my waist, then I went looking for a fire. I preferred to find a fire, or make one, where I couldn't be seen; but I soon realised cooking the rat would be difficult, and I would have to wait until after dark.

I did not want to waste any time. So I took the liver from around my waist, stuck it on a stick, and wandered around hoping to find someone else with a fire. Eventually, I found a fire, and they let me cook the rat.

After that, I caught rats night after night, and the following evening I would find a fire to cook them on. Everyone knew I had chicken blindness, so they let me cook on their fires. But they would never stop asking to taste my food. I would share the rat meat with them, so I had something to negotiate with, but I always begged the owners of the fire not to share the liver. The negotiations were always tricky.

As time passed, I caught fewer rats. Sometimes the rat got away, and sometimes my rat was stolen. One day my rat-trap was also stolen, so I had to design a new one. This happened after I had eaten a lot of liver and my blindness was mostly gone.

One day about April 1976, the village leader called everyone to the dining hall.

'In a couple of days,' he said, 'we will have new people. We will welcome them and let them live with us.'

This was the first time since we arrived – nearly nine months before – that others had come into our village. They would have news and things would be different.

A couple of days later they did arrive, and I met one of the new boys, an orphan called Huor. He was short and kept his head down when he walked. His voice and accent were also different from everyone else's, because he was of Chinese parentage but born in Cambodia.

Huor told me that his family of five had all died of hunger and sickness, but he had been saved by a KR family. His eyes were red when he told me this. He was now staying with the family of a deputy village leader. Everyone showed Huor respect because of where he was living. He was allowed to leave the teenage boys' camp and stay with his adopted parents whenever he wanted.

Huor was modest and humble, and we became good friends. He was my first real friend since Thon, whose wicked eyes now circled around whenever he saw me, because he thought he was my superior.

One night, our whole village was invited to hear Huy-Meas, one of the newcomers, who was a very popular singer. Most people had only heard her over the radio or on cassette, but now she would be singing in one of the other villages.

The village promoting her had set up electric lights, run by a generator. She sat in the middle, and her singing was heard through a loudspeaker across the villages. Although still only about thirty, she had been a popular singer under both the monarchy and the republic. Now, she was forced to sing all the communist songs, but she sang them to older Khmer music. She had a beautiful voice, but I didn't pay much attention, because I wasn't much interested in the words. Though I was trying to get along with the Khmer Rouge, I was losing interest in communist beliefs, because my thoughts were focused on food and survival.

On the Khmer New Year, known now as Victory Day, we were invited to the Wat Chrey district celebrations. In the morning we lined up, all dressed in black, many of us with caps on our heads and kromas, and marched to the communal town hall for a meeting.

There were many villagers here, and we listened to a number of leaders speak. Then a military group came to join with us. Carrying AK-47s over their shoulders and wearing ammunition strapped around their bodies, they arrived on bicycles, with their leaders coming in on motorbikes. Many of them came from different places. They stayed in their own groups and watched each other.

A dancing demonstration followed, then a meal provided by the Communal Cooking Committee. But there wasn't enough food to go around, and we were only given half our normal helping. We had to sit in the sun from morning till afternoon, talking and singing revolutionary songs. At about five we headed off back to camp to a bland meal of rice and rice soup. The size of the meals was being reduced again, and I was constantly hungry, still lacking nutrition. I wondered where it would all lead.

It was April, still too early for replanting rice, and we continued to build dykes and dig canals. Sometimes we had banana tree soup mixed with smelly fish pickle, or some bananas were fried for us.

I became more and more unsettled. I just couldn't get the orphanage camp out of my mind. It had been an easier life with more food to eat, and I was the leader: there I felt I was someone, and I wanted to return there.

One morning, while we were walking to the fields, I saw a small crowd gathering on the edge of one of the fields, on a dyke where trees grew. They had found the dead body of Huy Meas, the singer.

Samamit Von led us past quickly. He was smiling as he said, 'This is an example for people who are lazy and only using their charm for themselves. Angkar has set a new rule that says everyone has to work hard and not rely on other people. If no work, then no food!'

He was happy and made us sing as we walked on. No-one dared make any comments about Huy Meas' death. We all knew the same could happen to us.

Chapter 10
The Prison Camp

'WHAT IS YOUR problem?' my group leader snapped.

'I have a very severe headache; my head is heavy on my left side,' I mumbled.

'Stay,' he said, 'but soon you come to work.'

I didn't know if I was really unwell, but I was miserable.

I had grown to hate our village. My dreams and thoughts filled my head so full that I hardly thought of my own wellbeing. Mostly I missed the orphanage centre.

I was lying down on my hammock when I suddenly got up, packed my belongings, and left. I didn't even think about saying goodbye to my brothers or the rest of my family.

I sneaked out and hid behind some trees, then walked in the canals, vaguely hoping to go back to the orphanage centre in Battambang Provincial Town. I took roads where I thought I wouldn't see many people. Hours later, I found National Road #5. It was very quiet, and I walked on it bravely.

I walked north for almost fifteen kilometres without having to speak to anyone, without really seeing anyone. Then I reached a patrol post: the guards were having lunch and didn't see me. I saw other people, villagers, near the road and then on it, but I stiffened my body and looked straight ahead as if I was sleepwalking.

As I continued walking toward my destination, a Khmer Rouge man on his bicycle came from a village and stopped me.

'Where are you going, Samamit?' he asked me.

'I don't know. I … I'm Angkar's child and I am going to the orphanage centre.'

'What. Your parents are dead?'

'Yes.'

'Where are you from?'

'From Chrey commune. Sahakor Seven.'

'So do you have any papers to prove you can travel?' he continued.

'No! But I have been at Angkar's orphanage centre in Battambang town.'

He told me to follow him. He took me to a long house like a school but built on stilts about a metre from the ground. It was made of wood with a zinc roof.

'You wait here.'

He pushed me in. The door closed behind me, and everything was dark. I knocked into someone, and hands pushed me away. I stumbled over feet and fell onto legs. The place stank with the smell of filthy bodies. I heard scratching and shuffling as some of them moved to make space for me.

I sat and leaned against a wall. I realised this was a prison camp where the KR held educated people – officials, professors, teachers, doctors – before interrogation, re-education or execution.

My dreams died as I waited for someone to speak. I waited and waited. I hadn't had any lunch, but no hunger grew within me. Hours later, in a silence that was broken only by the occasional shuffling or distant murmuring outside, I fell asleep.

I awoke to more shuffling. The men were taking turns moving to the centre of the room. 'Go on,' I heard someone whisper. Between turns I saw sunlight coming through small holes in the wall.

Then I heard footsteps – 'Bang! Bang! Bang!' They grew louder, closer. The door opened, and sunshine raced in. It struck our eyes, blinded us.

'Here is your dinner! Come out one by one and line up,' a voice said roughly.

We squinted as we filed out and lined up. There were many trees, and a dirt road, and hills. I counted twelve others who had come from that small room. There were other rooms, other houses or huts. They all remained closed, except one. From here more prisoners came out and lined up beside us.

Five or six Khmer Rouge soldiers with weapons stood around. Two girls dressed in black carried a big rattan basket full of plates. The plates were distributed, one in front of each of us. We were then told to sit down. The two girls returned with rice and dried fish. Each of us was given a piece of fish and a large spoon of rice porridge; it was only one spoon, but the rice porridge was solid. I saw a man use his hands to spoon his food into his mouth. Another man did the same, and I followed his lead.

It was getting dark, but soon we had finished.

'Back to your own cell!' a voice ordered.

I suddenly felt I had to go to the toilet. I asked for permission from one of the Khmer Rouge, who was busy lighting up his tobacco-leaf cigarette. He looked at me.

'Samamit! Take this boy to the toilet behind the house,' he instructed one of his men. Everyone else turned and stared.

The toilet was located down a path, past some trees and behind the houses. Along the way I noticed there were wooden boxes near the doors of some of the huts, and inside these were foot-chains. It was getting darker. I saw a house nearby lit with a kerosene lamp. A number of Khmer Rouge were sitting on the veranda, smoking and talking to each other.

After I came back from the toilet, when they opened the door for me to go back into the room, I saw there were only about five people there now. Some leaned back against the wall, and others lay down on the floor. After the door closed, I could not see to find my belongings. While I was feeling for my pack, someone grabbed my hand. 'Here is your bag,' he said.

'Thank you! Do you know where the rest of the people are?'

'Go to sleep,' he said. 'Tomorrow you will know.'

I slept. Then there were noises. Someone was opening the door, and the sound of liquid was falling near me, running into holes in the floor – it was someone pissing! I moved to one side as the door opened.

The men with me rose and walked through the door and out into the darkness. I followed as they marched down the steps to line up in front of our small room. There was freshness in the air and the gentle breeze felt good: our room had been so stuffy and smelly from piss remaining on the floor and the faeces underneath.

One of the Khmer Rouge brought out the chains from the boxes and started to attach them to everyone's legs. But they did not chain me. We marched off in a line, and it was clear the others knew where they were going. Over by a wall, they picked up their tools – hoes, baskets, spades. I picked up a hoe. We walked along a track to the main road, then along the road to the rice fields as the sun started to rise.

The work was not much different from what I was used to – digging and repairing canals. But this time the people I worked with were in chains and were being closely watched by the armed Khmer Rouge.

I looked around – no-one else dared to. Two men with torn clothes were straining to pull a plough as though they were cattle, while a man dressed in black with his gun slung over his shoulder steered them with a whip. There were others working, men and women, others pulling ploughs, and many guards with whips and guns.

I could hardly believe my eyes. How cruel they were to these people! My hands started to shake and my body started trembling, so I stopped looking.

That night, I wondered why this was happening. Why were all these men here, and what would happen to us? I had my eyes closed, but I heard murmurs. The others were awake and seemed to be worried about something. I did not know what and I fell asleep.

'Samamit Virak! Please come out.'

The light blazed in, and I raised my arms to my face. The others were cautiously alert, their faces tense. The guards rushed in and grabbed one of the men, then bang, the door was closed again. Everyone was quiet. When prisoners were taken for interrogation, I later observed, some would return and others wouldn't.

The next morning, I was up early. I wandered around the walls of the room, peering into the cracks, and for the first time I noticed I could see into the room beside ours. Upon entering or leaving my room, I had noticed the next room's door was always closed and bolted with a lock. Now, as the sun outside rose higher, some light shone through other cracks. As I spied into the room next door I saw a man.

He lay on the floor in the middle of the room, unmoving. He looked more like a skeleton with only a rag covering him. Was he dead? But I couldn't smell him. Then he moved. Well, I thought he moved, but it was hard to tell in the dim light shining through the cracks.

I sat down again. Picking up my courage, I finally spoke softly so that only those nearest could hear.

'Look, there is a man lying dead in the other room next to ours. I wonder what he did, and why there is only him in that room?' I said. 'Please tell me.'

'He's like us.'

'But why is there only one person there? Who is he?' I persisted.

'He is a high official from Battambang province,' came a voice beside me.

I stood up and looked through the crack once more. The sun was rising, and more light peeped in through the walls, so I could see him more clearly. His head was bony. His feet and ankles were chained to two pieces of wood. His hair was so long it wrapped around his neck for a pillow.

I turned. 'How long has he been there?' I whispered.

'The whole time. More than a year.'

'And you?'

'The same.'

I was with men who would probably be executed, but I too was a prisoner. Really, they knew I was no criminal, but I had lied and run away. They must be deciding what to do with me.

But in my Sahakor I had also been a prisoner, not much different from this. Here we all knew we were of the same kind – survivors – and everyone was friendly enough in their own way. Yet we never knew each other's personal histories, whether we were a teacher or a farmer or a student or what, and we didn't know which villages we were from.

Two meals of hard rice porridge with a little fish were provided each day. It was sufficient. I enjoyed the work building the dykes along the main road, cleaning up canals. There were no propaganda meetings at night, and I was glad of that. The main disadvantage of this prison camp was that my room was very small, and my eyes always hurt when we had to leave. There were no showers or water for washing, and the other prisoners knew that sooner or later they would probably be executed.

After I was there a couple of weeks, a nearby village requested assistance. They were mostly Khmer Rouge in that village and had been treated well because they had been liberated before 13 April 1975 and volunteered to join the Khmer Rouge. Now we started to work for them in their fields.

A couple of weeks later, some time in June 1976, a prison official took me aside as we ate our morning meal.

'We have visited your Sahakor Seven,' he said. 'We have decided to take you back.'

I didn't know what to say. Within the hour, that official was carrying me on a bicycle back toward Sahakor Seven, eighteen kilometres away.

I was tired and could hardly stand when we arrived. I was passed immediately to the village leader, who handed me over to the teenage boys' leader. It was Samamit Von, who had been promoted.

'What happened to you?' he asked.

'I do not know.'

'You do not know?'

'No. I think I was sleepwalking.'

'Sleepwalking! Children of Padevat!'

I was lucky. The man who brought me back was not the one

who first found me, so he did not report that I had told him my parents had died.

I had no idea what excuse to give, but I told Samamit Von, 'I did not know what had been going on but I felt as if I might have been sleepwalking.'

Samamit Von laughed when he heard this story. He teased me and accused me of being lazy. 'You just wanted to return to that old place,' he said.

He did not know it was Angkar's orphanage centre. I did not bother to explain, but maintained my silence and felt very guilty. The rest of the team in the camp all laughed at me. But the village leader intervened; he said I had been a hardworking child in the prison camp.

Von continued to tease and threaten me: 'So you were sleepwalking? Ha. Did you mean to escape or what? If you go sleepwalking again, you will be dead.'

'You believe or don't believe,' I said, 'it's up to you.'

After dinner, we had a meeting. One of the issues raised was about whether I needed to be watched. Samamit Von wanted me to be watched. He said I was unreliable and couldn't be trusted. The other leaders discussed the matter. In the end, I was told to be careful.

Stories about me soon circulated around the village, and children were making jokes about me sleepwalking.

Finally, my family came to see me. They had been so worried. Keeping their silence, they prayed I would be excused. Otherwise, they would get into trouble as well. At the same time, they thought I was very lucky to still be alive. I had been in a prison camp from which people didn't usually return.

Two weeks later, we were told new leaders were being sent to us. I hoped this would bring about a change for the better, but meanwhile matters became worse.

One day – a day with black clouds in the sky that I will never forget – my group was called to a meeting before dinner. This was unusual, and the meeting was held near the dining hall, in front of everyone who was waiting.

One of the boys in my group had complained to the cook about the food. It wasn't the first time.

Samamit Von called him over, grabbed him, tied his arms and beat him till his face was bruised and his arms and legs were broken. He dragged him by the hair through the watching crowd until there was no life left in his limp body.

'This is an example of people who dislike our rule and who want equal share,' Von announced, still holding the boy by the hair. 'We are the ones who liberated you, and you must remember the difference between you and us.'

In front of women and children – there must have been more than a hundred of us – he took a knife and stabbed the lifeless chest he held. He opened up the boy and cut out his liver and gall bladder.

'This will be the same for anyone who opposes us,' Von declared.

He took the liver and gave it to the cook.

'Cook this for me,' he said, 'and I will share this with everyone.'

Von walked to the side and talked with his colleagues. The rest of us stood in silence waiting for our meal to be distributed. I saw the faces of the children – they were all in shock.

The cook chopped the liver and threw it into the wok. It smelt nice, but the liver bounced on the wok. It was full of energy and anger from the person who had died.

This was the only day I could not eat my food. I think no-one ate more than a few spoonfuls. Some of the women fainted, and I was shaking.

Nobody spoke much after that. We just lined up obediently and worked. The death weakened everyone's minds. When I saw Samamit Von again, I saw in his eyes the liver he had eaten. He always looked evil to me, but I bowed and behaved respectfully to him out of fear.

In August, two new leaders came to replace some of the old Khmer Rouge in our village and immediately introduced new regulations. One of them, Samamit Khon, was tall and talkative and seemed well educated, but he kept Samamit Von as the leader of our teenagers' group. We were sad at this, and we became more careful than ever.

The killing continued. Our village was next to the one where Huy Meas had been executed. The Khmer Rouge left her body unburied under a tree as an example to those who missed the old ways. That tree was near the rice fields where we worked. I never forgot the tree, and I remembered Huy Meas.

I witnessed further executions. In the same village, I saw a woman who had been taken. It was far away, but I saw a man kneel behind her and hit her with a stick until she didn't get up.

No-one talked. Everyone who had supported a republic or monarchy was threatened. I was so scared of the horror. The methodical killing made me focus on one thing only – staying alive. There was no time to think about anything else. When I tried to recall the past, my mind went numb. I couldn't even remember my birthday or everyone who was in my family. All I could do was focus on my work, and what I was told to do.

The rain pelted down onto the fields of mud. It was like being under a waterfall, and it hadn't stopped all morning. My legs were heavy as I lifted them and took another step. I looked across to my friends, but it was hard to see them through the sheets of falling water. They were still there, so we hadn't been called back yet, as we sometimes were after hours and hours of rain. Maybe soon? Maybe the message was still getting through?

I lifted my feet again and again, stepping onto higher ground. The water was only knee-deep as I approached the next island of mud. I replanted the young rice I was carrying, parting the mud hastily with my fingers, compacting it again with my palms. If they did call us in, it would be because the mud was too wet for the plants to hold – no other reason.

My arms empty, I began walking back to the dyke with rivulets of rain tumbling down from the top of my forehead to my soaked shirt then to my shorts. I noticed the mud on my thighs. I didn't mind having my legs covered in mud, especially dry mud, which covered my leech wounds. Some of my wounds were about the size of my thumb, but to us the wounds were a lesser worry. Food and staying alive by working hard according to their rules was the utmost concern.

The leeches bit everyone, especially the women, it seemed. I had sores all over my legs, and they were getting bigger. I wasn't healing quickly because of inadequate nutrition. It was only the mud that gave my sores any relief, the mud that was being washed off my thighs right now.

I was angry. Why didn't they call us in? Or had they called and we couldn't hear, couldn't see because of the rain?

I still worked with the teenagers in the monsoon season. The parent groups ploughed the fields, and we planted the rice. There was a growing shortage of food. It would increase again at harvest time, but that could be months away. And our clothes? They said, 'Angkar will provide new clothes soon.' The promise echoed through my mind like my lunch bowl – empty – as the monsoonal rain continued to pour down. We'd been wearing the same clothes for almost a year. They were full of holes, and the black dye had faded.

There was no pleasure in working so hard three hundred and sixty-four days a year. We were soaked and we were bothered and we were wondering about our food, which was late again. We continued to replant the rice under the dark sky, sloshing through mud often thigh-deep and sharing it with the leeches. There were more leeches than I'd seen before. We called them buffalo leeches because of their size.

We had to work every day and meet every night. We met to criticise those who didn't work well enough and who didn't achieve their goals. At these meetings, we were also given future plans: 'In the future, you will have a better life, if you work hard now. Three or five meals a day, whatever. You will travel in a luxury vehicle. You will have meals on a turntable spinning around so you can all choose what you want to eat.'

The new regime was praised endlessly, but we had already seen the executions and the disappearances. We grew more and more discontented, but we all kept quiet.

I heard the whistle blow. Exhausted, I climbed up to the dyke and walked along. I fell off into the canal on the other side, but picked myself up quickly. Everyone was gathering just a little further along. We had no shelter from the pouring rain, and by the time I arrived, the large containers of rice and soup were already mostly empty. I saw the grim look on everyone's faces. It wasn't just the soaking rain.

When I peered into the pots, I was shocked. The rice, like a porridge, had stuck to the bottom of the pot and was burnt. We could smell it. And taste it. But we had to eat it with morning glory soup – there was nothing else, only this soup that had no flavour except for the dead larvae from the pickled fish that floated on top. Some of the larvae had already grown to the size of caterpillars. Were we going to fight for these?

We sat in our groups, trying to touch our heads together as we ate in an attempt to make a shelter, but the rain continued to fall and pour into our food. After eating we had twenty minutes to rest. There was no shelter, and I was so tired. I lay on the dyke with my head under the leaves of a young palm tree that didn't even reach up to my knees. When would we have a better life, or was this the best I could hope for? I fell asleep, and immediately dreamed of Mother.

I worked for about a month until we had almost finished replanting the rice in every paddy field. We worked through very heavy rain, sometimes for a whole day from early in the morning, sometimes for several days. Many workers contracted colds, hay fever and flu, and other diseases no-one understood.

Occasionally, work was called off if the rains were too heavy. The soil on the dykes would be slippery too, and that's when we fell off. We would slide down into the canals or the fields. It could get cold, and no-one had any shoes. I often looked for excuses to go back to camp for dry clothes, or just to wipe off some mud or examine my sores. One day, while I was doing this, I checked the new rat-trap I had made, and it was gone.

I had learnt a lot from Banh, my young colleague at the orphanage, and became confident at killing lizards. One day I killed a good-sized lizard, enough for more than one meal, and took it home as I often did, strapped to my waist and hidden beneath my shirt. Stepmother was boiling water so I started to cook. But the smell was strong and she found out what I had.

'Quickly, take it off!' she said. 'They will come and punish me.'

I took it from the fire, wrapped it around my waist again and returned to my camp. Surviving was difficult. I would eat what I found, whether it was cooked or not. I ate the lizard half-cooked.

Despite my resourcefulness, I continued to lose weight. I was given two spoonfuls of rice in a working day and one when I was sick. Like everyone else, sometimes I ate what we called the rice dust, which gathered sometimes after the husks were removed. The fresh dust tasted very nice, but once it was stored and ridden with insects it tasted horrible. Normally, they used the rice dust to feed pigs, ducks or fish. If humans ate too much, they would get yellow fever or blood in the urine. I was still eating anything else I could find: crabs, shrimps, fish, snails, lizards, grasshoppers, frogs – anything. It was amazing how well my body could adapt without getting sick again.

As time passed, the rice grew. It was November, and the birds came to eat the rice that was ready for harvesting. I was one of many children selected by Angkar to chase them away. We would shout, scream, wave our arms around and make loud noises. We would bang drums or hit buckets with bamboo. Many of us did this, and it meant running through thick mud, or climbing trees to watch the flocks before they arrived. Others built small huts or shelters in the middle of the muddy fields, or dressed up scarecrows to look like old men. Usually it was a dull job, but often the birds would come in flocks so large that we would all suddenly jump up and yell and run through the fields like a pack of dogs.

We continued to move from one field to another. When harvesting was busiest, I was taken from bird watching to join the harvesting teams. The parents and girls did most of this harvesting, and then during the night we did the smashing and grinding and helped transport the rice to the village for storage.

After all the rice was collected from our village, the village across the river requested help, and I was chosen to go along. This village belonged to the Khmer Rouge military people. They were not considerate. They expected us to work hard for them, but only gave us rice with pickled turnip to eat.

While assisting with the harvest, I saw a big rice-field rat. It ran when it saw me, but I chased after it, following as it darted in and out of the water and between clumps of rice. At one point, I thought I had lost it, but then I saw it out of the corner of my eye going into a hole.

I blocked the hole and looked around to make sure there were no other holes nearby, then I put my hand in. I felt the tail of the rat. I pulled, but the tail was slippery. I lay down with my legs in water, my chest in mud and my shoulder resting on a clump of rice. I was in the hole up to my armpit now, my head turned to the side and my eyes facing a bright sky. This time I got it. It was still slippery but I managed and I pulled it out.

It was a poisonous snake! I smashed it down and killed it quickly. I looked around, but no-one had seen me, so I skinned the snake and kept the body. Then I put the snake to the side and tried to break open the hole, bit by bit. I put my hand in again and snap, the rat bit my fingers. I grabbed it around the jaw and pulled it out with my hand bleeding. I killed it, and as I was cleaning it I found babies – it was pregnant.

The babies were so small their eyes weren't yet open. I had to keep this to myself, of course. If the leaders found out I had the rat or the snake, I would be executed. I hid the snake but knew I probably wouldn't be able to return. I grabbed the baby rats and the mother, and wrapped them in my shirt. I found a place on the dyke behind some bushes and pulled some matches from my pocket. I gathered twigs – there wasn't much – and started a small fire. Quickly I topped it up. It wasn't enough to cook the mother rat, but I cooked the babies. There was no-one nearby. I was hungry and wondered how long I had before someone would see me or notice the thin billowing smoke from my fire. I knew I didn't have long so I took one of the babies, rubbed it against my clothes to remove the ash, and ate it. I ate three, then lost the fourth when someone shouted.

'What are you doing? You're eating something, aren't you?'

It was one of the deputy leaders of my group. He came over and kicked my fire, looking for food in the ashes. He didn't find the baby or the body of the mother, which I had already hidden nearby.

'There's no food here,' I said.

'Then why are you playing in the ashes?'

'Just to put on my bites.'

I showed him my sores from the bites of the leeches, and rubbed ash across them. He stared for a moment, then shrugged and walked off.

I was almost throwing up now. I had never eaten anything like this, and I had swallowed the last baby whole. Luckily, the people in this village were lazy, which was why they needed us. They weren't vigilant either, just happy to use us for any help they could get.

I went back to where I had hid my mother rat. That night I sneaked out to where the fires were for the cattle, cut the rat in half and cooked and ate it. After that, I felt content.

After a month, we were returned to our village. I asked for permission to visit my family. Permission was granted, and I was told I had two hours. I saw Father sitting on the steps outside the house. He was fat and smoking tobacco wrapped in some kind of leaf.

'You're here,' he said.

'Yes Papa, I'm here.'

He was staring.

'There is rice and other food inside a container. Eat.'

There was no greeting of love any more, just an offer of food.

I went inside. I found a plastic container with rice and pickle, and dried fish that he had brought from the lake. It was very tasty, and I ate quickly, not even stopping to swipe at the mosquitoes buzzing around my ears. I was ravenous.

I returned to Father on the steps and sat with him.

'You've put on a lot of weight,' I said.

'Yes, we have been very lucky. We find a lot of fish in the swamps near the Tonle Sap Lake.'

'OK. Good.'

'I saw your brothers before, and your sisters. I gave them fish. Do you want some fish?'

'No thanks. It's no good. If I take fish back everyone will find out. Maybe better to leave it here. If I can come, then I can eat here.'

'That's fine.'

'I'd better go.'

I got up to leave. It was late when I returned to camp, and Samamit Thon called out to me as I approached.

'We have a meeting,' he said. 'So why are you late? You asked for two hours. What happened?'

'My father, he's come back. Just had a long talk with him.'

'What were you talking about?'

'Oh, about … oh, talking about how we were doing well. He really likes Angkar and he said that's the way to improve the system, by working and living in a group.'

'Really?'

Thon left.

There were times when he or some of the other leaders interrogated me.

'Your father,' they said. 'He was a film producer in the old days?'

'I don't know.'

'He's wealthy. You're missing your home town very much?'

'No.'

I wasn't concerned. I was aware of these types of questions. I knew to respond only positively, and otherwise keep quiet. But I knew Thon wouldn't be asking these questions if I hadn't told him a bit about my old life, back when we were friends.

As we continued to work on the canals, I noticed the village was becoming quieter. There weren't as many of us. Some who were of Vietnamese background had been sent back to Vietnam, or so I thought. Others were executed or died from ill-health, overwork or starvation.

I personally didn't see much killing, but I came across many dead bodies in the rice fields or in the area between the camps and the fields. I also saw many uncovered graves.

We didn't speak of any of this. When we were given more food, we forgot a lot. At the meetings, we would sing songs of the revolution and condemn the capitalist governments for treating poor people badly and supporting the rich. The songs guided people to forget the past, forget other people, forget our backgrounds: they taught us to be grateful only to Angkar.

I didn't think much about what was happening, but we were all being watched. The chlopps were given even more authority to spy around the village, and it was common to be confronted and questioned by them. They demanded answers and demanded them quickly.

Families were disappearing and nothing was said. Individuals were sometimes taken from their work or their camp and interrogated or arrested. 'What is your family doing?' KR officials would ask. 'What are they planning? What have they done in the past?'

Sometimes the leaders or the spies would do things differently. They would give a boy extra food portions and allow them to do less work, and then they would sit beside him and draw out any information they could, which usually meant everything he knew.

I looked on. I spoke to no-one about anything. I focused on my work, and on my food, and on putting from my mind anything that didn't help me to survive.

Thon was involved with all of this. I had done the work he was doing, and I knew how he operated. He knew I knew, and eventually he left me alone. But I knew I had to get away from him and the terrible mood that was gripping our village.

Chapter 11
Smashing the Temple

ONE DAY IN March 1977, our leaders called us together and said, 'Our group is requested to assist in the building of a dam on the Sangkae River. In three days time, a truck will arrive.'

I had longed for a change, but I wondered if it would be for the better. I scratched my head. I felt my scar again and wondered how it looked. I wondered how I looked: so skinny, dirty and worn.

Most of the harvesting was finished. Everyone was collecting rice, removing the husks and storing it. We had been very lucky with our crop, and now I had the opportunity to leave the village to build a dam across the Sangkae River in Battambang province.

The truck picked up about forty of us from the Wat Chrey villages and we travelled the whole day. Chandy was there with me, but we didn't talk. I was alone now, no matter who was with me.

We arrived just before dark to a construction area that was full of activity. Thousands of people from many districts and provinces were gathered in dozens and dozens of camps along the road near the Sangkae River. I'd seen nothing like this before. It reminded me that places could be different, circumstances could be different.

It was a military camp, and Khmer Rouge soldiers and officials were everywhere. The Sangkae was a wide river. I raised my hand above my forehead to block the sun and gaze at the dam wall that stretched before my eyes. It was enormous. The area they were working on must have been well over a hundred metres wide.

Our group of forty was divided into two, and we joined existing groups. My camp was based next to the river, where temporary

Left: Here I am in the middle, at age three, with my older brother Chandy (right), and cousin Vuth, who now lives in the USA

Right: Back row: Father, Mother (holding Puthea) and Vanny; Front row (left to right): Sivanchan, Sophea, Chandy, me and Sokha. With Dad being a film-maker we often posed for the camera

Seven days after my mother's funeral in 1966. The girls are on the left (from the back): Vanny, Sophea and Sokha; boys on the right: Father (carrying Puthea), Sivanchan, Chandy and me. My mother meant more to me than anyone, and her memory comforted me throughout the four years of Year Zero

In front of our bookshop on Kampuchea Krom Street in 1967, about a year after mother died. Father sat on the bench. Standing (left to right): Vanny, Chandy, Sokha, me and Sophea

This pic was taken in 1971. Father looking sophisticated wearing his sunglasses. I'm the one with the big grin standing in front of him. Puthea is standing in front of me with Sophea far left. Vivath is on the bike. On Dad's left is Vanny, Sokha, Sivanchan and Chandy

Taken sometime in 1973. Clockwise from left: Chandy, Sophea, Sokha, me, Vivath and Puthea. In the background, if you look carefully, you will see Ar-Peng standing on steps behind the fence that separated our houses. The jar in the foreground is what we would sell in our family business

This photo was taken inside our house in March 1975 just before Vanny went to the airport to go to Australia, and right before Year Zero. Back row from left: Chandy, cousin Suor, Dad, Vanny, Stepmother, Sophea and Sokha; front row from left: Sivanchan, me, Puthea, Mealea, Dasy and Vivath

Phnom Penh residents sheltering from a Khmer Rouge rocket attack
Françoise Demulder © The Image Works

The mountain where I was deployed to work, and taken to be executed

In front of my family's hut in the Khao-I-Dang camp, Thailand, early 1980. Back row (left to right): Chandy, Cousin Vuth, Sophea, myself, Cousin Rom, Uncle Chhoeun, Sokha, Cousin Rothmony and Father. Front row: Cousin Tontoo, Vivath, Stepmother, Dasy, Aunty Lay and Puthea

Inside my family's hut in Phanat Nikhom in 1980 while waiting to migrate to a third country. I am standing in the back next to Sokha. Squatting on my right are three Filipina nurses, Linda, Betty and Roza. Sitting (left to right) are Dasy, in front of Chandy, Father (in the black shirt), Sophea, Vivath and Stepmother (in the white shirt with the long sleeves)

Working at the Catholic Relief Services clinic as a registrar in August 1980 before I became a doctor's assistant. (I'm in the foreground taking notes. Possibly the beginning of my journey to becoming a school teacher!)

Sitting next to Dr Margaret, the visiting head of Clinic, who promoted me to the position of doctor's assistant. The man standing on my far right is Lim Suor, now known as Richard Lim. He now lives in Melbourne and together with his wife runs Lim's Pharmacy in Springvale

This photo was taken with Sister Nurse Mary at the Phanat Nikhom refugee camp, October 1980

Working in the Catholic Relief Service clinic in the Phanat Nikhom refugee camp, September 1980

My friend Huor and I learning to use the apparatus

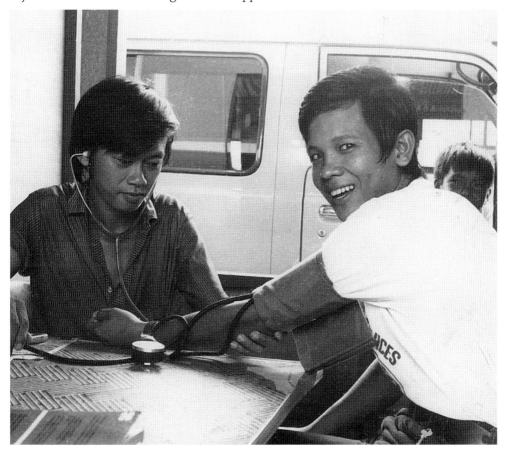

This photo was taken with Sister Nurse Mary at the Phanat Nikhom refugee camp, October 1980

The Wiltona Centre in Melbourne, March 1981. I was moving from the hostel to live in a rented house in East Melbourne

huts had already been built. We had new leaders from other provinces as well as one or two of our own, but not Samamit Thon or Samamit Von.

Everything was different. Nearby were rice fields, but there were lakes and ponds too. Behind the dam wall, a large lake was forming. Many rivers entered this lake. At the foot of the wall, a river flowed steadily through an outlet beneath the dam, feeding the fertile valley, which supported many villages as well as providing a great source of fish. The dam had to be completed before the rains came, so the work went on twenty-four hours a day, each group working two four-hour shifts.

My job was to carry soil upstream in bamboo buckets while others worked with metal or broke down rock. I carried soil for about a week to build up the dam wall. To get the soil, I had to wind my way along a narrow path into a large hole about fifteen metres deep. I was scared. I didn't trust that hole. We all hurried to leave it as soon as the buckets were full.

The hole grew steadily deeper until it reached below water level. When it reached the right depth it would be filled with concrete, which had to be poured immediately, to form the foundation of the dam.

We had different tasks. Some of us had to lay wire along the foundation, some brought the rocks to lay down between the wires, and some had to break large rocks into smaller ones so they could be used for the foundations. The foundation was about a hundred metres square, so they needed an enormous amount of rock. My group was pulled out to break the rocks, which were brought in by truck.

'Here, these are your hammers,' a Khmer Rouge official announced.

He and an assistant threw a couple of bags on the ground. Another assistant showed us a cubic wooden box a metre on each side. This was the standard – every day we had to fill one of these for each person in our group.

Breaking the rocks involved rotating shifts. The rocks had to be smashed to the size of a fist. We did not get any safety materials to protect our face or our body. Each of us was only given the head of a hammer, and then we had to make our own handles.

They were ordinary hammer heads about the size of my big toe – nothing special for breaking up rock. Some rocks were tough and couldn't be broken with a small hammer like this, but the demand for a cubic metre of broken rocks per person per day was not negotiable. We knew we had to do as we were told. We were not Khmer Rouge, and the penalty for disobedience was death.

I soon found my hands swelling and hurting, but we had to keep working. Blisters began to form, and my hands became red and bruised. But we couldn't complain or get any medical aid to cure those blisters or bruises.

One day, a leader came over. He came from one of the other villages, but he wasn't Khmer Rouge. He was looking at his own hands. Some of the other boys sat and listened as all three of our leaders discussed what to do.

Different ideas were shared before one of the boys caught everyone's attention.

'Let's get sticks. Tie them to the hammer, and swing the sticks to bang the hammer down on the rocks,' he said. 'There's rope back at the camp, with the other tools. Over there,' he pointed to a nearby group of tall trees, 'we can get the sticks.'

The leaders thought about the idea.

'If they're green,' another boy added, 'they will bend easily when we swing them.'

We tried this, then made the sticks longer. Finally we worked out a method. It wasn't just the impact that had been hurting our hands, but it was the vibration of holding the hammer as it pounded into rock. Now with a long, thin, flexible stick we were protecting our hands and adding force to the whack of the hammer.

We became experts at our work, and soon the rocks were breaking easily. I was grateful. Whenever I thought about them, I was fearful of the Khmer Rouge: keeping busy helped me hide my fears, and I came to enjoy the work. But it still wasn't easy, and we were stretched to our limits.

One day, I heard a terrible shriek from one of my room-mates, Samamit Vy.

The nearest leaders ran to him.

'Here, put this towel on your eye,' someone said.

But nothing helped and he was crying hysterically.

I ran over.

'Help me, Samamit Ra!' he said when he saw me.

'Samamit Vy! What is happening to you? What is wrong?' I asked.

'It's my eye. It's my eye.'

I saw his hands covering his right eye. I saw blood flowing down between his fingers.

'Let me have a look!' I shouted.

'Help me, Samamit Ra. It's hurt.'

Forcing his hands apart, I saw his eye was badly cut. I spoke to a leader and was given permission to take him to get help. I took him by the arm. He was crying and screaming and staggering. Nearby was a house where many KR cadres were hanging around, and I headed there.

'I can't open my eye,' Vy said. 'It feels as if a piece of my eye has gone.' He sobbed some more. 'A splinter of stone hit it and took it away.'

'Don't say anything, Vy! Wait till I find someone to help you.'

I encouraged him not to cry. We reached the house, and a man sitting on the veranda leaned forward and shouted to me. 'What is his problem, huh, Samamit?'

'This Samamit's eye was hit by a stone.'

'How did it happen?'

'He was working at breaking the rocks into smaller pieces, and accidentally a sharp piece of stone snapped off from the rock and hit his eye.'

'So he worked without any safety gear?'

He took Vy inside the house and had a look at his eye. He told me to return to work and said he would call if he needed me. As I was leaving, he asked my name and what group I was in.

I returned to the rocks and took a deep breath. Our lives were so fragile. I wondered when it would all get better. Would we ever get back to a normal life like the one I was brought up in?

'It's in his eye,' I heard our leaders say. 'He'll lose it.'

He would lose his eye, I thought, and he would lose his mind and he would lose his life. This couldn't happen to me. This could never happen to me. Mother, please help me, I prayed, closing my eyes for a moment.

We worked on and on with the rocks at the foot of the dam wall. We were given special meals three times a day, because we were now working in engineering and construction: we were elite. We worked hard, but it was good.

We had been working for about a month when I began to wonder about my brothers. A year ago, we had been told that Sivanchan was working somewhere in an elite construction group, but I'd discovered it wasn't here, and I didn't know where Chandy was. Chandy came to the dam with me, but our group was separated into two on the day we arrived, and I hadn't seen him since. I wanted to look for them now. I wanted to ask questions, but I didn't know who to ask. I dared not ask the Khmer Rouge.

Next, we were ordered to Ak-Phnom district to smash some rocks.

We carried food and woks and other implements as we walked. The bright sunshine soon became oppressive. We had a cook accompany us as we marched along the dirt road.

It took us almost the whole afternoon to get there and when we arrived it was like walking into a jungle. It was not a jungle, but an abandoned village. As we walked deeper into the empty village I overheard the leaders speaking. I realised it wasn't a quarry we were going to, but a temple, the Ak-Phnom Temple, which was about a thousand years old.

'Quick,' one of our leaders shouted. 'We need to set up our camp before it gets dark and the rain comes down.'

'Put your things under the rock over there,' another leader commanded.

Then I saw the temple. It was a mighty ancient temple hidden in the middle of a forest. By the time the rain began to fall, we had almost finished building a makeshift tent to protect the food. It was common to encounter unusual weather at this time of year, a sign of the coming of the monsoon season. When the rain came, it fell quickly and hard. All around me I could see water streaming from the plants as soon as it touched them.

It was difficult to see through the rain, and the combination of rainwater and sweat made me uncomfortable. But I was overwhelmed by Ak-Phnom Temple. It was so old and it was huge. There were trees and vines growing all around it, even seeming to grow into the walls themselves. Through the rain, I saw someone among the trees. It was an old man, and he was watching us.

'Build your own tent,' I heard one of the leaders say. 'In the morning we will smash rocks.'

But first I looked around. I saw the old man again. He had grey hair and a beard, but he looked fit for his age. He seemed to be some kind of caretaker. There was no-one else around in this amazing temple. It was quiet and peaceful, except for the squeals and screams from the animals in the forest and the constant whistling of the birds. I spotted the old man again around the side of the temple, where he seemed to be sweeping leaves into a pile.

The next morning, the sun was shining. I overheard one of the leaders say the temple was built between the tenth and eleventh centuries. Our task, we were told, would be to demolish it.

That first day, we built huts in the morning, because the tents would not be enough to shelter us against the rain, then we began breaking rocks. We worked in teams of about a dozen, which included three leaders in each group. At least two of these were Khmer Rouge. We searched for loose rocks first, and found rocks that had fallen from a broken wall outside the perimeter. As we did, the old man I had seen yesterday hurried across.

'This is the Ak-Phnom Temple,' he said. 'It is protected by guardian gods. If you continue to destroy the temple's rocks there will be a curse on you all. Then, if you persist, you will become ill ... headaches, diarrhoea ...'

'Nonsense!' said one of our leaders.

'And once you get sick, you will die.'

'Go away, old man. Let us work.'

We started to break the rocks. It was easy. We gathered and broke so much in that afternoon. It was quite a soft rock, and we didn't have to go to the temple to get it; the rocks had fallen from the walls of the temple and were sitting in piles, waiting for us.

When we completed our day's work, I went with some friends to explore the area nearby for food. We found a huge beehive on a tamarind tree.

'We have to be careful! Does anyone know how to get this big beehive down?' one of our group asked.

Samamit Kaet nodded his head and waved his hand. He was short but strong, a dark-skinned native of the northern part of Battambang province. Without saying a word, he placed an empty bag between his teeth – an old sack used to carry rice – and climbed confidently up the tree.

When he got near the hive, Samamit Kaet took his scarf from his waist and covered his face. He took the sack and stretched its opening wider, placing it over the beehive, then squeezed the beehive into the sack. He tied up the mouth and dropped the sack down.

I was hiding behind another tree and looking up nervously. When the sack hit the ground, it opened up, and the bees got out. They flew back up the tree and attacked Kaet. He was brave. He climbed down with his scarf over his face and ran to a nearby stream. The bees chased after him, stinging and buzzing, but the insects that persisted drowned.

Back at the camp, with the leaders' permission, we all began to eat the honeycomb and the honey. We tried to chew but the honeycomb was too tough to swallow. I realised they were not bees but something more like a wasp. We sucked out the honey nevertheless, and it was delicious. Then we took out the dead wasps to fry in the big wok and ate them.

Cooking in the wok, the insects gave out a most delicious smell. I just couldn't resist, so I put a spoonful of them into my mouth.

'Oww!' I cried.

'What have you done?' one of the oldest boys said.

'It hurts. It bit me. It's still alive.'

'It's not. You must remove the sting from his butt first before you eat. Don't you know that?'

I didn't know. I held my mouth wide open, blowing as if I was trying to extinguish a fire.

The other boys were laughing and happy with their food. Rice was coming now, and the rain had stopped. I learnt to remove the sting from the insects, and I still ate quickly until I received my last spoonful. The soreness in my mouth eased, and I enjoyed the fried 'bees'.

The next morning we all lined up in our camp. It had been raining, but the sun was shining now, and as usual it was hot. As we approached the temple – around the side of it this time, near a major entrance to the hidden city inside – one of the leaders saw something.

'Stop, wait here,' he said.

We stopped, and I glanced up to see the old man again, walking among the trees beside the temple.

The leader went ahead by himself, then off the track to the left. He glanced up, and the old man met his eyes. They stared at each other before the leader returned.

'There is something here. It's a pattern in the grass.'

On his signal, we all went and looked. A rounded grassy hump extended out of the ground. It was about a half a metre wide and looked like the roof of a tunnel, and extended across the surface like a meandering snake. We were all shocked. We'd never seen anything like it.

'Here. We'll take the rocks here,' another Khmer Rouge leader in black uniform demanded. 'Start working on the fallen rocks on the ground near the temple, but outside the main temple area.

We started to pick up the smaller rocks and made a pile of them in a dry, flat clearing. We took our elongated hammers and began banging, the sound of our tools shattering the peacefulness of the forest.

'Stop! Stop!' a voice called from the forest.

We all turned to listen. It was the old man who had been watching us. He ran over. 'You'd better not break any more stones, or tonight one of you will get sick. Keep breaking the stones and you will die.'

A chill ran down my spine. I had already sensed the guardians he had mentioned earlier. The banging on the stones slowly stopped as two of our Khmer Rouge leaders confronted the man.

'Bullshit. That's a lie,' one of them said.

He looked over to us.

'Don't worry about it,' the leader shouted. 'Let's continue. Back to work!'

The Khmer Rouge ordered the old man to mind his own business, but there was some hesitation when they told us to start breaking rocks again. The leader who had spoken grabbed his own hammer and began setting an example for us. He raised the hammer and ... bang.

After a few more bangs, we all started working and breaking stones again. Our enthusiasm began to return, and soon we all stopped believing what the old man had said.

After a couple of hours, I noticed that the KR leader wasn't there. Another KR man who had been standing near him was watching us working. We continued breaking stones. These stones were not hard to break, although they looked hard and had holes in them like volcanic rock.

After a while, another KR called: 'Samamit Daek! Where are you? Are you OK?'

He was looking for the one who had spoken to the old man. We found him lying down on the ground. He looked up, and I saw his mouth move. He spoke softly, and we came closer to hear what he was saying.

'Please help me,' he whispered. 'My stomach is so painful. I've eaten something bad.' He sighed and groaned. 'But I don't know what. I've only eaten the same food I had yesterday.'

We looked on and listened as he caught his breath.

'I've got a stomach ache. Very bad. I can't go to the toilet and it's getting worse and worse. Please help me.'

I thought of the old man's warning. This KR leader was stubborn, and this is what he got for smashing up the temple's stones.

We lifted him and carried him to the camp. There we waited for a nurse. I left and went back to work. No-one dared raise their hammers, but sweat poured freely down our backs. Only some Khmer Rouge leaders continued to break the stones, wanting to prove they did not believe in superstitions. As for the rest of us, we began to believe. In our hearts, we prayed to the guardians not to curse us, for we had only been doing what we were told.

We gathered together, about twenty of us, and discussed the problem with our leaders.

'Last night, the guardians came out,' one of my comrades explained. 'I dreamed of the old man, and he warned us not to harm the temple, otherwise we will get hurt. Maybe killed.'

Then a third Khmer Rouge man came and insisted we return to the camp. It began to rain again. I was shaking. I think we all were. None of us wanted to die like this.

At camp, we found that many of our comrades were sick. They had persisted in trying to hammer away at rocks. So we rested, waiting for our leaders to tell us what to do. Our fear kept us quiet, then I heard a voice.

'Ahhhhh,' it cried.

Those sleeping were woken up.

'I saw them,' one of my comrades screamed.

'It's only a dream,' someone answered.

'No, I saw them too,' another called out.

'And I did,' a third one shouted.

The camp leader, who was Khmer Rouge, went over to a comrade who was ill.

'If we don't get out of this place, we will all get sick and die here – including the leaders,' he said quietly to his comrade.

He went and spoke with the other Khmer Rouge, then came back and spoke to us.

'News from the dam's construction HQ has come to us,' he said. 'We are to immediately stop our action of destroying the temple. It is an historical temple and our top leaders in Phnom Penh were not happy when they heard the news of its destruction.'

Our thoughts of death suddenly disappeared, and we felt alive again. Our camp leader announced that we would pack and leave the next morning. We were very pleased.

Chapter 12
The Wall Breaks

WE WALKED BACK to the construction camp the next morning in heavy rain. I had never seen as much rain as I had those last few days. It was a slippery walk, with puddles everywhere turning into streams.

Finally we saw the camp through the mist of the rain, and everyone was frantic. People were hurrying, running. There was shouting, but it came softly to my ears, muffled by the noise of the water that fell from the sky. It was as if there was an ocean up there, and it was falling over the edge of the world.

A KR soldier ran up to us. He had been waiting at the end of the road.

'Hurry,' he said as he pointed wildly. 'The water is rising. Take your belongings to camp and then report to the construction office.'

Soon we discovered the cause of the panic. Days of rain had filled the reservoir, and it was feared the water would spill over, flooding the village below.

Everyone was hurrying to the bottom of the wall to bring more soil to higher ground and stop the water from spilling over the dam. We were enlisted at the top of the wall, emptying buckets of soil. The outlet low in the dam wall couldn't release the water fast enough, and the water level rose steadily. From where I was, near the top, I could see water starting to flow over the other side of the dam. It looked as if the level on that side was lower than where I stood. The top of the wall – we called it a road – was about eight or ten metres wide, and little streams were running across it.

A KR engineer called a soil-carrier group over to the road. They raced over and poured soil there, and another group tried to press down the soil. But it didn't work. The water continued to run over the dam-road, and the streams grew wider.

'Get out from there and let the water flow over!' another KR engineer with a loudhailer shouted out to that group. He was dressed well and sounded as if he was in charge of this construction. I had the impression he knew the dam was not big and tall enough to withstand two days of heavy rain.

We had been back for an hour. I was exhausted, but the rain continued. My comrades were hurrying everywhere, and I sensed the urgency among the Khmer Rouge.

The rain continued to pelt down. Finally, an alarm sounded, but music was playing over a loudspeaker, and not everyone heard. Those who could hear the alarm were racing away from the bottom of the wall, but some workers were still there laying down reinforcing rocks. They couldn't hear the alarm or the cries of the engineers calling out from above.

'Get out! Get out!' the engineers shouted.

But the workers were still trying to reinforce the wall. 'More soil! More soil!' they called to us.

We stood there watching, listening. We didn't move.

Then there was a crack. I could see water leaking through the wall.

An instant later it happened.

The water made a mighty roar as it broke through the wall – the wall that was about two hundred and fifty metres long and ten metres thick at the top, much thicker below. The sound of the flowing water was frightening as it poured over the broken wall to the foot of the dam, crushing everything in its path. Some workers rushed to climb up the side of the dam, but for many it was too late.

Many people were working at the base of the dam, and now they were all in a panic. The ocean of angry water washed through the valley onto the plains and into the villages. Frames made of metal poles were carried along by the rushing waters. Rocks and people and huts bobbed up and down in its wake.

Everyone fought hard in their own ways to stay alive. I felt sad for those who could not make it to shore, but there was nothing I could do to help them. I thanked my mother for watching over me and directing me to stay back. I had no idea what else to think or do. There was no time, no room in me for any feelings. Most of the construction area was covered with water now, and people were screaming as they were carried along by the water.

It all happened so fast. The water washed away as we looked on. It had gone into the villages and under the houses before flowing downstream. The rain also stopped. Then we saw fish. Some were quite big, up to about eight kilograms, and we collected them for food.

Only one part of the dam had been destroyed. Within hours, the Khmer Rouge were organising us to rebuild. Part of the foundation was holding, but it was covered in mud. We had to dig the mud out and replace it with stone. The work started immediately.

I began to feel as if a weight was falling on me. People were killed and still missing, everything had been destroyed, I was hungry and we had been wasting our time.

The next day, I found out more than two hundred people had been found dead or were missing. It was like a slow execution for us. We were working harder and harder each month, and it was killing us.

We had been working for weeks, and now the rain was falling steadily each day. The engineers instructed us to make the sluice gate wider and detour more water around the dam. Other areas had already had heavy rains, which were now flowing into the lake.

It was important to divert the water away from the dam wall, and many groups were assigned to do this.

There were about two thousand of us working at this site, despite the deaths and others who were missing. My group was working long hours carting soil and carrying supports that had been made in other places. We had to stop the water as quickly as possible, and more workers were called up from other districts and villages.

We were bringing more soil. Workers hesitated to work at the foot of the wall, but they were ordered to go there. It was very slippery, and the revolutionary music played on through the loudspeakers.

One day, a Khmer Rouge engineer told me to go to headquarters. 'Go and see Samamit Khom,' he said. 'Go and get me the measurements.'

The headquarters was a large wooden building with two offices, a kitchen and a dining area. It was surrounded by a veranda and had many windows. Unfortunately, Samamit Khom was not in. There was only a cook there, and he told me to wait. He didn't ask me what I wanted. While I was waiting, he started cooking, and the aroma mesmerised me. It was rice cooked in a special way, and grilled fish.

'Samamit Bong,' I said, 'do you need help cooking while I am waiting for Samamit Khom to come back?' I asked him humbly, with the most sincere look on my face. I was hungry and I saw an opportunity. If I could offer assistance, I might be able to eat some of the food.

He stared at me for a moment, holding his spoon just above the wok. He was much older than me, but still young. I could see he was well fed.

'Yes, all right,' he said. 'Take off the rice and pour it into that bowl.'

I lifted the saucepan with the rice and poured it into a big bowl. The bottom of the pan had rice stuck to it. I scraped this out, and started washing it. 'Show me how you want me to do this,' I asked.

I tried hard to show him how capable and interested I was. He was working alone, and he wore the Khmer Rouge uniform. I was wearing black too, so I suppose he thought I was also Khmer Rouge.

As the minutes passed, he began looking pleased. I was so nervous, being in the camp headquarters of the Khmer Rouge engineers. Many of them were older men, and I could tell they had been with the Khmer Rouge for many years. Some were military and wore their weapons, but others were just engineers. And they all wore black.

'You take the fish,' he said as he began cutting the vegetables. I saw he had a plate of pork near him too, probably to make some soup. 'You look after the grilled fish,' he repeated, and he came over and showed me how.

When he went outside to get water, I pinched some rice and put it in my mouth. It was hot and almost burnt my tongue. While I was taking care of the fish, I looked around. I cut a portion of fish and put it in my pocket, then I changed my mind: I just ate it and kept quiet.

The cook came back with a bucket of water.

'Cook more rice for me,' he instructed. 'I'll just clean this pan first.' He pointed to the one used for the cooked rice before. 'I don't have another pan like this,' he added. He gave me a few more instructions, then left with the pan.

I noticed someone looking in. Then the back door near me opened. It was the Khmer Rouge engineer who had first instructed me to go to headquarters.

'Oh it's you,' he said. 'Why are you still here? Why didn't you get the measurements for me?'

'Sorry. I was told to wait for Samamit Khom to come back. He's not here and I don't know where he is. The cook asked me to help him.' I was nervous and waved my hands around as I talked.

'OK. That's OK.'

He came in and looked around, then he spotted the rice. It was grilled golden brown and hot from the bottom of the wok. It looked crunchy. I had already prepared some with oil and onions on top and placed this on a plate.

I took a piece and asked him to try. He tasted it and started to smile.

'Do you need me,' I asked.

'No, that's OK now.'

I felt relaxed and pleased to know these KR engineering people were reasonable and understanding, but then I had to return my thoughts to my work. I had made tasty, crunchy rice the first time

I had cooked rice in a big wok. I had seen people cooking before, though, and I had used my initiative in preparing good food.

I continued cooking, put more wood into the stove and placed a lid on the saucepan. The cook came back, made the soup and came over to check my rice.

'How is it?' he asked me.

'I don't know. It's still cooking.'

'Let me have a look.'

I lifted the lid. He wiped his hands on his apron, took my spoon and scooped out some rice. He lifted the spoon to his lips and blew on it. I was so nervous. I sensed this was an opportunity for me. But I kept thinking nervously that I'd never cooked before.

He tasted the rice and smiled.

'Wow, this is great cooking; the rice is just right.'

'Thank you.'

'Well, this is good rice because it is crunchy on top and crunchy underneath. It's perfect.'

As the afternoon progressed, I started to spoon out some rice and eat it. The cook didn't say anything at first. Then he said, 'You can have some if you want.'

Later he told me, 'Tomorrow, if you can, come to help me again. I will be pleased.'

'Yes,' I said, and he gave me a portion of the food he had cooked – rice and fish and vegetables.

I went back to my group.

'Where were you?' asked one of the leaders appointed by the provincial construction task force. 'I'm sorry,' he added, 'but we didn't know where you where and we've eaten your share already.'

'That's OK.' He looked surprised. 'I was asked to help the Khmer Rouge engineering team with their cooking.'

'Did you eat?'

'Yes, and tomorrow they want me to help again.'

'That's fine, good. You go ahead.'

He was happy because he then could take my share. I was pleased too. I had brought back rice and dried fish to eat that night, and I knew there would be more. I was pleased also because I had a special job now. I only hoped they wouldn't find out that I was just a peasant, or wouldn't care. I had done well today, I thought, but I really didn't know how to cook.

I went to the engineering headquarters again the next morning. The cook was pleased to see me.

'OK,' he said, 'now we have to make a special dish. I need you to cook rice and chop vegetables.'

He showed me green papaya.

'And this is the fish.'

He had already cleaned the fish: he had three of them lying in a basket.

'And morning glory.' He showed me another basket, full of the morning glory plant.

'That's fine,' I said. 'I can do that.'

I started to do the work he wanted, then he had to go out. He said he would be back, but something kept him. I washed the morning glory and made the whole meal by myself before he returned.

At lunchtime, some of the officials saw me as they came back from outside.

'Oh, you are the new cook,' they said.

I was dressed in black and they thought I was a part of their team. I served them hot fries, rice with vegetables and morning glory, and papaya sour chilli soup. They enjoyed it, and from that point on I became a cook for them. It was easy in some ways but difficult in others, because I would risk my life if I made a mistake. The environment was friendly though, despite the disaster we'd had. They didn't seem like killers.

There were many Khmer Rouge around, and I was happy. Mother was looking after me, I knew. But some of the workers were less fortunate. I was on the west side of the river, and other groups were on the east. I don't know why, but I often saw people on the east lined up and killed. And they didn't get as much food as us, or so I'd heard. They were from villages that had very little Khmer Rouge influence until now – villages that had not been working hard in a disciplined way like us.

For three weeks I worked there as a cook, eating well and enjoying many different kinds of food. I hadn't paid much attention to the progress of the dam, but I noticed that the rain had poured down constantly for two weeks. I didn't think about it because all my thoughts were taken up with what meals I must cook and how much I enjoyed this job. As well as me, the cook had an assistant. He was friendly and had many ideas about preparing different meals, so I was kept busy learning from him, as well as from the cook.

Then I heard bells begin to ring. I could hear the propaganda music but also the alarm. I lifted my pot from the stove, and we raced outside.

Heavy rain was still falling. Everyone was running, and many people were falling over in the mud. Someone turned off the music, and the workers beneath the dam began scattering in every direction like frightened ants.

Then the dam burst. It was like a gigantic explosion, but it didn't go up, just out from the wall, into the valley and toward our camps and the village. Fortunately, canals had been dug to divert the water this time. The angry water rushed out in many directions, but no camps were washed away, and no houses in the village were damaged beyond repair.

Many of us ran down to the river, hoping for fish to be left behind as the valley flooded. The water flowed over the dam very quickly, and nothing could stop this flow now. We were soaked and shaking as we lined up on both banks of the widened river, watching the strength of the water, feeling despair, gazing at the water flowing over the remains of the dam wall, then watching the supports float downstream.

I wiped water from my face and put my hand up to my forehead so I could see more clearly. But I was looking into my mind: I couldn't see how the wall could be rebuilt this time. I couldn't see how I would be able to go on surviving in this world.

Later, back in the kitchen, I looked for a place to get warm. After I returned to camp that night, I sat in silence. We all did. The rains continued through the night and next morning. Then there was a whistle for the group leaders. They instructed us to remain in the camp and they all left for a meeting. It was a strange feeling, watching the leaders from over a hundred camps making their way to the dining hall while the rest of us were confined to our huts.

I'd already folded up my hammock for the day, but I pulled it out again and tied it up from one pole to another. I was never good at sleeping on the floor. I climbed into my hammock and slept.

An hour later, we were all awake, wondering about the leaders' meeting. Our group leaders soon returned and gathered us together. My group met under our hut, where we always had our meetings.

'Some groups will be going back to their villages, and some will be staying here until further notice,' they announced.

I looked around at my colleagues. What would happen to us?

'We will stay here?' someone asked.

'Yes, we will stay here, for now. Our village is well organised, and we are able to carry out our work without assistance. In the meantime, we have been asked to help some of the villages nearby to clean up from the floods, the heavy rain and the breaking of the dam.'

'And then do we go home?' It was someone from another village who asked this. I knew he wasn't happy here.

'We help clean up, and the dam engineers will be looking at the damage. Then they'll decide if the dam can be rebuilt.'

We were given instructions to stay put and wait. I could not go to the headquarters kitchen, but I could at least relax. I lay down on my hammock again and listened to everyone.

A few hours later, we lined up and started to walk down to the villages. But the rain became heavier, so we turned back. I lay on my hammock again and listened to the pounding of the water against the bamboo sides of the hut, and pulled my blanket closer to my neck.

'Wake up. Wake up.' Another boy's hand was on my shoulder. 'Pack, pack, pack. We all have to go back.'

Chapter 13
Eating Flesh

IT HAD RAINED without stopping for five days, and it was raining now as we sat in the truck. We'd packed quickly and rushed down our lunch. The rain blew in, and I waited for the trip to be over. Many thoughts ran through my mind.

I didn't like my village, but I was looking forward to seeing my family. It was now September, and I'd been away for more than six months. It would be harvest time soon, with plenty of rice for everyone.

'So would it be a good time to return home?' one of my friends asked me. 'What do you think, Samamit Ra? Is it time for the harvesting?'

I closed my eyes for a moment, then opened them again and counted slowly on my fingers. 'Oh, ah! Not yet. Two more months for the rice to be ready. But I guess the replanting is almost done.'

When we arrived, Sahakor Seven was empty, dead. There were few people and those we saw didn't speak: people saw us arrive but didn't care. Our first meal was only three spoons of rice porridge. This explained the sour faces and the sick, tired bodies.

I went back to the teenagers' camp, but it was now known as the Elite Teenage Boys Group, a separate group. Samamit Von was the leader of all the teenagers, but he didn't bother us. No-one did.

But Thon mocked us and seemed to think it his duty to make everyone feel dejected. I didn't know why. He was only one of us, not Khmer Rouge. Our group leaders felt all this too. They told me Thon had talked to the village leaders to try to remove our group leaders so he could take over our group again.

Everyone and everything was miserable and mean. It was like

a sickness. On returning to Father's house, I saw Stepmother and she cried. She didn't say anything, just wiped away her tears. I thought she was excited because I had returned.

'Where is Father?' I asked.

And then I saw him, walking over.

'Are you back?' he said.

I saluted him with both my hands then I gave him a big hug. I held him so tight.

'It looks as if you've been taking care of yourself.'

'Yes,' I said.

'I have some bad news,' he said. He sat me down on the step of his house. 'Your uncle's father-in-law has been executed.'

I looked at both his eyes. They were red but I knew there was something else hiding inside of him, something he did not want to share with me.

'What about his wife?' I asked.

'She's all right.'

My uncle's brother-in-law had been in the special forces to build the dam. He would be shocked.

'We have nothing to eat,' Father added.

Food. Death. I didn't know what to think or feel.

'We have nothing to eat,' he repeated.

'That's OK.'

He was cautious and tense, and he didn't say any more.

The next morning, we lined up to go to work. The rain was so heavy that it hurt our faces. It was difficult working through the monsoon season, and we often had to stop. Whenever the torrential rain eased, we would leave camp and march out again, on those dykes that were cold and slippery as ice.

There was less food and everything slowed. Without the right food, our bodies didn't work properly. We had trouble seeing, trouble with our muscles and with our stamina. It became hard to control our steps, to walk carefully and not slip and slide into the canals or the flooded fields.

Many people died during the monsoon season. I constantly feared being executed for finding my own food. Nonetheless, those fears always faded in the face of the greatest priority – fighting hunger. I think we all believed we would rather be executed and die with food in our stomachs than die of starvation. No-one dared disobey the rules by gathering or cooking food in front of the KR, but in secret we did not deny our needs.

Months passed. Every day could have been our last. Our living situation was chaotic, and this enabled the Khmer Rouge to gather information from us: it only took the promise of a little food to satisfy someone too lazy to scavenge for their own.

One morning, a camp leader spoke to me when I woke up.

'Sovannora,' he said, 'go to the hall. Get the salt and the pickled fish for our group.'

As I approached the dining hall, I heard a woman screaming. I stopped. She was shouting and swearing. I ran to her voice and saw the Khmer Rouge dragging her from her house.

'Release me! Let me go!' she yelled. 'It's my own business, it's none of your business.'

They tied her up.

'You have your own meal to eat – why can't we?' she screamed.

She continued to yell as they dragged her between the huts, her hands tied tight behind her back. There was no doubt they were going to kill her. I didn't want to look and kept walking without turning back. When I reached the hall, people were standing outside, talking about her.

'What's happening?' I asked one of the ladies.

'This poor lady,' she answered, 'she's crazy.'

It wasn't easy to talk. There were spies in the village, and I didn't know what would get back to the leaders. Another lady came over, and so did one of the cooks.

'What's she done?' I asked the lady.

The cook looked interested. He wanted to know too.

'She has been eating her own children.'

'What! That is crazy,' I said. The cook shook his head.

'Yes. She's insane. But she's worked hard, never stopped for one day.' She looked at me and at others nearby who were talking, 'Who are we to judge her?'

'Why?' I asked.

'She was a widow with one girl and three boys. Her girl was about a year and a half, just walking. Her boys were, let me think, about three, five and seven. They needed more food and she could find nothing to feed them. One day her youngest one got sick. Eventually she died. We didn't know. We wondered where she got her energy from.'

'You knew her, didn't you?' another lady asked.

'We worked together until I was reassigned to work in the kitchen. But when we were together in the fields she was a nice lady. Friendly, educated. Her husband was a medical doctor from Battambang. She was a teacher.'

More people had gathered now. The Khmer Rouge stood away from the hall talking as their comrades dragged over the woman they'd bound. One of them smacked the woman in the face every time she yelled.

The women and the cooks gathered there told me the whole story. Her youngest child, her daughter, had died. They asked her to bury the body, and she went away to do this. But in the days after there wasn't much food. Her children were eating only a small portion of rice and had no energy. So she went back to the grave and dug up her dead baby and brought the body to her house. Later, around midnight, she woke all her children to come and eat, and the food smelt very good.

'They've only given us rice and salt,' we imagined her saying. 'Here, eat this.'

'What is it, what is it?' the children would have cried.

'Just eat it.'

The children did eat, and it would have tasted very good. But she had the bones to bury, and she collected these while she cooked the meat, night after night, and left them under the house. Her house was built on stilts but sat only about a metre from the ground. Underneath was messy and smelly, but she hid the bones there in a plastic bag.

Later another child became ill – her third youngest – and eventually died. This was the five-year-old boy. She said she was going to bury the body, but she didn't. She hid it and cooked it, as she did with her baby. Later, the three-year-old died, and she did the same with him to feed her remaining child, who had now turned eight.

She didn't kill any of her children. She had no other resources, and she was desperate. In her mind she had no choice. When they arrested her, she said all she was trying to do was keep her children alive. It was a tough time. She knew she had to do everything she could.

They had caught her because of her son. After his three siblings died, he woke one night and saw his mother skinning the body of his brother.

He was shocked. She would have said something to him like this: 'I hope you understand. Please, we are living a nightmare. We are living in a world in which we have no room to move. If we don't do this, we all die, and I don't want you to die because you're the only child I have left. Please understand.'

The boy didn't say anything. He went back to sleep. But he didn't eat the meal. A couple of days later, one of the leaders overheard him talking with the other children. Spies looked under the house and found the bag of bones. They interrogated her yesterday. From her point of view, her acts were justified. To those of us talking, they were insane.

This poor lady had no skill except teaching and helping her husband. She had no ability to work on farms or in the fields, to catch fish or crabs or other things. I had seen her with snails, but anyone could catch snails.

I shook my head and grabbed the supplies I had come for. It was rice, just more rice and salt. On the way back, I saw the woman's house. Her eight-year-old was standing out the front.

At that moment, the Khmer Rouge dragged the woman past

the house. I noticed their guns. One had a machine gun and the others had revolvers. Those guns would be used on her.

The boy still didn't cry.

She stopped screaming and looked up at him.

'Wait!' she said to her captors, and she called out to her boy. 'Stay strong. Don't cry. I will always be with you.'

They dragged her away and he continued to stare, but not after her. He didn't move and he didn't talk. The Khmer Rouge lady who was the leader of the children's group came and took him away.

I passed by the house after everyone had left. I climbed up the porch and looked inside. It was totally empty – no pillows or blankets, just a pan and some plates all messy on the bamboo floor.

I couldn't say whether she had been right or wrong. She must have suffered so much as her children died. In her situation, I would understand, I decided. She had to help her children, and she saw their dead bodies as reusable.

Chapter 14
Starvation

IT WAS THE old routine at harvest time: chasing away birds, finding rats and fish when I could. But late one afternoon, I was given permission to go to my father's house.

He was very sad. He spoke Sanskrit, and then translated it. 'You must remember these words,' he said. 'Say them to yourself if anything happens. You have to learn it by heart. Use them when you are in trouble, or when you cannot sleep, or when you need to be protected. It will make you feel better.'

He wrote it down for me. It was partly Buddhist wisdom and partly a spell you repeated to keep evil spirits away. I didn't believe anything like this, but I saw no harm in taking those words Father wrote for me and I placed them in my pocket.

'Come back,' he said as I was leaving. 'It has been more than a year now since Sivanchan has left us. Some that went with him have returned. They said he was removed from the Special Teenage Elite Force to join another provincial force.'

'What do you think?' I asked. 'I was hoping to find him at the dam on Sangkae River in Battambang, but he was not there.'

'I don't know. There's nothing we can do,' he said, shrugging.

The next day, I packed my things for an assignment scaring the birds away from some fields that had not been harvested. It was far from the village, and I had to sleep in the fields because the birds were everywhere when the sun rose. I would return for meals. Mostly I would return for evening meetings too, although sometimes I was given permission to stay with my scarecrow.

We were always hungry, and I knew I would find small ponds with fish or frogs, even though we were always being watched by the Khmer Rouge. My body was eager for the protein in the fish and lizards. I had to do this. I needed protein to survive, even at the risk of capture and death.

Huor, the Chinese Cambodian who had been adopted by the deputy leader, was assigned to work with me. It was the first time he had joined in any work in the fields.

We became very good friends, and whatever we found to eat we shared, even the smallest fish. If he collected six fish as long as my finger, he would save me three, and I did the same. We shared our secrets too. This mainly concerned hiding our food.

He was shorter than me and one or two years younger. Like me, he was determined to stay alive. His stepfamily couldn't help. They cared for him, but he now had to work like everyone else his age. I got along very well with Huor. Sometimes we argued, but we kept each other's secrets.

It was a good season – less rain, calmer and warmer weather – and it was the season when we had most food. It reminded me of the way I had often felt at home. I thought about my life in Phnom Penh, where I could walk freely down the boulevard and go to the shops or the market, and sometimes to the movie theatre.

Daydreaming under the hot sun, I became sleepy and dozed against a tree.

'Get up!' It was Samamit Thon. 'This is not a suitable job for you any more. You come and we will get you to help in processing the rice.'

I followed him back to the camp without saying a word, and there I was introduced to the processing. After the rice stalks were harvested and tied in bundles, they were taken to a flat, cleared area where the ground was firm and clean like a floor. The bundles were placed on top of each other, then spread around in the shape of a circle six metres in diameter and two or three bundles high. Two bulls were then brought to the circle and led round and round, breaking the grains of rice from the stalks.

People worked day and night in the processing area. Those of us not bundling the rice for the bulls to trample were busy smashing the stalks against a board. So much rice was collected, much more than would feed the people in our village for a whole year.

Despite working every day from 5 a.m. to about 6 p.m., we still had propaganda meetings. These went as late as 9.30, and were sometimes followed by guard duties.

After we finished harvesting the rice, we were sent to fix canals, dykes and dams in the fields, just as in previous years. We worked quickly, and often alone.

The number of people in the village had declined tremendously. Some groups didn't exist any more. I was still in the elite force at the teenagers' camp: this meant that if the provincial leaders needed extra help from our village, we would be the first to go.

In March 1978, our leaders told us, 'We've got to go and help another district up near the mountains. On the Phnom Tapadae. We have to help in building canals and dams, because they don't get enough water during the monsoon season.'

I was excited to be going. I thought this might give me a chance to look for my brother.

We were given a meal early the next morning, then we packed and left. We marched in a line along the dykes toward the main road. I felt good. Huor was walking behind me, and I was thinking about my brother. I hadn't seen Sivanchan for more than two years. We had a ladies' line following us too. My brother Chandy was with me, and my two sisters were in the line behind. I looked around, paid more attention, and discovered most of the village was there.

We all had baskets on our backs and tools in our arms, except for Samamit Thon, who didn't carry anything. He walked alone with his cheeky smile and his kroma.

The sky was blue and bright and the sunshine hot. It would

be a long day and a long hike. The dyke took us to the main road. We travelled along National Road #5 for much of the way, and soon we approached the area where I had been caught and jailed. Rice fields were near the road and men were working there under armed guard.

I saw the man who carried me back to our village on the bicycle. He was standing beside the road, watching us. I called to him. He looked puzzled, then smiled back.

'Where are you going?' he shouted.

'We're on our way to Phnom Tapadae.'

'OK, good luck.'

Thon heard me talking to the prison guard. He hurried up to me and smiled.

'Did you know that guy?' he asked.

'Yes,' I replied. I didn't want to say any more, because I knew he would mock me. But his memory was good.

'Is that the place where you ended up as a prisoner while you were daydreaming?' he said. 'Well, this time make sure you get to Phnom Tapadae – no more daydreaming.'

I didn't say anything. Huor came from behind me and patted my back.

'Keep walking. Keep walking,' he said, to interrupt our conversation.

It was good to have a friend – it had been so long.

We had been working for the past two and a half years now. We survived basically on toughness – the will to survive. Many women in particular had slowed down. They were pale and undernourished. Men seemed to be stronger, but they died more quickly when they became sick. I'd noticed one lady looking pale for the past year, but she didn't get worse.

We kept walking. It was very hot. Our line had broken up, because some weren't feeling well and others had less energy. We still walked with the leaders, but we stopped at various places. Huor and I found some shade under a tree and looked around. Other groups were far ahead, some far behind. Across in the distance, I could see people from other villages walking. Further along the line, I saw Samamit Thon and Samamit Von talking and laughing. They weren't weary like us – they had been walking empty-handed.

Huor and I continued to walk together after lunch, and I caught up with Chandy. He just looked at me. He had lost so much weight since we left Phnom Penh. We walked together for a while. We could see that the soil in this area was red and very dry. To the side were many trees I didn't recognise. I only knew orchard trees and palms; these tall trees seemed as if they belonged in a national park.

It became hot and more than a little windy. I was tiring. We did not have any water ourselves but relied on ponds, rivers or lakes that we passed, or drank from the paddy fields. We came across paddy field water along the side of the road. It was milky brown, but we were thirsty, so we both scooped up the water and began to drink. Then the Khmer Rouge leaders pushed us on, because we weren't at a designated stopping place.

Finally, we stopped again at an empty place designated for us by a Khmer Rouge man on a bicycle. 'You can rest here,' he said. 'Rest and then you will work.'

Many groups were spread across a wide, dry area of forest. I still didn't know yet what type of work we would be doing. There were fourteen in our group, including three leaders, two of whom were Khmer Rouge. We shared our food and our cooks with three other groups. The cooks were healthier than the rest of us. If you were a cook, you were probably related to the Khmer Rouge, and you knew how to please them. The cooks ate more and travelled by ox-cart with their equipment and the food.

I sat back against a tree and watched as our cook made his stove. He dug a hole and placed wood and stones in it. The wok went on top. I spoke to Huor. Soon we had the wonderful smell of rice cooking and morning glory being fried in pork fat.

'Call the group leaders to bring their bowls. Tell them the rice and morning glory is ready,' the cook announced.

We sat around and ate, but the amount was so small it hardly touched our stomach. After the cook cleaned up, many of us went to the cooking area to search for anything that had spilt from the wok or the rice cooker.

Then a leader came over. 'Welcome to the Tapadae Mountain area,' he said. 'Tonight you are camping here. Tomorrow we will choose a proper place for building your camp.'

He went on, 'Tapadae is a remote area, which is important to us. The Khmer Rouge have been here for a long time, since the beginning of the revolution. Now we have brought people from all the provincial towns, including Phnom Penh city, to come and live in this area. We need more good land here, and there's not enough water for the crops. That is why we have called you all here.'

We camped in the woodlands beside people from other towns. As night approached, I heard animal sounds I was not familiar with. After our meal, we tied up our hammocks, then were called to another meeting. We were warned not to wander to other groups or to houses in the nearby villages. We were told again the consequences of sneaking off to find additional food. And the leaders explained the irrigation system we were going to build, and how it would impact on the rice fields. They spoke about great revolutions of the past, and about defeating the Americans, and about doing our work well.

'Irrigation is so important,' they said. 'Irrigation is the way for the future.' There was clapping, but not as much as in the past. 'One day, one day we will have five meals a day and Angkar will have a better life for all of us.'

When the leaders left, we spoke among ourselves.

'This is like execution,' said a boy from another village. 'Just another way to execute us without weapons.'

'But we have no choice,' someone else commented.

The first boy spoke again. 'It really is another form of execution,' he said. 'They work us too hard. We don't get enough food. This is how they kill us so they don't have to feed us all.'

I didn't say anything. I knew this boy would be dead soon. I thought about our village, where so many had died. The Khmer Rouge didn't care.

The next morning, we went into the forests. It seemed as if

everyone was working there; some were cutting down trees, others using machinery to chop them into smaller pieces, which we then carried to trucks and ox-carts. We worked very hard. It was like a test, and only the strongest, the most determined, survived.

Apart from work, there were many interrogations. People – even whole families – were disappearing every hour, and there seemed to be no reason why. I didn't think much about anything – I just wanted to survive, and I kept my mind focused on that. I knew that if I allowed myself to feel too much, it would weaken me, and I wouldn't survive. If I missed my family too much, would I still be able to work hard? Would I still be able to eat any food I found, no matter what it tasted like? I had to survive, that's all I knew.

Thon had his eyes on me all the time now. When I felt his stare it was as if his eyes were speaking to me, telling me I was in danger and he would hunt me down. But I tried to ignore him.

We boys watched each other's backs. All of us teenage boys – I was still only seventeen – tried to get along as well as we could. We worked at trying to build our huts, then we joined other groups digging canals.

Ticks were a problem. They all sucked human blood for their meals. They were spread by animals like lizards and armadillos, or they fell onto us as we passed bushes and trees. We couldn't fight off the effects of the ticks if they attached themselves to our skin: our bodies weren't strong enough. We would get fevers initially, then become weaker and weaker until we died.

There were also sand-flies that stung us to suck our blood. They were tiny flies that didn't do any serious damage, but their stings were painful. These flies were most annoying in the early morning and early evening. They bit any part of our body that was uncovered.

Here in this dry area, it was hard to find any extra sources of food. At first, the local villages supplied us with pumpkins, cucumbers and other vegetables, but that lasted only a week. From that point on, we were given only rice soup with dried fish and tamarind leaves. Fever and fatigue affected all of us:

sometimes we went to work, sometimes we couldn't. We still had our propaganda meetings every night, and each group took turns guarding. I ignored the death all around me – or I did until Brother Doeun died.

Doeun was Thon's second cousin and was like an uncle to him. Doeun was also a good friend of Samamit Khon, who had been brought to our village in 1976. They both grew up in the same village, but they were separated in 1970, during the civil war. Doeun was in Republican territory, but Khon was captured by the Khmer Rouge. Then Doeun was brought to our village and they were reunited.

By this time, Khon had been assigned to be a leader on the same level as Samamit Von. Khon had proved to the village leader that he could be trusted and was committed to Angkar. He worked very hard and always accomplished what was assigned to him.

Back in the village, Samamit Khon and Brother Doeun were never in my group, but we were assigned to the same group on this mission, and I had the opportunity to meet them. Doeun and Khon were the same age, about twenty-three. Doeun was well-educated, kind and worked very hard. He was friendly to me. We had to do as much work as the men, but we were slower. When his work was finished, Douen would sometimes come and help us as we dug canals or carted rice.

Since Doeun and Khon had been reunited, their relationship was very close. But Samamit Von became jealous of the privileges given to Doeun, who was not Khmer Rouge and was not allowed the same rights and privileges as Samamit Khon.

One day, Samamit Khon was asked to return to the village, and while he was away, Doeun was executed. No-one knew where Samamit Von executed him, only that he had gone away for a long time with some Khmer Rouge soldiers.

That night, Von returned from the forest with meat attached to his belt. He asked the cook to make a meal for him and his team, but not for us. Fortunately, our mealtime had passed, and it was time for our propaganda meeting.

One day I started to explore around the forests. There would have to be some food there, I thought. It would be a different kind of food, but I would eat it. I pretended I was going to the toilet but I was looking carefully everywhere, behind trees, under logs, on the sides of hills. There were no ponds, but I dug in the ground with my fingers.

Then I heard flies buzzing. There must be food nearby, I thought. I brushed past bushes following the buzzing of the flies, and I saw a body. I was shocked and frightened, but walked toward the corpse. It was Mr Doeun. He was on his back. His chest was open, and flies and larvae were feeding off it.

I almost collapsed. When I saw his body lying on the ground like an animal's corpse, I was terrified. I ran back to the camp and found Huor.

'I saw Mr Doeun,' I whispered in his ear. 'He is dead. His body has been given to the insects.'

'Ohrr,' he replied with his Chinese accent, 'don't say anything. Just keep working.'

It surprised Huor and me that Thon did not seem to take any notice of this incident. He still stayed around Samamit Von, even though he knew Von had executed his second cousin. But somehow I understood. Thon had to betray his own conscience and ignore what had happened, or he would lose his life too.

The work continued – the same amount every day – but the rice became even less. We had to find other sources of food or die. I ate leaves and a thick kind of edible grass.

We all watched the cooks seriously every time food was divided. Groups of about ten of us would then sit around a large bowl of food until someone called 'Start!' Then we would each fill our spoons in turn. Some people ate without taking a breath. Others didn't want to chew, just swallowed their food quickly. The rice or the soup might be burning hot, and someone would choke and die. No matter how many times we saw this happen, others still did this. I didn't think about it. It was a matter of survival and I was surviving.

In July, the wet season arrived and the rain began falling heavily. Only strong people remained alive. We felt good now, because water was everywhere and it would be easy to find food in the fields and forests, though our meals continued to be cut more and more.

We began using what we called kduch, the root of plants we found at the foot of the mountains. It was like a black-skinned yam but larger, and had a sticky substance inside. It was brown inside and had to be soaked in water for at least seven days to dilute the bitter and poisonous sticky substance. After soaking, we chopped it into small pieces and boiled it. It was tasteless, but we mixed it with rice when we cooked.

When the wet season started, canal construction and dam building stopped, and we moved our camp closer to the village to help them with their rice. 'Everything belongs to Angkar,' we were told. 'It doesn't matter where you help. All the rice production will go to the one place. It will go to the provincial town, then it will be redistributed to the villages equally, according to the number of people in each village.'

Being on the young elite force, we were told we would be kept strong with enough food. It didn't happen, but we held on to the promise. We had our dreams of what was possible.

Chapter 15
Execution

FOR MANY MORE weeks we worked on rice production as the monsoon season seemed as if it would never end. In August, we were finally told we would be going back to our village – the work in the mountains was over.

I longed to return to our village, where there were fruit trees, and lizards, grasshoppers, rats, frogs – but instead we were sent to another village, deeper into the Khmer Rouge country. Our task was to work in the rice fields. We continued to work hard, always focusing on our next meal.

The leaders spoke to us in our meetings about families who had been wealthy in the past. 'Stop dreaming,' they told us. 'Behave. You will never return to that capitalist lifestyle you once had.'

We currently faced the worse possible standard of living and felt as if we were living in hell. Yet we tried to hold on to the promise that our lifestyle would change for the better if we worked harder to produce rice.

'The village has instructed us,' Samamit Von said, 'that some of you are from wealthy families. There are too many people who do not believe in the Khmer Rouge way. They pretend. They live among us. But we will find these people. We have been instructed to execute more people, to weed out those who might oppose us.'

They had been watching me. I had tried my best to oblige the Khmer Rouge – rising early, working all day, eating what I was given without complaining, attending meetings, guarding when it was my group's turn. All I got on my plate was two spoons of rice, just enough to cover the palm of one hand. With my spoon I would scoop it into my mouth and it was gone. Then I would walk away and lie down, my body aching for more food.

The village we were sent to strongly supported the Khmer Rouge. Often, newcomers were taken away and executed – sometimes whole families at a time.

One evening that September, I returned all wet and sweaty from replanting the rice. It was about 5.30 p.m., just before dark. I was so sweaty. I washed, ate my two spoons of rice with a little fried morning glory and attended our meeting. The meeting finished around ten, and we returned to camp.

It was my group's turn to guard all four groups, and the leaders were deciding the shift times.

One of the leaders turned and spoke to us.

'Samamit Chhay and Veth will guard from 11.30 p.m. to 12.30 a.m. And Samamit Ra and Huor will guard from 12.30 a.m. to 1.30 a.m.' So go. Better be off to sleep now before your turn.'

I was tired and fell asleep quickly until one of the boys shook me. 'Get up, it's your turn.'

I woke Huor. 'Huor! Get up and go to the front of the camp, and I will go to the back,' I explained.

'Hmm!' he yawned. 'You come and remind me when it's time to change guards. Make sure.'

At the back of the camp, there was a post. I leaned against it, looking up at the stars. My eyes closed from time to time and I yawned. Soon I fell asleep.

About 4.20 a.m., Huor found me.

'Hey, get up.' He shook me nervously. 'I fell asleep too. You forgot to wake everyone. It's too late now.'

The roosters were crowing. Others would be up soon. I jumped to my feet.

'What do we do?' I whispered.

'Nothing.'

'Huor, that was the first time I fell asleep guarding. What are we going to do?'

We waited. At 4.30 a.m. whistles began to blow in other groups, so we started to wake people. We lined up with everyone else and began marching into the fields. Samamit Thon walked past, hurrying to take the lead. He glanced across and frowned. He was dark-skinned and shorter than me, but solid: he had been eating well.

I stepped down into the rice fields and worked as usual. Late in the afternoon, I lined up with everyone else to return to camp.

'Tonight we will start our meeting at eight o'clock,' one of the leaders announced just before we ate.

After the meal, I lined up to walk to our meeting. We were always lining up, so obedient and well-trained. We did everything for the Khmer Rouge. We even died for them. It made me angry, for they were nothing without us.

Then Thon came up to me.

'You will come with us,' he whispered.

My stomach dropped. What did Thon want? He was just playing games again, I thought. That must be it. But there was last night. I had slept on guard duty, and he must have found out.

Then I saw two Khmer Rouge soldiers. They were dressed in their black uniforms with their knives and guns holstered on their waists and AK-47s strapped across their shoulders. They nodded to Thon and he pointed. They walked straight up to me. Grabbing my arms, they twisted them behind my back, pushing me to the ground. They tied my hands and arms – my two elbows joined behind me – and covered my face with a cloth.

'Get up,' Thon called. 'Follow me.'

I stumbled as he led me by the arm. I told myself to stay on my feet, otherwise they would drag me. I knew my group was watching, but they remained silent. I thought I would never see my family again, but I kept up, and I kept my footing as I was marched along.

'What's happening? Where are we going?' I asked.

Thon didn't answer. Suddenly he stopped and took off my blindfold. It was night-time, but I could see we were about to enter the forest. I turned around. There were others with us, but they were silent. All of them covered their faces with kromas but I knew who they were. I saw Thon, Von, and Khon, plus the two Khmer Rouge soldiers who had grabbed and tied me, and other Khmer Rouge from the village.

Thon let go of me. The two soldiers grabbed me again and led me further into the forest. This place was only used for killing: I could smell the rotting corpses and hear the buzzing flies.

Someone pushed the back of my knees. 'Kneel down,' he said.

I knelt, with my hands still tied tight. Von began to question me with his arrogant voice. 'We know you are connected with the enemy. If you tell us what your connection is, then we will let you live.'

I was confused.

'We are trying to be free of the enemy. We don't like it when the enemy revolts against us. You tell me about the enemy, then we'll let you go.'

'I'm sorry,' I said, 'I can't understand what you're talking about. I do not know what you're trying to ask me.'

'Oh yes, you know. You just tell me, what did you do last night?'

I told him. 'Last night it was my turn on guard duty. While I was guarding, I fell asleep. And then I could not ... I could not wake up the next guard to do his duty.'

'That is your problem,' he said, 'because you have stolen rice crackers from the kitchen. Because you were guarding at the back of the camp, you stole them?'

'I did not. I did not know where the rice crackers were.'

Thon interrupted, 'Yes, you do. I saw you many times walking around the kitchen, staring at where they keep the rice crackers.'

'No. I did not stare at the rice crackers, because I did not know where they are. I only ... the reason I was going around the kitchen was I was looking for any rice that might have dropped from the wok.' I felt ashamed but I had no choice if I wanted to stay alive.

'Oh, so,' Von said. 'We gave you food, but that's not enough? That's why you're doing that.'

'I was still a bit hungry!'

'So you are hungry. That's why you have to disobey Angkar's rules, and steal the rice crackers.'

'What? No, I did not steal the rice crackers. Last night I fell asleep, as I told you and … and I did not take any rice crackers.'

'You bargain too much. You talk too much. You'd better let us have the rice crackers back.' Von spoke firmly, stressing his words with an angry voice. 'You know the situation. At this time of year we are short of food, and we use the rice crackers to feed everyone when we run out of rice. If you do not bring them back to us, you know the consequence to your life.'

'I do not have … I cannot say any more. You can deduct my meal until the crackers have been fully recovered. I am doing this because I take full responsibility for falling asleep last night. I do not know how much was taken, but I'm happy not to eat if you think I have stolen the rice crackers due to falling asleep during my guard duty.' I thought about not having my meals, and I couldn't imagine being able to do that, but I was fighting for my life.

Thon spoke again.

'I saw you. Your eyes search the kitchen. Is that true?'

'No, that is not true.'

'You steal the rice crackers so you can survive, and let other people die. Right?'

'That is not true. Anyway, I have already told you the truth. You can believe it or not.'

'Oh, I know you. I know your father, your family. They're lazy. They come from the rich. They do not know how much we have been struggling in this war. You would like to get some energy and feed the enemy among us and try to defeat us.'

They walked away from me. I heard them whispering, then I heard the footsteps came back.

'Samamit Thon, leave here now,' Khon said.

The other soldiers came over. It was hard to see them in the dark, but I saw their guns. One of them bent down. He suddenly put a plastic bag over my head. I felt his hand holding the plastic bag around my neck while another soldier held me tight and still.

I could hardly breathe. The bag was tight and the plastic covered my mouth, stuck to my lips whenever I tried to get air. My hands were still tied up, and I knew what was going to happen. I began to struggle as hard as I could, breathing in and out quickly now as I began to panic.

The hands tightened around my neck – he was strangling me.

I couldn't get my breath and I was starting to suffocate. My back hurt, and my legs, my arms. I had a sense of something swinging through the air, and I felt it. It came down hard and hit me on the head – a blow that was meant to kill me. I struggled and thrashed around. One man was trying to hold me still while another one was whacking me on the back of my head with a stick, just as I had seen done to others. But I was fortunate. The man holding me released his grip as the stick hit my head. Perhaps he was afraid. Perhaps he thought he might get hit by the stick if he wasn't careful. Still I collapsed. They released my arms and my neck as I fell head-first into a hole in the ground.

For a moment, I blacked out, but I came to as I was falling down into the hole. I felt something soft and heard footsteps walking away. Then the plastic around my neck opened up. I began sucking in air, but the plastic stuck to my nose. I breathed in and out through my mouth. I thought I was probably on top of other bodies, and they were warm. They must have been recently executed, just like me. But I was only guessing. The uncertainty made my heart pound as if it was going to explode.

It was so hard to get air in with the plastic stuck to my nose but somehow I did. As I battled for my life, I heard someone shout, 'He's still alive.'

One of them came back and pulled me up. He pulled me out of the grave. He held me by my hair. My legs wouldn't straighten, and I stayed still in his grasp like a puppet.

They pulled off the plastic bag: I sucked in and breathed out in a rush. 'Hoo, hooo, hooo!'

I was crying, not because I was hurt or scared, but because it was so unjust to try to take my life in such a cruel way – and without any proof of my crime! They had no right to manipulate my life as if it was a joke. I took another gasp and another. I was so weak that I just fell to the ground and lay there.

'What are we going to do with him, Samamit Von?' the man beside me asked.

Then I heard Khon's voice. 'Let him go,' he said. 'We've already executed him, and he didn't die. According to our regulations, he must be given another chance to live if he can survive his execution. Put him in the rice fields. Punish him there. When he completes his work, allow him to return to the camp.'

Von agreed. 'I look forward to seeing you tomorrow morning, Samamit Ra, huh!'

I continued to cry. I was miserable. I was alive but devastated by what was happening to me. I didn't want to be strong any more.

One of the Khmer Rouge soldiers came over and untied my hands. 'Follow me,' he said.

My sobs and groans just wouldn't stop. Why couldn't I die? It was so unjust that I did not steal the rice crackers, but I got this punishment.

They dragged me to the rice fields and pushed me in. It was dark and wet and I had a terrible headache. Both my hands were hurting. My eyes were itchy from the tears, and I could hardly think. I sat there in the swampy fields for about ten minutes beneath the shadow of one of the soldiers standing on the dyke. We didn't speak, and my crying slowed.

The other Khmer Rouge soldier brought rice plants – about ten bundles and then another ten – and told me to replant the field. I had to. I could hardly move now and felt dead in my heart, but I had to work, though there was so much pain in my body.

Then the flies came. They were small flies, beginning to bite me on my neck and face and arms and elbow and everywhere else. I was very tired and just kept splashing water all over me as I stumbled, but the attacking flies showed no mercy. It was as if they were trying to wake me up. Under the attack, I put my face in the water. I wanted to drown myself and die, but I couldn't.

I recalled an old saying: 'If you go down to the water, there is a crocodile. If you go up the hill, there is a tiger. If you are not

strong and smart, you will not know how to resolve this obstacle.'
So I had to use the mud from the bottom of the field to cover my
body so that the flies would not attack me so much. I worked
fast, frantically, to cover myself in mud and plant the bundles of
rice-plants.

It was a long night. All by myself I finished the task. Then I
crawled onto the dyke and slept.

The sun rose, and everyone lined up and marched toward the fields
as usual. They saw me and walked past, or over me. I didn't move
or open my eyes. They mumbled, and I could tell they thought I
was dead – accused of stealing rice crackers and executed as an
example for everyone to learn from.

Then I felt a touch and heard a voice – it was Huor. I opened
my eyes as I heard his words and felt him lift me by the shoulders.

'Hey. Get up. You better line up with us. Let's go to work.'

I followed his lead and stood, then walked, but I couldn't walk
straight. I was very tired. When we reached the fields where we
had to work, Huor helped me. He did what he could to support me.
Samamit Von and Samamit Thon watched, but they left me alone.

Then Chandy came. 'I thought you died last night,' he said.
'They came and warned me. "Don't try to be like him," they said.
"He stole the rice crackers from the kitchen."'

I didn't want to respond. Then my tears started to fall again. I
kept staring at him, but I didn't say anything. Huor dragged me
away.

'You'd better go to work,' he said to both of us. 'Stop talking.'

I followed Huor and tried to work. I was in a daze. The day
passed slowly at first, then quickly like a dream. I was imagining
all sorts of things before it became time to walk back to camp –
things about pain, death, Mother.

Mother sustained me. Whenever I thought of her, I felt her
presence, and I could feel her love in spite of everything.

Back at camp, I feared they would cut my meal, but they still
gave me the same amount as everyone else. I couldn't eat, so I gave

it to Huor. I rested in my hammock and looked up into the sky. Where would I be if I had died last night? It would be better than living and suffering like this.

The next day, I felt too sick to go to work. Samamit Khon came to see me.

'What's wrong with you?' he asked.

'I'm not feeling well, Bong.'

He looked at me and studied my face.

'All right, you can stay.'

When the others returned from work, I was only given half my usual meal, but Huor was very kind. That night, he caught a snake and a crab and passed them to me, and I ate all of the meat over the next few days. Gradually I regained my strength and felt better. I worked on. We worked as usual for many weeks, watching as the weaker among us struggled to cope, then eventually died.

Chapter 16
Nothing is Perfect

AFTER LUNCH ONE day in November, when we were about to return to our work, a new leader arrived from the provincial town. He gathered all the teenagers who were working in the rice fields.

'All of you,' he said. 'We have new orders from Angkar. You all have to pack and leave this village and work on canals, dykes and a dam in another village. Angkar acknowledges how good your work has been in this village, but now there is a need in other villages near the Mong Russey River. So please return to your camp and pack your working gear and your belongings and be ready to leave tomorrow. Tonight there will be no meeting.'

Everyone applauded this news. Huor came up to me with a big smile and touched my shoulder.

'We will meet our families, huh!' he said.

'We aren't returning to our village,' I told him. 'We will go to work in another village near the river.'

'But at least it is near our village, isn't it?'

'Well, I'm not sure, because we don't know how long the river is, right?'

'Hmmm! Well, at least we've finished in this horrible place. We can leave behind your bad experience that you have gone through.'

I said nothing, just gave him a smile as we picked up our working gear and walked back to the camp.

That night, a special dessert was prepared for us – a rare event. It was a sticky rice dessert called nom kriep, which had sesame seeds and coconut sprinkled on top. I was so excited that I couldn't control my feelings. Still, I didn't eat it straight away. I hid it while I went to the toilet, but when I returned, it was gone.

The despair was as strong as the pleasure I had anticipated. I remembered the old saying, 'Never leave good food for tomorrow and never let a beautiful person out of your sight.' But I wasn't happy.

In the morning, we left for the new village. When we arrived, I realised that Huor wasn't in my group. He'd been selected with others to return to Sahakor Seven before us.

After the leaders met among themselves that night, a new leadership structure was announced. Many new leaders were promoted, and the cooks were removed and assigned to work in the field. Samamit Von was demoted from deputy camp leader to a deputy group leader. Samamit Thon was also demoted. Only Samamit Khon was still in the same position.

I could tell Samamit Von was bitter about this. Once he had been leader of all the teenagers, but now he had to work like us, with the same portions to eat. He had made many enemies in our teenagers' group, and other leaders started to tease him.

It was the dry season, and our job was to work on irrigation, extending canals from the river to the fields. This new village was located in the western part of Mong Russey district, not far from the Mong Russey River.

We were given special rules. The leaders said, 'If you leave the camp, then you are the enemy. We are close to many enemy areas now. A number of people have run away and escaped. If you leave the camp, you will become the enemy and you will be shot.'

We no longer had guard duties. The provincial guards were there with guns, and only our group leaders were asked to assist them.

We were happy working on the irrigation because the new leader was Samamit Vichet, who treated us well. He was one of us, not the Khmer Rouge. He was part-Chinese and well educated, and he had been badly treated by Von for several years.

One morning, I heard that Samamit Von had been killed. He had left the camp without permission the previous evening to visit his parents. When he returned, the guards had told him to identify himself, but he didn't answer. He was arrogant and couldn't accept that he was now answerable to others. He had never listened; he always did the talking.

The guards arrested him and tied him up, then brought him to the camp.

'I'm Von. How dare you touch me!' he said. 'I will report you to the camp leaders.'

There were rumours that Von had been discovered another time going home without permission. Samamit Vichet had warned him to stop it, but Samamit Von did not take any notice and continued to disobey Angkar's rules.

When he was caught this time, he was bringing back some extra food from the village. He argued that he and his family had fought against America during the revolution, so why couldn't he have his own food?

But his arguing did no good. Vichet said, 'Von in the past has misjudged many people and mistreated many others.'

After the death of Samamit Von, Samamit Thon was placed under close surveillance because he had been involved with many of Samamit Von's cruel acts. He became afraid and attempted to escape back to his village. Unfortunately he was caught. He was tortured until he died because he refused to confess the truth. When I heard this news, I thought of Huor, who would have been delighted.

The new Khmer Rouge leaders – the teenage group leaders, the camp leaders, the village leaders – all seemed more reasonable. They treated us more as equals. They worked beside us to inspire us to continue working.

In January 1979, after two months working on the dykes and canals, when our work was almost finished, we were ordered to return to Sahakor Seven. I longed to see my family and my friend Huor, and let them know of the deaths of Von and Thon.

I lined up as we marched into the village. The villagers were friendly and happy and I soon saw why – the management was different. The new Khmer Rouge leaders were from the capital and other provinces, and they treated the local Khmer Rouge differently. They were suspicious of these people and accused them of misbehaviour. I assumed this was because they had not treated us fairly.

When I got back to the village, the first person I saw was Sophea. She was very pleased to see me, but she was anxious too. I told her I did not have time to talk.

'Later, then,' she said. 'Come and meet me tonight right after dinner, before the meeting. There is something I have to tell you.'

I nodded. I wanted to see her as well because I had not spoken to her for a long time.

After dinner I went to her camp, a women's camp, and then I saw Sokha. She looked so tall but it was really that she was so thin: she used to be plump.

'Bong Ra! You are back!' she said.

'I came to see sister Sophea. Where is she?'

Sokha led me to her at the far side of the camp. Sophea asked me to have some food; her share was left over and she had made soup with green leaves. No way would I refuse any food, so I sat with her.

A girl came up to us. 'What are you doing at the women's camp?' she demanded.

Still no-one trusted anyone, but the girl was satisfied when Sophea told her that I was her younger brother. Sophea encouraged me to eat faster. With my mouth full so that I could hardly talk, I said: 'Boonnng! Whhat ddoo you wanna tell mme?'

She handed me some water and asked me to move closer.

'Did you know what happened to Father while you were away? We are very lucky, I tell you. If anything had happened to our father, we would not be sitting here.'

I gulped down my food. 'What? What happened to Father? Tell me. Quickly.'

She looked around her, then back at me. 'While you were gone, Father was taken to be executed.'

'What?'

'He was taken one night. They questioned him till about four in the morning. Mother was so worried that she did not sleep all night.

'Father told me all this only a week ago. He wanted to tell everyone so that we would be aware of the execution system, and of how he overcame this deadly obstacle.'

I listened. This is Father's story as Sophea told it to me:

It was the third day after he returned from Tonle Sap Lake. It was about 7.30 in the evening, soon after the meeting, and just as Father was lighting up his hand-made cigarette after washing, there was a noise at the door. One voice called out, then another.

'Samamit Nhar! Come out! Come out now.'

Father went to the door with his towel wrapped around him. Two Khmer Rouge men stood there, one with an AK-47 strapped to his waist. 'Put your clothes on and come with us!' he shouted.

'OK, give me a moment.'

Father left the door open, but turned quickly: 'Mother, you must take care of the children if I don't come back tonight and you must stay strong,' he whispered. 'And don't question them, only work harder. And if you have any trouble or need to swap food or goods, only trade them with people we know. Be careful, OK!'

'Hurry up, Samamit,' the KR soldier called.

'I'm ready now, let's go!'

He had dressed and strode out quickly, showing his keenness to go with them, trying hard to indicate his life had already been dedicated to Angkar with no regrets and that he was ready for whatever Angkar wanted.

Mother, with the two children, Vivath and Dasy, looked on in despair. There was nothing they could do. Mother held back her tears until Father disappeared from sight. Vivath cried too. Dasy just lay on Mother's lap.

Father was keen to go with them wherever they pleased, so they did not tie him up. He saw others who were being taken too, but Father was kept separate and sent to the edge of the village to the old Wat Chrey Pagoda. There he was taken into a room. As he walked in, they covered his eyes with a blindfold and led him to a chair.

Father remained calm and patient. No-one spoke. He didn't know if he had been left there alone or if someone was there guarding him, watching him in the darkness. Many minutes passed before he heard footsteps again. Someone came in. There was a conversation between at least three men, but Father heard mostly whispers. Then one of them said, 'Question him as much as you can. Make sure he doesn't get out from here, not easily!'

Still blindfolded, he heard a bang on a table; they had put their guns and ammunition there. Then someone came around behind him. 'Tell me the truth. What did you do before the revolution, before 1975?' he whispered.

As his blindfold covered his ears as well as his eyes, Father hardly heard him, and wondered if he was speaking to a colleague. He didn't answer.

'Hey! Samamit Nhar! Are you sleeping? If you want to live, better tell me the truth. We knew what you were doing during the American regime!' the man shouted.

Father sat straight, vigilant and ready as always. His life was going to end this night, he knew that, unless he could change the Khmer Rouge officials' minds during this interrogation. 'I'll tell you anything you wish to know, Samamit Bong!' he promptly responded.

'You were a film director and a producer, weren't you?' The KR man shook Father. 'We also heard that you were very rich, huh?'

Father started laughing. 'A film director and producer! Me? A film director. You think I… me… I was a film director?'

He laughed with his blindfold on. What a sight he must have been, if only they could see him clearly in the dark room.

'Wow! How fortunate I was!' he added.

'Why are you laughing? Do you think that we don't know anything about you? And you think you can fool us?'

The man went on, 'Samamit Nhar! We decided to carry out this interrogation because the details of your occupation during the Lon Nol regime have been reported to us. Now, are you telling us that you were not a film director and producer, huh?'

'Samamit Bong! What I was saying … I am not denying that you have a right to be questioning me.' Father addressed them firmly. He was too smart to beg for mercy. 'However, I want you to put yourself in my position just for one minute. After you hear what I am going to tell you, if it is not true it will not be too late for you to kill me. Your interrogation of me is to hear the truth from me, right?'

'Of course! That's why we brought you here! We'll give you time – one minute. Talk.'

Father suddenly felt free and confident, as if the spirit of Shakespeare was in his veins and he was back to being a real film producer again. He took a deep breath.

'Samamit Bong.' (He used the respectful term for older brother, even though they were younger than him.) 'I am not as clever as all Samamit Bong, because I don't know the difference between an AK-47 and an M-16. All I know is they are guns. How are they different?'

'Yes! Of course they are different; one made from China and another made from America. But what do guns have to do with your position as a film director and producer?'

'Thank you, Samamit Bong! I will explain about my position. Whether I was a film director and producer, or the assistant of a film director and producer, doesn't matter. Whenever anyone saw me working with the director, they would immediately think I was a film director and producer – they couldn't distinguish the difference between being the director and the assistant. You know about your AK-47 and M-16 – I would not be able to tell which was which. If you showed me an M-16 and then an AK-47, I would say they were both M-16s. I would not know which is which.'

The Khmer Rouge interrogator was quiet. He stopped mocking Father. Father continued.

'Before April 1975, people saw Samamit Bong dressed in black only on TV or in newspapers and thought they were very bad people. It wasn't until we were released by Samamit Bong from the evil American puppet government that we started to realise how wonderful our lives had become. Only then did we begin to be grateful to Angkar Padevat for giving us our new lives.

'It is easy for people to judge without knowing the facts, but if you want the truth you have to probe deeper, is that right? Because people could not tell if I was a film director and producer when they saw me involved in shooting, guiding or directing actors and actresses. I don't think it was wrong of them to think that I was a film director and producer, but my question would be the same question I started to ask Samamit Bong about the two types of guns. Those people who reported to Samamit Bong – did they know there was such a position as the assistant to the film director and producer?'

'Cough! Cough!' One of the interrogators cleared his throat. 'So what is the assistant to the film director and producer?' he asked Father.

Father was inspired.

'Being the assistant to the director and producer of one of the film production companies in Phnom Penh was a hard and slaving job. I had to comply with what I was being asked to do. Sometimes, I had to be away from my family for months while shooting the film. Sometimes, I had to work day and night in order to complete the film for the film industry as demanded by the public market. When I was sick, I had no family nearby to look after me. So I was used to all that. That is why my family has devoted and committed themselves to Angkar.'

When Father stopped speaking, everything was quiet. There was no sound or movement for a long time. Then one of the KR men rose from his chair and moved closer to Father. He left both Father's hands tied, but removed the blindfold, which had made Father's eyes sore. Father only had one working eye: a traditional doctor cheated him of his wealth and his other eye when he was only seventeen. When he opened this eye, he could hardly see.

A kerosene lamp now sat on the table in front of Father. He squinted, then began speaking again. His interrogators listened. Father spoke what they felt, what they believed. The two Khmer

Rouge interrogators who questioned him began to share their own feelings. This made it easy for Father to flow with them and convince them that he was the assistant to the film director and producer and was living as a poor person with ten members of his family to be fed. Father had told them how many stories he had worked on, and how many he had changed to show the poor overthrowing their bosses when they were not treated fairly.

Father also criticised the American puppet government on their poor administration under their capitalist regime. The poor people were treated unequally. The rich families got richer and more powerful, while poor families got poorer and lost the power to help themselves.

Father kept responding to questions from the Khmer Rouge about poor families struggling hard to stay alive under the American puppet government. He kept flattering Angkar Padevat for the positive outcomes in helping the poor and defeating the Lon Nol government.

Around midnight, they left him alone for a time. He drifted in and out of sleep until he woke to the first cry of the roosters, and to approaching footsteps.

One of the men came to Father and began to untie his hands. 'You can go home now.' he said, 'but now you must work harder in order to prove yourself. And … the fish you caught at the lake were very tasty.'

Father could hardly believe it. While he had been dozing and waiting for his death sentence, he had dreamed of being executed. He remained sitting on the chair, as still as he could be, waiting for his spirit and soul to re-enter after his dream. Then he began to sob. A short while later he stood up, shaking, and walked slowly out from the dark hall. He walked directly to his house with inspiration for his new life.

As I walked back to my camp, I kept telling myself that Father and I were very fortunate to have new lives again.

The next day, I was very keen to find Huor. I kept asking people if they knew where he was. I wondered if he was away with another group. I'd heard that he had already come back. I doubted it, but I went around the village to look for him. While I was looking, I ran into Samamit Chay, who was in Huor's group to return to the village.

'Have you seen Samamit Huor?'

'Ar-Huor, huh?' Chay replied in an uncertain voice. 'You mean a small Chinese boy walking with his legs far apart, huh?'

'Yes! I was told by your brother Im that he was assigned to stay back with your group. Is that right?'

'Oh! Ar-Huor did not come back.'

He began to walk off. I grabbed his arm and pulled him back.

'What did you say? Huor did not come? What do you mean?'

He shrugged off my hand. 'I am in a hurry to report to the village leader,' he said, so I let him go.

Chapter 17
The Colonel

ONE EVENING IN late January, before dinner was distributed, we were given new orders from Angkar: a number of us would be chosen to go to the mountains, but this time it would be near the Thai border.

The next day, we lined up. I was among seventy who were chosen. The assignment was to go to Phnom Chraok Thlang. I didn't know where this was, and none of us understood why we were assigned to go there.

We marched for several days through remote areas and forests. I walked side by side with Samamit Sri, who had helped me when I had chicken blindness. While we were camping on the road, I tied my hammock next to his. I felt warm, because to have a companion was a good thing. One night, Sri asked me whether I knew what happened to Huor. He startled me – I had been daydreaming about old times at school.

I sat up quickly. 'What happened to Huor? I have been asking around about him. So where is he, do you know?'

'I noticed he was your good friend, right?'

'Yes! Huor is very kind to me and always helpful. He's always busy, always singing to himself, always doing things. Anyway what did you just say … what did happen to him?'

'Oh no! You don't know? Huor is dead!'

'What! Huor is dead? How did he die? When?' It was as if Sri had yelled at me. I began to shake, and at the same time I wanted to know exactly what had happened.

Sri was upset. I got up and held him, then I shook him vigorously and demanded he answer me quickly. He shook off my hands and asked me to calm down and sit back in my hammock so that he could talk to me properly.

He knew Huor was a nice person, and very innocent. 'Well,' he said, 'nobody really knows what happened, but the night before we all had to return home, he must have eaten something he shouldn't have. He had diarrhoea, and left the camp for the toilet. On the toilet, which was a place behind an anthill, he heard a wild dog and began imitating its sound. He wasn't afraid – he wasn't afraid of anything.'

The guards must have heard him. They made the dog sound – 'Hool oooo ooo!' – and Huor kept on answering. The next morning, he was found shot in the back.

I was shocked. How ridiculous this was. I could not stop shaking my head. Huor did not deserve to die like this. I lay down on my hammock, and tears filled my eyes. I couldn't believe this could happen to a person who committed no crime but made a simple mistake.

I had been fond of Huor. He had been the only child left in his family, and now there was no-one. He had been my only friend, and now I was alone. I prayed for him to sleep in peace and hoped he would find his family now and be happy with them in heaven.

After a whole day's marching from early morning, we arrived exhausted at a camp around dusk. We were surrounded by thick forest in the middle of a jungle with tall trees. Beyond the forest, the jungle was even thicker.

'Build your camp first,' we were told. 'Cut trees, make a frame for the houses and dining halls, then wait for hay to come for the roofs.'

It was all virgin forest with many leeches and ticks on the leaves and branches, and our voices echoed from the trees. Hidden among the trees were other tents and huts. How many I did not know. Ox-carts soon brought food and hay, and I slowly realised that people were scattered everywhere. We built our camp hastily, and then we were asked to clear the bush. We still had no idea what was going on.

I had a strange feeling settling in my stomach. Why were we here, and not working on the canals near our village?

Problems arose immediately when we began clearing the land. Apart from the leeches and ticks, I heard from others who came to work near us that there was malaria too. As we worked, the leeches attacked us. These were not the larger river leeches, but small ones that made their homes on the leaves of bushes and trees. Their bite was soft, and we couldn't feel them, so we had to look for them all the time. They would crawl everywhere over our bodies and suck our blood until they had had enough. Women were especially scared of them. They would crawl into the women's vaginas.

Many people in the camp were already sick. There was no medicine at all in the jungle. Nevertheless, over the next few hours I met many Khmer Rouge who were easy to get along with. Most had migrated from Kampong Thom province. I met a couple who had just got married. They were medical people who worked as nurses supplying hot water to us workers.

Soon we settled into this camp. Day after day, we worked on the clearing, fighting the mosquitoes and malaria, the leaves and leeches and ticks.

One day I got sick. The glands on my neck began to swell, first on my left side, and then a few days later on the right. I told my group leader I couldn't go to work. At this time we were rebuilding our camp to raise it higher from the ground because of ticks. While my colleagues worked, I lay on my hammock and became feverish.

We were still only getting two spoons of rice, but we were getting other food too: pumpkin soup, fried morning glory, cucumber soup. I lost half my food because I was sick, but it didn't matter. I couldn't eat much anyway.

One day, the nurse came and checked on me. She was in her twenties. Her long hair was tied in a ponytail and she was strong of character. I tried to talk to her but she wanted me to listen.

'There's no way to cure your glands,' she said. 'We have to

experiment. We can burn your glands. This type of illness might be cured by burning, but the only way to know is to try it.'

They did not wait for me to agree with them but forced me to lean on a thick low-lying branch of a tree, where my head and neck were easily available to them for the operation. They tied my neck to the branch, then my hands and my back, my whole body. I couldn't move my head. I heard them talking, three or four men and the nurse. They made a fire nearby, and then I heard only the nurse's voice.

'Here, these are the glands. See them?' she said. 'This is where you burn.'

I heard a man respond – I didn't know any of the men who were there – then I heard the men around the fire. I felt the warmth of the fire. It must have been close.

'Hold him now,' someone said.

I felt strong hands at my head and my shoulders.

'I've got it,' another man said.

'There. Now!' the nurse squealed.

I screamed and screamed as I felt a hot knife on my neck. In fact it was a piece of stick but sharpened like the point of a pencil. I went crazy. I couldn't think. All I knew was pain.

They took the burning stick away, then brought another, then another, and poked them into the same hole they had made in my neck. Then they moved to my right side and burnt the glands there in the same way. I sweated with fever and continued to scream until I fainted.

When I woke up, the pain in my neck was terrible. The nurse was sitting beside me. I was in a different camp, her camp, which was more like an administration office for the leaders.

'So you're awake,' she said.

My neck was shaking. My whole head was shaking.

'Did I die?' I asked.

'No.'

A man came over when he heard us talk.

'Help him up,' the nurse told him.

'Can you get up now? I think you should get up,' the man said.

I was able to get up. The shaking eased, and I was led outside to a log. I sat down. I felt cold, although the sun was shining, then I remembered we were near the mountains and wondered if everyone felt the cold.

'This is your meal,' the nurse said, 'from one day when you didn't eat. I made porridge for you.'

I ate slowly as the nurse spoke to me. She told me I had slept all day and night. After eating the porridge, I was helped back to my own camp, where I lay down on my hammock. As I was lying down I saw a man walk past. He was old but seemed strong; his skin was fair; his hair, moustache and eyes were grey; and beside him were two bodyguards with AK-47s. The old man had a kroma around his neck, and he was going from camp to camp, checking everyone who didn't go to work. He had black trousers but wore a dark green shirt.

He passed everyone – there were others there, because many of us were sick – and came to me.

'What's wrong with you?' he said.

I couldn't open my mouth because my neck was so sore. He leaned closer. I just pointed to all the spots where I got burnt.

'That's nothing,' he said, 'compared to my leg after I ran through landmines. So it's only a problem with your neck? Your hands should be all right. Why are you lying down sleeping?' He rolled up both his trousers and showed me the scars made by the mines. They were deep and long.

I opened my mouth and raised myself on one arm. 'When I feel better, then I will go back to work,' I mumbled.

'Well, we need a lot of people to help. You see my hut there?'

He pointed across. I turned slowly with my sore neck and saw a hut, the commander's hut. About four metres wide and ten metres long, it stood tall and impressive on its stilts. The side facing me opened on to a veranda that was reached by wide steps. I saw a desk and a chair inside, and a hammock, among other things.

Then I saw steam rising.

Beside his hut was a much smaller one. There was someone there, a woman. The steam was rising from a pot under her hut, and I realised she was boiling water. The water in the mountains was cloudy. We all had to drink boiled water or we would get sick.

I felt the old man's eyes as he looked at me.

'You better come and help the nurse boil the water. Is that a problem?' he said.

'No, I can help,' I mumbled.

'All right, because your hands still work. Go on then, go and help Samamit Theary.'

He left me then, but I heard him whisper to his bodyguards, 'Why did they have to burn so many holes? Poor boy, hmm!'

I rolled on to my side and got up. I went to the hut and started helping the nurse, loading wood into the fire, making sure it was always hot and making sure the water was properly boiled. When the water was ready, she took it away.

Beside the boiling water there was a wok. I stared at the embers. They fascinated me, and I dreamed of having something cooked in the fire.

The nurse came back and saw me working hard pouring the water, bringing the water from the well. I helped her store it for cooling, and then she carried it to the workers. Once I finished boiling the water, I came back to my own hut.

A couple of days later, the old man with two bodyguards – I now knew he was a colonel, and the camp's manager – was watching me from the window of his hut as I was speaking to the nurse.

'Can you bring me some water?' he called.

The nurse looked up at his voice. 'He has his own kettle beside the wok,' she said. 'Can you bring it to him?'

I picked up the kettle from a small table. There was hot water with something mixed in it, like the root of a plant. I brought it to the Colonel in his hut. As I walked inside, I saw another man, who was even older but of lower rank. He was sitting at a table working on business of some kind with pen and paper. Earlier, I had seen ox-carts arrive bringing food, rice and fish. This man was organising how to distribute the goods to each group.

I walked through as the old man sat at his table in his room, listening to the radio. I didn't intend to eavesdrop, but I listened from outside the open door. I heard the announcer say, 'The Vietnamese have invaded Cambodia' and 'Battalion Number Three and Regiment Number Eight have been defeated. Now we have moved our lines to the second front.'

I knocked on his door. He turned off the radio.

'Yes,' he said.

'Your kettle, your water.'

'Come in.'

I entered.

'Leave it on that table.'

He pointed to a small table, where he had a cup made of coconut.

'Would you pour it for me?'

I poured from the kettle into the cup.

'Just leave it there.'

'Is there anything else you want me to do?'

'That's OK. Just go and help the nurse.'

I started walking out, but he shouted to me, 'How is your neck now?'

I returned and told him. 'Now it is better. Thank you, Om!' (Big uncle.)

'Can you bring this plate and wash it for me?'

On the plate was some rice and dried fish left over from last night.

'You can eat it if you want to,' he added.

'Thank you, Om.'

I walked out carrying a tray of plates with his food. I noticed I could not see his bodyguards, but the older man was still sitting at the table calculating the distribution of food and other items. I glanced at his calculations, because he didn't seem to mind. Then I noticed he had made a mistake and pointed it out. He turned and stared at me, his eyes unfriendly.

'Do you know how to do calculations?' he asked.

'A little,' I said, 'but I need to take this plate and do some washing.'

'Go,' he said. 'You've done enough for the Colonel.'

I left him and took the plate to the well. Before I got there, I went behind the hut where the wok was boiling water. I quickly ate the leftovers, which were more than my normal meal.

I ran to the well and washed the metal plate, using ash as soap. I brought the spoon and plate back to the hut and left them on the roof to dry. Grabbing more wood, I broke it into pieces and brought them near the wok. I didn't see the lady – the nurse, as the Colonel had called her. She had probably gone to the fields with water.

Then one of the bodyguards returned. He seemed friendly and said he came to look for a light for his cigarette.

'Now you're coming to help him here?' He pointed to the hut where the commander was.

'No,' I said, 'the Colonel just asked me to boil some water.'

He lit his cigarette and began smoking. He was a little older than me and carried an AK-47.

'No! I mean Samamit Khoeun, the man who organises the food distribution. I heard he has requested the Colonel to ask you to come and help him. So if you can stay, it will be good.'

While we were talking in the shade of the hut where the water was boiling, the Colonel's assistant called out to me. I didn't hear him at first. Then the Colonel walked out.

'Would you be able to help my logistics official in dividing food distribution and the meals?' he asked.

'I'll try,' I said.

I came in and I saw the logistics man smiling. That pleased me: when he had first stared at me, I had become nervous. I looked at his book, and began to work it out – how many cans of rice each group would have, how many pumpkins. I made allowances for the sizes of each group and the numbers of men and women. I looked at the special needs of the elderly people who took care of the twenty ox-carts that travelled up and down the mountain with logs or supplies.

I finished the calculations, then went to the store with the logistics man. We grouped the food, and then we waited. Each group came up for their supplies. My group leader was not happy when he saw me at the Colonel's camp, but he didn't dare come and talk to me.

We finished distribution, and the Colonel came over. 'Why don't you bring your stuff and stay in the shed behind my hut?' he said.

I went to grab my belongings. Everyone looked at me.

'Ahh, are you no longer in my group?' the group leader said.

'I don't know, but the Colonel said to stay close to him. So I don't know.'

I grabbed my things, which wasn't much: my hammock, my bag, my clothes. I brought them to the open shed behind the Colonel's hut and tied up my hammock from pole to pole.

'Boy, come and get your meal,' the logistics man called after he had eaten his own.

I came in and took my food, brought it to the cover of the hut and ate it near the fire. It was getting dark. While I was eating, the nurse came and grabbed a pot of water that had cooled.

'Can you put some more water on?' she asked.

'Yes, I will,' I replied.

She left, then the bodyguard returned. His hammock was tied on the left side, mine on the right. He untied his hammock.

'Tonight you have to help me guard this place,' he said, 'because I have been asked to guard the store.'

'OK.'

'People might come. But there is nothing. Only some vegetables to be cooked tomorrow.' He pointed to a bag near the fireplace. 'Just guard the water and the vegetables. Keep an eye on the Colonel's hut.'

I finished my meal and took the plate to the well and washed it. I brought it back, dried it, and lay on my hammock.

I could hear the Colonel's radio. It was very soft but I could hear the words. It was about the Vietnamese invasion of Cambodia. They were now approaching Siem Reap province.

Then my hammock moved. Someone was shaking it. It was the logistics man.

'Do you know how to use this?'

It was a gun.

'No-oo,' I said.

'Well, it's not hard,' he explained. 'All you have to do is pull the trigger.'

He began to show me.

'You have to have this. Otherwise there is no point in standing guard.'

'OK,' I answered, and I took it.

It was a long gun, not an AK-47, but a rifle with a knife attached to the end. He left, and I fiddled with the gun. I was scared. I sat on a log, leaning against a post, and flipped the knife in and out. Finally I decided I had better leave it out. I held the knife, sharp side up. I ran my fingers along the blade, turning it around. Then I placed the rifle between my legs as I sat in the darkness at the edge of the shed, guarding.

I just held it there.

I leaned back. I could hear the bats and a couple of birds. I imagined the bats flying around. I thought I could see them cast shadows in the dull light of the last flickering embers of the fire.

I fell asleep and dreamed of Mother. My dreams were full of her, living in a better world, telling me I would be there with her one day. My sleep was restless at first, but it became peaceful. Then something disturbed me. I woke was with the sense that someone was there.

Quickly I turned around.

'Who is this?' I whispered.

It was one of my work colleagues. He was trying to light up his cigarette.

'What are you doing at this hour? You are not supposed to be here!' I said. 'This is a prohibited place.'

'Do you have anything I can share?' he asked quietly. 'I was hoping you would have something I can eat.'

'No, I don't have anything.'

'Can I have one of those potatoes there?'

He pointed to a bag. It was dark. I could hardly even see the bag.

'The potato in the bag,' he said. 'The bag that's torn.'

Even in the dull light, he had guessed food was there. Or had he been here earlier?

I reached down and felt the bag. It was torn. I reached in and pulled out one potato and gave it to him.

'Now, don't come back here again,' I said.

I had to speak very softly, because the Colonel's hut was right beside us. After I gave him the potato, he left. I lay down on my hammock and pulled up my gun. I held it beside me. I felt a cool breeze and huddled closer into my hammock. It was about one o'clock, and I was half asleep, half awake, my mind and my dreams focused on Mother. Then my ears pricked to attention.

I heard someone walking very softly, sneaking behind my hut. It was so dark I couldn't see, but I heard the crackling of leaves under feet: the intruder was getting closer.

I held my gun tight and waited. Then I turned and quickly jumped off my hammock.

I pushed the gun into the darkness and probed hurriedly: in and out, in and out. I knew someone was there. Then I touched him.

'Who's this?' I demanded. 'You'd better stop. I will kill you.' I was very nervous, and my hands were shaking.

I held the rifle against him and pushed the point of the knife into his body.

'It's me. It's me,' a voice shouted.

'Who is "me"?' I shouted back.

'Colonel.'

'Oh, Colonel.' I lowered the rifle. 'Sorry, Om, I didn't know. What are you doing?'

'I came to check on you, to see if you were asleep or still awake.'

'Sorry, Om, I did not know.'

'That is good. You almost ripped my stomach. You have a very sharp knife.'

'Well, I did not know. I don't know how to use it. I just… only wanted to scare you, but I do not know. The knife was already there.'

He tapped me on my shoulder.

'Good,' he said. 'Keep up the good work, and I'll see you tomorrow morning.'

He left and I was relieved. I lay back down on my hammock and didn't care about anything. I fell asleep immediately.

In the morning, the nurse came and started to make the fire. Some wild roosters woke me when they started to crow.

'Hey, wake up,' the nurse said. 'We need water to bring to the fields by seven o'clock.'

'OK.'

I got off my hammock, tied it up and put it in my pack. I heard the whistle call for everyone to line up for action in the field. The main activities were to clear the forest and stack logs. There were two reasons for this. We had to clear land for agriculture, and we had to prepare barriers for defence in case the enemy attacked.

I helped the nurse make the fire and carried water from a well for her to boil, before I heard a voice calling. It was the Colonel.

I went inside his hut, where I heard the CB radio. He was talking and trying to tune it to get a clear sound.

'What is it, Colonel?'

'Get yourself ready. I want to go and check the work fields. Come along with my guards.'

I went outside and saw one bodyguard, the man who was friendly to me when I first met him. 'I'm coming along,' I said.

He nodded and we waited. The Colonel came out with his stick, and we followed him. It hadn't rained for a while, and the sky was blue. It was a cool morning, but the sun started to push through the tall trees. We walked through the forest all the way to the fields, where a group was working. They stopped and turned around. Many eyes were staring at me. They were shocked to see me with the Colonel, walking behind as he smiled and tapped everyone with his stick.

'Good work,' he would say, or 'Well done, keep it up.'

The leader of the work group came to greet him and told him about their progress. The Colonel looked around as he listened.

'You don't seem to have many people working today,' he replied.

'Many people are sick,' the leader replied. 'They have been

bitten by ticks or leeches, and some contracted malaria, as we have no mosquito nets for them. We do not have enough medicine to help them.'

'Hmm,' the Colonel mumbled.

He walked on, away from the group. As I followed, the villagers reached up and tapped me, or put their thumbs up quietly and whispered, 'That's good.' I wasn't pleased. I felt self-conscious.

We returned to the camp.

'You'd better help my logistics man in your spare time, then also go to help the nurse supply hot water, and help her clean up the wounds and see what else you can do for her,' the Colonel ordered. 'Go and help her with her patients when needed.'

I did help her, and I continued to work with her and the Colonel while my comrades laboured in the fields.

Chapter 18
Flight to Freedom

A MONTH PASSED quickly. I was appointed the assistant logistics officer. I was well and healthy, living closer to the store. My days were easy enough, despite the very hot weather, which bred monster mosquitoes.

One morning in March, the Colonel sent for me at the store. Food had arrived, and I was doing some calculations. I had a pen in one hand and a hot potato – my breakfast – in the other.

I came to the Colonel's hut immediately. Climbing the steps to the veranda and gazing across to the tall forest, all I saw were trees, but I knew that in among them were many huts, and many more being built for Khmer Rouge soldiers, who seemed to increase in number each day.

I couldn't see the Colonel through the open side of the hut. I waited, then entered. I heard the radio from his room as I approached, and caught the words: 'The Vietnamese have now reached Siem Reap and plan to reach Battambang by tomorrow.'

A tremor shook my body. I had no idea the Vietnamese were so close, and I wondered what they were doing here in Cambodia.

I knocked on the Colonel's door.

'Come in.'

When I entered, he turned and faced me with a stern look.

'I have a letter. This letter is confidential, understand? I don't have anyone else to deliver it, so will you take it? Take it to your Sahakor Seven. Hand deliver it to your village leader. And don't let it fall into anyone else's hands. If that looks like happening, you must destroy it, understand, huh?'

'Of course,' I replied.

I was given a bicycle – now I would be seen as high-ranking – and I got ready to leave. It was about 8 a.m., and my lunch was packed for me. I placed the envelope in the same bag as my lunch.

I was anxious about this task. I had been told the Khmer Rouge had many enemies. We knew the Vietnamese were in our country – boys had overheard the Khmer Rouge talking about it on their walkie-talkies, and they had told other boys what they knew. But the Vietnamese were so close! What had been happening?

I was thrilled to think the Khmer Rouge revolution might be coming to an end, but I was worried I would be seen as Khmer Rouge when this happened.

It was a long ride, and I had plenty of time to think as the hot sun pounded onto me. Much of the road was sandy, and it was hard to ride the bike through the sand. In some places I had to get down and wheel my bike. Then my heart beat faster – I was in the middle of nowhere. I also had to push the bike through areas where there were many spiky roots. It was very quiet, and another warm day. The shade from the trees helped, but it was a difficult journey.

Finally I saw some decaying houses, but no people. The sun was very hot and straight above, shining on the top of my head, but I dared not stop for my lunch. Eventually I reached other houses in Mong Russey district, and there I felt safer.

I reached my village about two o'clock. Villagers came up to me immediately and stared, wondering what I was doing there with a bicycle. Some Khmer Rouge took me to the village leader, who was sitting on his veranda. I rested my bike near the steps and walked up to him. He was a new village leader. He stood as I approached.

'Yes?' he said.

'This is a letter from the Colonel.'

I gave him the letter. He opened the envelope and started to read, then looked down at me.

'OK,' he said. 'You rest here tonight in my house.' He went inside.

I pulled off my backpack and made myself comfortable on

the balcony. He came out again and began to speak, but stopped, staring past me.

I turned around. Khmer Rouge soldiers were disciplining a group of teenage boys, who were screaming and shouting. Some were boys I used to know. They were being dragged and kicked all the way to the leader's house. Then I saw the nurse who saved my life when I was almost buried. She was also being dragged and beaten.

Other boys ran up to us. 'She has betrayed us,' they yelled. Everyone was gathering now. 'She has fallen in love with one of the villagers.'

'And the boys?' the leader asked.

'When the Vietnamese came near in their tanks calling for victory and liberation, these boys wanted to follow them.'

I stayed on the veranda and watched new Khmer Rouge faces dragging the boys I used to work with. There was one in particular they were beating. They had him on the ground and kicked him repeatedly. Another boy grabbed a duck cage made of wire. It was shaped like a box, only about seventy centimetres on each side.

They tried to push him in. They kicked him and pounded him and smashed him until he fitted into the cage. His arms and legs were broken, and blood was everywhere. They had broken his limbs for the sake of getting him into the cage.

I tried not to react, but I was shocked as I looked down on these events. For a moment, time stood still. As the stifling sun heated the camp – very few trees, just huts and dirt – I could almost smell the wood cooking. Stench was everywhere: the stench of the summer's day cooking the wilds, and the stench of what we had become. I thought of Mother again. She was always with me, yet I feared her spirit could not tolerate what I was seeing.

They dragged the nurse to the back of the village. They stripped her and yelled at her, then made a cross and tied her to it.

'Is this your sex fantasy? You want to betray Angkar? Then this is what you get!'

One of the Khmer Rouge walked over to her. He held a knife

and slashed her breasts as she screamed. I couldn't bear to see the torture. I couldn't stand the shouting and screaming.

I was shaking as I stood on the balcony, wondering if they would do the same to me. I wasn't sure if I was one of their workers or if I was now Khmer Rouge, but I reminded myself to stay firm: I was the leader's guest today.

My family were further down in the village and didn't see this. I didn't dare go to them, but stayed at the village leader's house. When food was brought to us, I was still shaking. I looked down from the house and saw the boy in the cage. He could not move. I could tell he was still alive because while I was looking he opened his eyes and stared at me.

'Eat,' the village leader said.

I ate with him. He didn't know my family was in the village. He spoke about how the Vietnamese had made a 'short tour' along the main national road with their tanks, passing through Mong Russey to Pursat then back to Battambang. A few foolish people got excited and wanted to revolt against Angkar. 'We have captured those people and executed them,' he laughed.

I nodded and complimented him on his appropriate action, and behaved myself by not leaving the house after dinner, even though I so much wanted to visit my family.

The next morning, there was a meeting. After it finished, I was told that everyone would be leaving. I hadn't read the letter but soon I understood: it was an order to this village to join my camp before the Vietnamese returned.

I spoke up. 'The Colonel would like me to return to the camp as soon as possible,' I said.

'All right, but I will send two of my men to follow you. And please inform the Colonel that we will be there as soon as we can.'

As I walked down, I saw the young man in the cage. His eyes were still open, and he stared at me. I turned away and saw the nurse on the cross. She was dead.

I took my bicycle and rode slowly back to my camp, followed

by two soldiers walking quickly. When I arrived, the Colonel came straight to me.

'The village leader will carry out your order and arrive here soon,' I reported.

'Good, good. That is a good job, boy. Now go help organise the food for them and make space for their dwellings.'

Night came, and I was still working when I heard the sound of ox bells and carts and hundreds of footsteps rattling in my ears.

The camp shook with the wheels of the carts and the tramping of feet. I ran out to the front of the Colonel's hut and stood behind him. They were already here, and I hoped my family was too.

It was an exciting evening. People came to the camp from Sahakor Seven and other villages, other provinces. My family was among them. I didn't know when they first arrived, because there were so many people arriving and I was so busy. But I soon found them. Everyone stayed with their own families now, but not me. I still had to take care of the store.

My parents soon had their own hut opposite the Khmer Rouge medical couple, who came to visit my parents with food and gifts. They liked me. They had seen me working hard at the store, trying to distribute goods fairly. But the woman was pregnant, and they did not fit in well with the other Khmer Rouge.

Father talked to the couple often. They had joined the revolutionary front in 1965, when they were both just kids. My family were good to them. The wife suffered from morning sickness, and Stepmother helped her. When the war was over, they said, they would return to their home village in Kampong Thom, the province where Father was born. My family fed them sometimes, but everyone still struggled to find enough food for themselves.

I didn't dare bring extra food to my family, only the food I had left over from my own meals. This caused problems with Chandy, who asked why I couldn't bring more home. I didn't discuss it with him. I just wanted to make sure we didn't do anything that might displease the Khmer Rouge.

The villagers built huts and cleared the forest. The camp had grown to three or four times its original size, then grew again as large numbers of troops arrived.

It was April 1979, two weeks after my family joined me. Summer was still with us. The sky was mostly blue, and every day was hot. But today was different. There was activity everywhere. Villagers worked, soldiers went through their drills, and it began to rain lightly. Then we heard shooting. The Vietnamese had come.

Reports came back to the Colonel. I watched from the store as soldiers and officers ran back and forth with orders. Several wounded soldiers were carried to the nurse. The camp became busier than ever and the Colonel more anxious.

A second front was mobilised, and the Colonel yelled out to me, 'Boy, pass this to the second front commander.' He handed me an envelope. 'Go with the medical team. They're leaving right away.'

There were soldiers everywhere around the Colonel now. I felt honoured that he trusted me to deliver the message. The medical team was waiting. I joined them and we hurried off. The second front was about a kilometre from the camp. The more important first front was a bit further out, but I could not see it for trees.

The rain stopped, but the sky was grey. Weapons fire was loud when we approached the second front, then it went dead and everyone stood still. There were eight of us.

'Down on your knees,' the medical team leader ordered.

I was already on my knees and now I began crawling. We reached the second front at the edge of thick forest. The soldiers were lying down, almost invisible behind the bushes and trees. I could hear shouting and gunfire from further away, but I couldn't see any movement.

A soldier looked at me.

'Where is the enemy?' I asked.

'There,' he pointed. 'They are now attacking the front line.'

I couldn't see where he meant. The first front was behind a thick forest about a hundred metres away.

'Where is the commander?' I asked another soldier.

He pointed but I couldn't see. I crawled closer to him.

'Where is the commander?' I insisted.

'Over there.'

I looked across and saw the commander, who was talking enthusiastically. Other Khmer Rouge were listening. I went over and passed the message to him. He read it and looked up. Two soldiers lay in the grass nearby and he nodded to them. They moved off.

I made my way back. Near me, two medics were carrying a soldier on a stretcher. As I crawled back, the gunfire suddenly began again, a hundred times louder than before. It was deafening. There was shouting and screaming, but the gunfire drowned out every other sound.

I hurried to shelter with the medics. We were a small group now, medics and wounded soldiers and a leader. We were forced to shelter behind trees, and we waited there for three hours. It seemed as if the first front was breaking. We weren't safe. One of the medics was hit in the arm, and I felt my body several times to see if I had been shot.

'Now!' It was the medical team leader. 'Now is our chance!' he shouted.

We crawled and ran haphazardly. I kept moving as people around me were shot. I bent low and ran as fast as I could. Eventually, we got beyond the range of the guns. I hurried back to the camp, then returned to the Colonel.

'Boy, tonight you'd better stay with your family,' he said. 'Whatever happens, stay with them. Don't come back here. I will see you some time later.'

When I passed by the veranda, the logistics man rose from his seat and tapped me on the shoulder.

'Take care,' he said.

I waited until dark and then went to join my family. They were all there. There was Father and Stepmother, Dasy, Vivath, Puthea, Chandy, Sokha and Sophea. Sivanchan was still away, but no-one knew if he was dead or alive.

Everyone was excited but scared. The Khmer Rouge couple came and stayed with us, because the husband was worried about his pregnant wife. Explosions and gunfire were constant. No-one slept properly that night.

When I thought about freedom, my heart pounded as if I was about to die. I was glad to be with my family. Somehow I knew my mother was with us too.

Then suddenly there was silence. I fell asleep instantly in a corner of the hut.

It was morning and the sun was beginning to rise. We heard loud explosions, which told us the Vietnamese had broken through the first front. We huddled in our hut, listening, staring out at the other huts and the sun shining through the canopy of the trees.

Suddenly villagers and some Khmer Rouge ran out of the forest.

'They're here! They're here!' someone shouted. 'They've broken through the second front and they're only half a kilometre away.'

Villagers and Khmer Rouge ran past. The Colonel and his team were gone.

'Follow them into the forest,' someone said.

Father called out, telling us to stick together. The Khmer Rouge couple led us across the clearing and into the trees. Carrying only basic clothing and a few cooking utensils, we climbed up the mountain with hundreds and hundreds of other villagers and Khmer Rouge. Around noon, we stopped moving. We were all hungry and thirsty. Others were near us, some with possessions, some with animals. We had seen people shot, and others had died recently in the forest.

We knew we had not gone far. We hadn't followed any paths or tracks, and we may even have travelled in a half-circle. Father told us to get up and continue walking further into the forest. We walked for another hour or so and then we saw many families: they had all stopped on a hill, resting, with no interest in going further.

Some started to light fires and cook. My family looked exhausted, especially my stepmother and my little brother and sister. We had used up all our water. And Chandy was not well. I was much healthier than anyone else so I didn't rest, but wandered around looking for water.

Nearby was a plateau where a swampy pond had formed. It was like a jungle, and I trekked into it, looking for clean water. Instead my leg knocked against something and I let out a squeal. What was it, coming out of the water? I swung around and it was a body. There were others – two more, floating in the water. I was shocked and began to tremble. I hurried out of there and retraced my steps back to my family.

'There is no water,' I yelled as I returned.

I sat down. Father put an arm on my shoulder, then he rose again. 'We must collect our urine,' he said, 'and be prepared to drink it. Otherwise we might die.'

The place was getting darker and darker. We all prepared. We burnt what we could to make steam. My brothers held up towels to catch the steam and then they squeezed out the droplets into a mug. We knew it wouldn't be enough.

There was some food, but very little rice. We each had only a sip of water, then sat or lay down around the fire. No-one slept. We were all so thirsty. We had to keep boiling murky swamp water all night. As I listened to the weapons fire far away, I wondered if we would die here. I felt the tension all around us from the other villagers and the Khmer Rouge. I watched some of them, their guns in their hands as they waited.

In the morning, we were greeted with another bright sunny day. And visitors. A few more Khmer Rouge came. They told the other Khmer Rouge to leave their guns and go back to their families in the villages. We all wondered if the Vietnamese were coming to liberate us or to kill us. However, my family talked it over with the others, and we decided as a group to stay where we were.

'We need some rice,' I said to Stepmother.

I had seen villagers running back to their families with rice.

'There's rice in the trench!' someone shouted out as he rushed past us.

I remembered the trench: it was an underground shelter built years ago, when the KR attacked the American planes. Now it was used for storing rice.

I yelled to Puthea to come with me. We took two bags back down through the forest to the edge of the camp. As we came closer, a voice called to us, 'It is not safe to get the rice in that underground trench. It is in the clearing, right in the middle of the battlefield.'

I didn't listen. I didn't care or think any more. I just ran down with others as fast as I could. Puthea was right behind me. I went down into the trench and we wasted no time filling our sacks with rice and placing them in baskets that were in the trench. Then we ran back out.

Suddenly there was gunfire. We ran fast, zigzagging all the way. Others around us dropped, but we held on to the rice and aimed for the forest. As we did, we passed many people running toward that trench. We finally reached the forest, ran a little further and then stopped and looked back. People were everywhere now, and the entrance to the trench was jammed with people trying to get in and out at the same time.

'The Vietnamese are going to bomb that trench,' a KR soldier warned through a loudhailer.

We ran further up the hill, but we hadn't gone far when we were almost deafened by the sound of explosions. I looked back. Smoke billowed up into the air: it must have come from the trench. Puthea just smiled at me. I don't think he had any idea what would have happened to him if we were at the trench when it was bombed.

It wasn't long before we reached our family.

Sokha rushed over. 'Did you see the smoke?' she asked.

'Is it still there?' Vivath shouted. 'It's coming from the village.'

Father greeted us with the biggest smile and immediately took some of the rice to prepare it: the husks had to be taken from the rice before we could cook it.

There was less shooting for a while, and no more bombs. We breathed easier, high up there on the side of the mountain at the edge of the jungle. The Khmer Rouge couple stayed with us and were grateful to have assistance for the pregnant wife. We worked on the rice, cleaning it and removing the husks. This took the whole afternoon and gave us something to focus on. Then we cooked it, waiting as everyone else did – waiting and hoping for freedom.

Early next morning, just before the sun rose, I was surprised by the silence. I wandered outside and looked into the forest.

Suddenly people ran out of the forest and came up to us. 'The fighting is over!' they said. 'Get out of here and go back to your home. The war is over and we are free! Hey! Hey! We are free!'

I could see a flicker of a smile on Father's lips. 'Go and get ready to go home,' he said.

Chapter 19
Liberation and Treasure

'CHEY YOO! CHEY Yoo! Chey Yoo!' ('Hooray! Hooray! Hooray!')
rang the excited voices. Families were crying out with joy, and
everyone was ecstatic. I realised that for the first time in as long
as I could remember, I was not being watched.

I saw the Khmer Rouge couple packing.

'The soldiers have gone,' the man said to me. 'The Khmer Rouge.
The Vietnamese. It's all over.'

It was May 1979, and the Vietnamese had defeated the Khmer
Rouge in province after province, helped by Khmer Rouge factions
who opposed the genocide. The Vietnamese had come to liberate,
but they didn't leave many soldiers behind. In some parts of the
country, the Khmer Rouge had been overthrown by the people
when the Vietnamese came.

The couple explained to Father the location of the village where
they hoped to stay in Kampong Thom province.

'We hope to see you again,' Father told them as they left.

It was another warm day. People all around us were cheering
and laughing. Every tree and plant seemed alive and vibrant as
we strolled down the mountain slopes and left that place.

When I reached the fields and looked back, I saw hundreds of
people coming out of the forest from all around. I looked for the
trench, but could not see it. All the people were walking around
its exploded remains. We still had no clear idea of where we were
going, but we left quickly.

We followed the ox-cart tracks that would lead us back to Mong
Russey district. Everyone smiled and greeted each other, but no-
one stopped. Everyone was focusing on their own business and

their own families, but some families took in others who had lost their own parents or relatives.

We arrived at Mong Russey District Town just before sunset. The place was packed with people already. We must have been one of the last groups liberated from the Khmer Rouge in this province.

There was a market with many people trading. I saw people exchanging food for goods, or rice for meat and other commodities, and silver or gold for anything.

We didn't go all the way back to Sahakor Seven. We had to decide: would we go to the provincial town of Battambang or return to Phnom Penh? Returning to Phnom Penh would mean a very long trip, but Father wanted to go back. He wanted to look for his relatives, including his two sisters. In the short term, however, he decided to stay here, because there was something he wanted to do before we left.

We found a place near the Mong Russey pagoda I had visited when I was sick. There was a lot of movement and activity. One thing we didn't see was the black-uniformed Khmer Rouge, though a few soldiers with a different uniform were always standing away in the distance, as if guarding us or looking over us to see what we were doing. They occupied only one building – the district office.

At night, I felt happy. I did not go straight to sleep, but stayed awake listening to the old music and melodies and the joy and laughter of people celebrating. I realised I was really free. But not everyone was rejoicing. Some families were quietly struggling to cope with their problems: many people were sick, and others had been executed or killed by starvation and hardship.

Father realised we would soon be running out of food, so he summoned Sokha and me. He explained quietly that we had a special task to fulfil. He had buried a treasure at Sahakor Seven. We were to go back to the village, dig under his house, find the treasure and bring it to him.

'The treasure is hidden under the house, directly below the stairs. I placed a big stone on top. You must be careful. Don't let anyone see what you are doing. What you will find is all we have now to keep going. And Ar-Ra, you must find it with your sister.'

The next morning, Stepmother cooked porridge for our breakfast, then we left. Sokha followed me with a small spade in her hand. We were going to the first house my family lived in at Sahakor Seven. It was never a home to me, because my time was spent in the teenage boys' group. With everything that had happened there, it was with confused thoughts that I was returning. But we needed that treasure.

Sokha and I walked for an hour along the canal to get there.

'There,' Sokha said. She was seventeen now. She was almost a grown woman, but she was thin and worn, 'There, I can see the river and the huts.'

It was far in the distance, but I looked where she pointed.

'Is that where we lived?' she asked.

Despite the sunshine and the heat, everything was grey. It was hard for me to answer her question, because it had been a long time since we had left the village. Bushes had grown. There was no movement, no life. The paddy fields lay untended. I knew they would be tended to soon. They had to be. Everyone needed the rice.

We walked on past the fields to the outskirts of the empty village.

'Look,' Sokha pointed.

The huts were ruined. Everything was dirty and messy.

'Over there,' she said.

The hall had been burnt, and many huts were burnt too. Others had been knocked down, as if a giant had walked over them. Each step we took revealed more. This had been our home, but now it was like a ghost town.

It was hard to recognise the village we had known, but I kept looking. Eventually, I guided Sokha to where we had lived.

The Vietnamese had been here. They had attacked and burnt everything. Father's house had collapsed. It was nearly unrecognisable, but we found it. We pulled away the branches and wood and found the place where the ladder up to the house had been. With wood that lay nearby, I started to dig.

I dug slowly, carefully searching for the rock that Father had mentioned. A couple of people passed: that was all. I dug and dug, right in the place Father said to. I thought it would be easy to find the treasure, but after two hours I had found nothing – no rock or stone or anything solid at all – and I stopped digging.

I began to lose hope. I wanted Sokha to go and ask Father, but she couldn't go alone. I was tired and it was lunchtime, but we had no food with us.

'Sokha,' I said, 'We have to go back and ask Father again.'

We rested for a while and then we walked back. An hour later, I was speaking to Father.

'I could not find it,' I said.

'No, no, it is there.'

'Then come, help us find it.'

I explained to him how the village was. I told him about our home, but he didn't want to return to Sahakor Seven.

'Try again tomorrow morning. One more time,' he asked. 'Maybe go to the left of the steps a little bit. Maybe you will find it, son. Rest and try tomorrow.'

He thought for a minute. I waited.

'Did you see anybody?' he asked.

'No, I didn't see anyone.'

'No-one?'

'Only a couple of people passing through.'

'I hope no-one else has been digging there.'

'No, not where I was, Father.'

Lights were everywhere that night. Some of the houses in the town even had electric lights. It was night, but people were talking all around us in their tents and makeshift shelters near the pagoda. In the distance, I heard music playing and the joyous celebrations continuing, but only for some people.

I woke the next morning when the cock crowed.

'You will have breakfast earlier today,' Stepmother whispered.

Sokha and I ate while the others still slept. We finished our breakfast as Father woke. He reassured me.

'The rock is there,' he said, 'and beneath it is the treasure. Just dig more to the left. I remember now, there were two bricks buried too, near the rock.'

'OK, Father, I will do my best.'

We left as the sun rose, colouring the fields in reds and yellows. We arrived back at the village, and again there was no-one nearby. I continued digging where I had been yesterday. When I enlarged the hole, I immediately heard a crack.

'Sokha, I've hit something,' I cried.

She jumped into the hole with me. With our hands we dug quickly and carefully. It was a brick. We had found a brick. A moment later we found another beneath it.

We removed both bricks and found a rock. I took out the rock, and then there was a bag. It was a cloth bag, a small one. I picked it up, and it was heavy. I squeezed it. Sokha took it and climbed from the hole. So this was Father's treasure.

I looked around. I could see no-one as Sokha opened the bag. Inside was jewellery.

'Oh, I remember this,' she said, as we rested on the edge of our hole. 'Stepmother used to wear this.'

She held up a gold chain to her neck.

'And this.' She held a ring this time. 'Now she can wear them again.'

The bag held rings, necklaces, bracelets, and diamond earrings.

'OK, tie it up again,' I said.

I looked in every direction to make sure no-one was watching us. On the way home, I thought of the past, and I couldn't stop thinking about Sivanchan. What had happened to my older brother? The sky was dark and it looked as if it would soon rain. We hurried home, but the rain came just before we arrived.

Father was happy and opened his bag of treasures in front of everyone.

'This is all we have got,' he said. 'We will have to depend on this to survive. I don't know how much it is worth now in US dollars or in gold, but it is time to start our lives again.'

Father packed up his treasure and gave it to Stepmother to keep safe. This was a happy time, but we had to wait, hoping for news of family members, hoping to hear from Sivanchan. There was Father and Stepmother. There was Puthea, now fourteen, Chandy, twenty, Sokha, seventeen, Sophea, twenty-one, Dasy, nine, Vivath, ten, and myself, eighteen. Only nine of us were left now that Grandmother had died and Sivanchan was missing.

For the next two days, Father wandered around the town while we stayed in shade near our camp. Father knew we needed additional resources. On the second day, he returned from town with a huge buffalo.

'We will look for my family,' he said. 'We will have to go to Battambang provincial town. Be prepared to leave once we have finished building a buffalo cart. We will be going to my old village.'

We traded for supplies and materials. The weather was hot and oppressive, but we built a cart. It was sturdy and large enough for some of us as well as our possessions. Five days later, we were ready to leave.

We left early, because buffalo only work early in the morning. By about ten or eleven, when the sun is getting hot, they tire and need to cool down and rest. Sometimes they will work again late in the evening, but now it was the end of summer, and the temperature was often over thirty degrees.

Along National Road #5, there were many people. Everyone seemed to know that we all had to do our best to survive now as we waited to see what would happen to our country, and many people approached each other for help.

'Do you have salt?' a man with a sack on his back asked Father.

'Yes, I have salt. I will give you a spoon of salt. What will you give me in exchange?' Father replied.

'Sorry, I only have a bag of corn that I have boiled for my children to eat tonight. I can give you twenty cans of corn, is it OK?'

We all had to help each other, and others helped us. Some families had sarongs and other clothes. Many families were attracted to our jewellery. In this way we steadily acquired more possessions to fill our ox-cart.

Days passed, and we continued to walk from early morning. Late each morning, we would rest and eat, sheltering in the shade of the trees or of the ox-cart. The buffalo would rest and cool down until about four o'clock. Then we would walk again, but only about three or four kilometres before finding another place to rest, usually close to a stream flowing down from the mountains.

One evening, it was overcast and cooler after a very hot day. We kept walking into the night, and it began to rain.

'We must find shelter or our belongings will get wet, especially our rice,' Stepmother announced.

We began hurrying. Soon, we stopped at a place where many people were gathered. Father made enquiries and came back to us sounding happy. 'I have found a shelter for tonight,' he said.

It was an old house, and we were allowed to stay in a corner.

The other family in the house gave us some firewood to prepare our food. In return, Stepmother gave them a meal. We ate and settled, but I felt uneasy. I did not know where I was, and yet I felt as if I should. During the night, I found out what it was: the spirits of the dead were there – ghosts.

We felt them when we slept, in our dreams. Then we woke and someone turned on a lamp. We saw them flying around the house and screaming. Many of us were there, sleeping in the one house, so we weren't very scared. But no-one spoke. Soon the lamp was off again. Surprisingly, no-one seemed to care, and eventually I slept.

Early the next morning, I went to the toilet. The rain had stopped, and I saw a number of graves in the yard around the house. Then I realised. It was the place where I had been captured and placed in prison. It was the place where all I did was march and work and sleep. Since I left here, I had pushed all thoughts of the place from my mind. But I remembered now: there were many executions here.

When the sun rose, I saw the place more clearly. I wanted to tell my family, but it wasn't relevant any more. All we cared about was our freedom. Now that it was morning, no-one even cared about the ghosts who had visited us last night.

We packed and left, pushing the buffalo so they wouldn't

grumble and get lazy. People were everywhere on the national road, going both ways, travelling by day and night. It was about sixty kilometres from Mong Russey District Town to Battambang Provincial Town. Everyone had been suffering from malnutrition and disease, but we had managed to move on, slowly eating more and more to build ourselves up. Still, with the heat it took almost five days to get to Battambang.

Chapter 20
Truck Number Seven

WE WALKED BESIDE the ox-cart through a Battambang in ruins. It was not just that the buildings had been destroyed. People everywhere were running around in a frenzy of activity. It had been only two weeks since my group had been liberated from the Khmer Rouge, but other people had been liberated a month or two earlier. The town had been reshaped by the Khmer Rouge and then destroyed by the Vietnamese. Now it was taking shape again.

We made a home in the ground floor of a building near a market, and we started to sweep up all the broken things. Father saw no more use for the buffalo, but others were interested. He exchanged it quickly, while Chandy and I went out to look around. We walked along the worn roads and looked at what people were doing. Everyone seemed like us.

'Look, Chandy,' I said. 'So many empty buildings.'

We explored deeper into Battambang Provincial Town and saw markets operating on busy streets. I watched as dozens and dozens of people on bicycles rode in from the north and the east. Chandy went and spoke to some of the cyclists.

I enjoyed watching what was going on, with no expectation that I would soon have to line up and work, or take lessons about this new system. It was quite a different feeling. People were happy, and they were doing what they wanted to do.

As I walked along near a pagoda I saw a young man sitting beside the road. He had people near him, and bicycles. I took a closer look – I knew him.

I hurried over: 'Is it you, Po-em?'

'Yeah?' He looked up from repairing a bicycles. 'Oh, Nora.'

'Yes, it is me!'

He stood up and embraced me.

'So where's your family. Is your family all right?' he asked.

'Yes, my family's fine.'

'What about your father?'

'He's good.'

Po-em was very happy. He packed up his things, and we went and found Chandy.

'Where's your father?' Po-em said. 'I want to meet him.'

Po-em's father had been our 'land watcher' before the Khmer Rouge came. We had a piece of land about ten kilometres from our home in Phnom Penh, and we gave him some money to look after it and farm it for us. We lost contact in March 1975, when the Khmer Rouge took over rural areas outside the perimeter of Phnom Penh.

We took Po-em to Father. When he saw Father, he ran to him. He held him very tight and started to cry. Po-em said we were the closest thing to relatives he had. He had been looking for his relatives, friends, and especially his father, whom he hadn't seen since April 1975.

He had been separated from his family during the fall of the Republic and was deployed to Banon district in Battambang. He was forced to join the elite forces and worked in a mobile team before the Vietnamese liberated his district. We asked him whether he had ever seen Sivanchan and described how he had changed, how he might look now. But the answer was the same as always – no, he had not seen him.

Father and Po-em talked happily about what was going on and what had happened. After a long chat, Father invited him to have lunch.

'What do you do now?' Father asked.

'Oh, I have a business,' Po-em answered. 'A small business where I pump up tyres and sell bicycle pumps. I repair tyres and bicycles. It's a good business.'

He told us more. Unfortunately, his business had no proper shop. He had to work on the main road under a tree near the fence of a pagoda, but it was indeed a good business. Bicycles were the most popular means of transportation. There were many more bicycles than motorbikes, ox-carts or other vehicles.

Father looked thoughtful, then asked: 'Do you think you can let Ar-Ra help you in this business?'

I didn't like it when he called me that, but I was happy at the prospect of working with bicycles.

I helped Po-em while he taught me how to repair punctures and tighten spokes, and what to charge, then he gave me work of my own.

I had only been working there a few days when he asked to speak with Father. 'I would like to go and look for my father,' he said.

Po-em had been away from his family for a long time, and missed his father very much. He had worked hard to save up so that he could travel back to look for his family in Kandal province, near Phnom Penh city.

'Would you buy my business from me?' he asked Father.

So Father bought his business and asked Chandy and me to run it, just days after I had started. Father gave Po-em some rice and gold so he could make his journey to find his father and family. The business wasn't much – some old tyres, some tools and parts – but I was excited when I went out with Chandy the next day.

We set up some shade around seven and started working. We had a rice bag and a can. When people came, they brought their rice, carrying it around as if it was money. They asked me to pump their tyres, and for each tyre they gave me a can of rice. There were many bicycles, and ox-carts also needed their tyres pumped up. Some days, we earned two or three sacks of rice.

Meanwhile, Father was looking for his family. He paid people to gather information for him.

One day in early August 1979, he finally met a second cousin and spoke with him for many hours. His cousin was working for the Vietnamese, who had put him in charge of some aspect of transportation, and Father asked him about getting information from Phnom Penh about his relatives.

'The truck will leave for Phnom Penh tomorrow morning,' his second cousin said.

'Ar-Ra, I want you to go,' Father told me. 'Go to our house and your aunt's house. See if your brother has returned. Look for your aunt and see if she has gone back. Look for anybody at all who you knew.'

I had to leave the business with Chandy. Puthea would help him.

The next morning, Father gave me three rings for trade and sent me off with about twenty cans of rice. He put me on truck number seven, as he had arranged, and I listened carefully to his second cousin's instructions.

'Hang on there,' he said, pointing to a rail. 'If anybody stops us and does any checking, let me do the talking. Don't speak at all.'

We left at five in the morning. The truck was in a convoy with about twenty others that had originally been made to carry soldiers. Now they were empty except for a few people who wished to return to Phnom Penh. I hung on tight as the truck drove north, then I fell asleep. Hours later, I woke when the truck stopped. I jumped down, stretched my legs, and found myself in a crowd. The drivers charged a fee – whatever they could negotiate – and now all the trucks were full of people.

Soon we returned to our places on the trucks, and I fell asleep again. We travelled for a whole day and into the night, then eventually stopped at Siem Reap River. The convoy was journeying around the north side of the Great Lake, Lake Tonle Sap, because National Road #6 had been badly damaged and many of the bridges had been destroyed.

The next morning, the truck left early. It was another beautiful warm day, and it was wonderful to see the open fields, free of the Khmer Rouge. After more than eight hours we reached a ferry at the Tonle Sap River. It took a couple of hours for all the trucks to cross.

On the other side, there was a checkpoint. Drivers and the convoy leaders had to be checked by Vietnamese soldiers to be sure each truck carried only soldiers' relatives or people who had travel documents. I kept quiet. My father's cousin told them that I was his nephew. I didn't really know this man. All I knew was that he was doing Father a favour and watching me to make sure I was OK.

After the checking, I jumped back onto the truck. It was beginning to get dark when we reached Kilo Six Market, where the trucks dropped their passengers off before they went into Phnom Penh city, because they were not supposed to be carrying passengers. The journey had lasted two days and nights. The distance was only about six kilometres, but there had been a lot of rain and the road was badly damaged.

The town was called Kilo Six because it was at the six-kilometre signpost, and now I had six kilometres to walk to the heart of Phnom Penh. For a place to stay, I settled on a big house near a river where many others were staying. Cautiously, I set up my hammock. I had no idea what to expect from people here, but in five days the truck would return and leave again for Battambang. That gave me five days to check my old house and find my father's family. I had five cans of rice and two rings, for I had misplaced one. I didn't know what the rings were worth.

The next morning, I found the market, which was huge. People were bargaining as I had never seen before. I strolled and watched. When the vendor and a buyer agreed on the price of goods, say for a pick or a motorbike or a bicycle, they would talk about payment being a milligram of gold or a gram of silver.

With gold, it is hard to tell how pure it is, so they had to depend on the goldsmith. He became very popular. The buyer would give the gold to him, and he would check it on his scales. The goldsmith had a black stone, which was used as an indicator. From scratching the gold on the black stone, the goldsmith could tell how pure it was. Sometimes, a goldsmith would just use his teeth. If the gold was soft, then it was probably ninety-nine per cent pure. If it was seventy per cent, it was paler and harder.

An agreement would then be made, and the goldsmith would weigh the gold. Everyone involved looked carefully to ensure the scale was perfectly balanced. Then he would pay the vendor in rice, or cut a piece of gold to pay with if the vendor wanted to sell something else.

The goldsmiths made a lot of money. Normally, people sold jewellery as whole pieces because it was not profitable to cut them. If they were cut, the goldsmith would gather up any small pieces that dropped, put them on a fire and melt them. The dirt and dust would burn away, and the remainder was gold.

At the market, I looked at the bikes. I sold one of the rings, and it was enough for rice as well as a bicycle.

I pedalled into a city that was dead. Paper money from the days of the republic was lying on the street and being blown by the wind. Weeds and plants were growing everywhere, and the old houses and buildings were demolished or closed.

I kept pedalling along the Russian Boulevard toward the airport, then I turned left into Mao Tse Tung Boulevard. I could not turn off to my aunt's house, as the Vietnamese military had blocked the street, so I continued straight to my old house. I was shocked. Bushes had grown up everywhere, and it was covered with branches and vines.

I couldn't get through. It was like a jungle, and I didn't see anyone.

I continued to ride along the boulevard to the other side of the city, where I thought people might be scavenging. I went along Monivong Boulevard to the bridge across the Bassac River, which I crossed. There, on the edge of National Road #1, which ran to Vietnam, I found a large market.

'Do you want to sell your bike?' a voice said.

I turned.

'Yeah,' I answered. 'How much will you give me?'

He offered me more than the value of the ring I had traded, plus fifty cans of rice.

'That's a good deal,' I said.

I sold the bike and carried the rice, but it wasn't easy. I looked around for another good bike and immediately made about twenty US dollars profit. I put my rice on the bike and pedalled back to where I was staying.

In the afternoon, I came back again. A short time later, someone tapped me on the shoulder.

'Bong Ra?'

It was Sopheap, the younger brother of a boy I used to visit after tuition in Phnom Penh five years ago. We spoke. He hugged me and cried.

'What's wrong?' I asked.

'It's good to see you,' Sopheap sobbed. 'The past is gone.'

'I know. I know.'

'And my family is dead. They're all dead.'

'Where are you staying? Why are you here?'

'I have no place to go. I've looked, but I've found no-one.'

'But where do you stay?'

'I live and work at the restaurant near the market.'

'Do you want to come and stay with me for tonight?'

We had dinner together and talked about our sad stories and bad times.

The next morning, Sopheap went back to work and I got on my bicycle and began pedalling around, looking through the areas I had once known. But all those areas were dead. There was no-one anywhere, except on the fringes of the city or in the small area that was being resettled.

When I returned to Kilo Six that afternoon, I met Father's second cousin.

'I have been waiting for you,' he said. 'We will be leaving tonight.'

'Really?'

'Yes. Get yourself ready, and when the truck comes, just get on.'

I sold the bike and waited for the truck. Then it started to rain. The first truck arrived in the heavy rain. Then came another truck, and another. I kept on counting until the seventh came by – that was my truck – but it didn't stop.

I ran alongside in the mud and the rain and shouted, trying to stop them. They shouted back – 'You cannot ride with us. There is no room with the rice. You must wait for the next one.'

A little while later, I got on truck number ten. I was worried because my father's cousin wasn't there to protect me, but at least the truck had a solid roof. I sat on the top because there was nowhere to sit inside the cabin. This truck too was full.

It was June, the middle of the wet season, and the rain was pouring down.

'Can I leave my bag inside?' I called.

The answer was yes, so I climbed down and looked inside. This truck was full of rice, with just a couple of families. I left my bag and climbed back on to the top, where I managed to squeeze under a cover so that only my feet got wet.

After an hour, we reached the ferry. It took another two hours to get all the trucks across. We drove right through the night. The rain started to fall heavily again, and it was hard to see the road.

After a few hours, I heard someone shouting, and the truck suddenly stopped. When I lifted the cover, all I could see was darkness and fog, and all I could hear was the rain. People were using their torches to look around. I saw our driver and his friends jump down from the cabin. The headlights from another truck shone bright. A couple of people hopped out of the back of our truck, but jumped back in quickly: the rain was too heavy, and the wind was strong. Our headlights shone ahead, and I could see a bridge.

The driver ran to the bridge. I jumped down and followed, and again I could hear people calling out. They were under the bridge. Some of them were in water, but I couldn't see them clearly in the darkness.

'Go and get the torches,' the driver yelled to one of his companions.

It was so wet that I could hardly see anything.

'The truck. It has fallen off the bridge,' someone yelled.

One of the men shone his torch down. People were calling out to us, and others standing near me were calling to the truck below. It was truck number seven. It should have been my truck. It had turned upside down and was sinking in water on the left side of the road.

Some of us hurried down.

'They're inside. They're inside.'

The water was deep and cold. The truck was sinking steadily.

Someone came up out of the water. 'They're trapped under the rice,' he said. 'They're drowning.'

We couldn't save them.

Only the people on top or in the cabin were saved. Three families inside drowned – a dozen or more people. At the start of the bridge, there were bomb holes, which had grown since we passed by four days ago. There were only two long planks of wood across them. Six trucks had got through by driving over the planks, but the sixth truck had knocked the planks as it drove off. Truck number seven didn't have a windscreen, and the rain was very heavy. It was hitting the driver in the face, and he couldn't see clearly. He didn't see that the planks were not positioned correctly. The truck tipped, then collapsed through the bridge and fell into the water metres below.

It took hours to get the remaining half-dozen trucks across the bridge. After passing the bridge, we stopped and waited. We would rest now. It was too wet to continue, and they were still dealing with truck number seven.

I had no place to sleep, because the rain was too heavy for me to stay on the top of the truck. I grabbed my backpack and went under the truck, where others were already lying, but the rain still blew in. I was wet, and so was my bag. I was tired and fell asleep quickly in the mud.

In the heavy rain and strong wind, I couldn't sleep for long. People near me couldn't sleep either. They talked. They were sad about the deaths on the other side of the bridge. I was freezing and couldn't sleep any more, but I tried to rest as I lay there listening to the talking and the sound of the rain pelting down on the canvas of the truck.

The rain eventually stopped. I heard noises and crossed back over the bridge to see what was happening. Dead bodies were now lying beside the road, and people were talking about the rice that had been lost. The truck was being pulled back up; eventually, another truck would tow it to Battambang.

'We should bury these people,' someone said.

I helped. Then the parade of trucks continued as the sun started to come up.

We drove all the way to Siem Reap before we stopped beside the river again. I had nothing to eat. My rice had become so wet that it was no use for exchange. Fortunately, a kind couple with one son invited me to share their meal. They were former Khmer Rouge who had trained in the city.

After we ate, the journey to Battambang continued. There was no more rain, no more accidents. I settled into my thoughts and wondered what would have happened to me if I had been on truck number seven. I knew I was meant to be a survivor.

We reached Battambang about nine the following night. I jumped off just before the truck stopped. I walked back to my home, happy to see my family again as they greeted me on the porch.

'Ar-Ra, you look so tired,' Sophea said.

She prepared a meal. Father and Chandy started asking questions. They wanted to know if I had found any family. They weren't interested in what had happened along the way. I didn't even tell them about the truck going into the river or the loss of the ring. It didn't matter. Whatever stories we had now were nothing compared to what had happened under the Khmer Rouge.

'No, I found no relatives,' I answered.

The next morning, I set off with Chandy again to work as a bicycle repairer. Then Father called. He needed Chandy for something else and sent Puthea with me. We became busy as soon as we arrived at our place beside the road. We did a lot of pumping – for a can of rice each time – and we repaired many punctures, either with hand patches or steam patches. Puthea was happy when I gave him some rice to exchange for ice-cream.

By lunchtime we had a whole sack of rice, which Puthea carried back to the house. Stepmother, Sophea and Sokha worked on cleaning the rice up, smashing it to remove the remaining husks. The value of the rice depended on how clean it was.

We worked like this for several days, and Sophea would always bring us our lunch. One day after lunch, I went for a walk around town. I would do this from time to time, when business was quiet, usually lunchtime when people rested because of the heat. There was no school, no systems except markets and trade, and I would watch the people, the children playing or their parents working, trying to rebuild the town.

Father came up to me while I was walking. As he approached, I saw he was walking with another man and talking loudly. They were excited and happy.

'Is this your son?' the man said as they reached me.

'Yes, this is Ar-Ra.'

I didn't know who the man was, but he was older than Father.

'Salute this man,' Father told me. 'Call him Great-uncle. He is my mother's cousin. I found him at the market. Do you remember your great-uncle who used to come and work for us before the Khmer Rouge took over?'

'You mean Great-uncle Searl?'

'This man is his older brother.'

Father put his hand on my shoulder.

'Our searching has prevailed,' he continued. 'Now, come on. Go back and pack your things. Great-uncle has asked us to go and stay with him while we look for more of our family. We will leave tomorrow.'

Chapter 21
Family Unity

MY GREAT-UNCLE CAME by as expected, but with another great-uncle, so there were two of them staying with us that night. Their area had been liberated some time ago and they had been looking for relatives for months.

At the end of that interminable Year Zero – a time of suffering that had lasted more than four years – everyone was focused on finding lost loved ones. Even if the news was bad, everyone was curious, everyone needed to know what happened to their parents, their brothers and sisters, their children and other relatives during that horrible time.

The next morning, my great-uncles left early. They had bicycles and went ahead to prepare a place for us. They lived at the border of the Siem Reap and Kampong Thom provinces, at a place called Kampong Kdey. We packed and loaded our cart, but this time we had to push it. We left Battambang and walked along an old, worn road to the Sisophon district north-west of the Great Lake, where the road turned toward Siem Reap province. We rested at Sisophon before moving on again.

We travelled on for another five days. Chandy and I pushed and pulled the cart, full of our belongings, and sometimes Dasy sat on top. She was now ten, but she was often very tired.

Eventually, we reached Kampong Kdey, and our whole family was at the roadside, waiting to greet us. Among them was a great-aunt I hadn't seen since 1974.

The cries of joy began as soon as we saw them. We greeted each other by putting two hands together and saluting, according to our traditional custom. We all saluted Grandma, my uncles and aunts and the rest of their families, who were our second cousins, by raising both our hands in front of our chin, a greeting that was forbidden under the Khmer Rouge regime.

We were so happy. We were taken to the village and given a place to stay in a building where bricks were once made. It was like a dome, and was situated next to a quarry. The area for making and drying the bricks was big, like a large hall. We were given half of the dome to live in: our half was separated from the other by two ovens.

Surrounding the area were many trees, and some even grew over the roof. The quarry was near the river, because a lot of water was needed for making bricks. The river was quite wide. I was a good swimmer and looked forward to having an opportunity to jump in.

My great-aunt had four daughters and two sons. I called the sons 'Uncle' and the daughters 'Auntie'. Ta Daek was Father's uncle, the eldest one, and he stayed near us. Father planned to find more relatives. He also hoped to find an income for our family.

I set up my bicycle business again with Chandy, under a tree alongside National Road #6. We also helped in Great-aunt's rice fields in the morning. In the afternoons, the girls sold goods at the market, where Father was able to get scales for their business. This made us like goldsmiths. Business was good: there were many smugglers that came this way by bicycle from the border of Thailand.

In the evening, we would often jump into the river behind the quarry. It was August, wet but still warm. One day, I had a break from my bicycle repairing and went to the rice fields. I loved the scenery. There was much more water here than what I had previously seen, and many trees along the dykes to provide shade.

We were two big families living together at the quarry. After meals, we all sat around in the candlelight and talked. We talked about the past, not so much about what had happened during the bad times, but about our memories from the good times before 1975.

Chandy and I had a shade now for our business, a cloth we erected above us like a tent so that customers could wait in the shade while we repaired or serviced their bicycles. It was still the wet season, but it was very hot, so we filled a big jar with water and offered it free to our customers.

People were always passing in trucks, a few on motorbikes, but mostly on bicycles, walking or pulling carts. One day, a large group came past us on their bikes. The last two in the group stopped and then rode back to us. They seemed to recognise Chandy.

Chandy smiled.

'Is it you, Chandy?' one of the men said.

'Yes, Uncle Koy.' They were about Chandy's age and he recognised them quickly. 'And Uncle Hean.'

'This is Ar-Nor, huh?'

'Yes,' Chandy replied.

'Wow! You are big now, huh!' said Uncle Koy. 'So where is your father?'

'We're staying with Great-uncle Daek and his sisters. We're staying at Grand-aunt's house at the moment,' Chandy replied.

They put down their bikes and asked about everyone, then came to meet Father and the others.

'We wanted to go to Kampong Cham,' Father said, 'but just now we cannot travel any further, as we have limited food supplies.'

'That's fine,' Uncle Hean said. 'We will come back, and bring more bicycles for you so the younger children can ride. And you can come to us later.'

When Uncle Koy and Uncle Hean left – they were on their way to return to other family members in Kampong Cham – they promised they would keep their eyes and ears alert for news about Sivanchan.

About two weeks later, Uncle Hean and Uncle Koy came back to get us, accompanied by Uncle Ngan, who was Father's cousin. They brought three extra bicycles. They rested for one night, and the next morning we packed. Only Chandy, Sokha and I knew how to ride, so the others would be riding with our uncles. Father sold the bicycle business to his great-uncle, then we said our goodbyes and left before noon.

The journey wasn't easy. All of our belongings were strapped to the back of our bicycles. Father and Dasy were with Uncle Koy, Stepmother and Vivath were with Uncle Hean, and Sophea and Puthea were with Uncle Ngan. Each of their bicycles had a ding, which extended out the back with bamboo sticks for our belongings and was designed to carry two people.

Sokha slowed us down. Chandy and I were told to keep our eyes on her because she was struggling. She was only sixteen and not used to riding. Chandy did not like to slow down, so I waited for Sokha.

'It's OK,' I called out to the others. 'Don't wait for us, we know the way.'

Late in the afternoon, we were stopped in the hot sun when Sokha began crying. She was tired and scared, but she was not going to give up. She got on her bike again and kept pedalling as hard as she could, because she had been told that it would not be safe after dark. The road was very quiet. Sokha tried hard to keep up with me, but her legs could not take any more. In the hot sun, I kept pedalling without looking back. Then, when I turned around, I couldn't see her.

I hurried back. She had stopped a long way behind and was crying again. I rode back to her. She did not say anything, just kept crying and rubbing her legs, which must have felt so sore. She showed me her muscles: they looked hard and tight. I felt sorry for her, but there was nothing I could do.

When we reached the next town, a place called Stuong, Father was waiting. There was another relative with him, his second cousin.

'Sokha! Are you OK?' he asked.

'I am fine except my legs have became so hard.'

'Ah, Sophea will bring some tiger balm and massage those legs. She will rub it into your muscles,' he said.

We went to Father's cousin's house. Sophea came to help. She massaged gently and Sokha was happier. Father turned to me.

'Ar-Ra, I am going to find my goddaughter and godson. Come along with me. This is where they live.'

I thought for a moment. He meant the Khmer couple we had been with when the Vietnamese came.

The rest of the family were getting ready to move on. Sokha stayed with our second cousin while Father and I went to look for the Khmer Rouge couple. We found them in a village behind Stuong town. They were happy to see Father. They had given birth to a girl, and asked him to give her a name. He also gave them the address where we would be in Kampong Cham Provincial Town if they wanted to visit us.

That night, Father was staying with me and Sokha at his cousin's house. Another cousin of his had already gone ahead with the rest of the family.

The next morning, Sokha wasn't well. She had a sore leg and was crying. She was also scared and didn't want to ride any more, and she had a fever.

'What is happening?' Father asked.

I told him how she was and explained she needed to rest.

Her head was hot, but Father's cousin told him not to worry. He said she was unwell due to the air flowing inside her body – this air we called 'Khol-Ch-Alle'. Father's cousin's wife started scratching all over Sokha's body with a coin and oil. It was very painful and made her legs red, but Sokha got used to it and did not cry. I knew she would be well, but we stayed there a while to rest.

After a couple of nights, Uncle Koy came with Chandy, and soon after that we said goodbye to Father's cousin and his family. Uncle Koy carried Sokha on his bike, while Chandy took Sokha's bike. We pedalled through Kampong Thom, Father's birth province, and reached Kampong Cham three days later.

We stopped at a big wooden house alongside the Mekong River. It was raining and very dark. As we approached the stairs to the veranda, I heard my father's second cousin, and we were called to come upstairs. I saw my aunt, Auntie U, her husband, Uncle Cheng, and their four daughters. Their sons were not there – some had gone to France, and the others were missing.

They took one side of the house and hung a curtain in the middle. I just stayed on the balcony. The rain was pouring down so heavily it sounded like drums happily welcoming our reunion. A candle was lit in the middle of the house, then Auntie U called out loudly, 'Ar-Ra Khmoy ('Nephew Ra'), Chandy! Please come to have your dinner!'

We had dinner by candlelight. After dinner, I fell fast asleep.

When I rose the next morning, it had stopped raining and everyone was going about their business. The house was surrounded by trees and built on stilts. There was a road in front, running next to the bank of the Mekong River. It was a big river, and the water level was high.

I stood on the balcony and looked at the other side of the river. There were many people using a large boat like a ferry to cross. I looked further along the riverbank: there were more people further up, and it looked as if there was a market at a port where people crossed the river. Along the street beside the house, there were many trees on both sides. I was seeing this place clearly for the first time – it was a beautiful town.

Later that day, Father told me he had a plan. He was going to go to Phnom Penh to find other relatives, mainly his two sisters. We were much closer to Phnom Penh now. I had failed on my mission there, so he would go himself.

I tried to think about what I could do to make some income for the family. One morning, I saw You Ren, my Auntie U's daughter, selling banana-cake rolls on the street. She had made a fire under a big tree and placed the sticky banana-cake rolls over hot coals to bake them. They smelt delicious as I walked past.

'Hey! Bong Nora, where are you going?' she called.

She remembered my name after almost five years. I remembered her name, but I was too shy to call it.

'Hi! I want to look around and see the market,' I replied. 'So you are selling banana-cake rolls, right?'

'Yes! But do you want some?'

'I don't have any rice to buy it from you,' I answered.

'It doesn't matter. Just eat it.'

'No. No. That's not good. You need to make money. I will buy them from you when I make some money, OK! Thank you anyway for your kind offer.'

She stood up and grabbed two cooked banana-cake rolls, held my arm and put them in my hand.

'Just eat them, and no need to worry about repaying me!'

I walked on with a smile and turned around to glance at her shyly. I thought how wonderful she was.

As I walked, I thought that I needed to find something to do to prove that I was now a fully grown person who would be able to take responsibility for my own future. And I thought about the Vietnamese.

Because we lived along the Mekong River, we saw many Vietnamese soldiers mobilising in their boats. Sometimes we also saw other ships or boats returning to Vietnam. We didn't know what was happening, but many Vietnamese walked around the town now. Their presence indicated authority, and they used this authority to govern us. They had their rules, and we had to obey them. They hadn't liberated us, they had invaded us – and now our freedom was being threatened again.

Chandy went with Father to Phnom Penh. I asked Puthea if he wanted to sell bread, and he said he did.

So I looked around town to find where bread was made. We started to buy rolls in the morning and deliver them to people's houses. We were paid in rice. The business was not very good, because now everyone was equal in what they owned, and the margin of profit was very low.

After a while I let Puthea sell bread rolls by himself while I helped my sisters with their business selling sarongs and skirts and scarves at the market. I collected the rice they were paid with and resold it at a different market after Stepmother cleaned it.

After several weeks of doing this, Father returned. He had found his sisters and their families. They were all still alive and had returned to Phnom Penh to look for us. He had brought them back with him. We were all reunited now and the house was full, but there was much talking and planning.

As the planning took place, our situation changed. Violence between the Vietnamese and Cambodians increased. Many rules were being forced on us. And people were disappearing.

I heard Father talk one evening.

'There is no real government here. Just the Vietnamese. We are all happy to listen to the Vietnamese now,' he said. 'But we must look to the future.'

Father asked questions around town and listened to conversations. A couple of days later, he called the family together.

'I have some information,' he announced. 'On the west side of the country, just next to the Thai border, there is a camp. It has been established for refugees. It is not only us who have found the situation difficult under the Vietnamese government. People say it will soon be the same as when we were under the Khmer Rouge.'

Father and my uncles and aunts kept talking. They all agreed they would lose their freedom and any future for their children if we stayed under Vietnamese rule.

'I am going to send Chandy and Nora away on a mission,' Father announced, looking at us as we sat on the floor of our home.

'Your uncle and I have decided you both must go with him and find your sister Vanny in Australia, or you must go to America and look for my younger brother.'

I hadn't dreamed of such a thing. How could this be possible?

'We have two people out of the country that we can rely on. We need to get their help so we can live elsewhere. Your uncle is going, because only he will be able to search for your sister or your uncle in Australia and America. Your assignment is to make sure he arrives at the refugee camp safely. No matter what happens during your journey, you must not leave him alone.'

Father's information was that if we could successfully escape into Thailand, then we would be given refugee status to go to a third country – Australia, America or other countries that would accept us.

After the Vietnamese invaded in January 1979, at first we thought everything was good. Nothing could be as bad as the camps the Khmer Rouge kept us in. The Vietnamese seemed reasonable. They let Cambodians travel anywhere we wished, especially when it came to travelling from one province to another to find lost family members.

But now the Vietnamese seemed to have changed their mood: there was no longer any free movement from one place to another, yet they expected us to settle down while they installed their government throughout the country. This new regime was showing its face, and it wasn't much different from the Khmer Rouge. We felt increasingly intimidated.

The Vietnamese said they wanted us to join them in the Vietnamese-installed government and to help rebuild the country. But Cambodians didn't want to work with the Vietnamese. We had never got along with each other since the Vietnam war.

Resistance groups had formed along the Thai border, and some Khmer Rouge were hiding there too. These were some of the reasons the Vietnamese gave – by word of mouth and at town meetings – to impose strict regulations on the people.

Father heard that the Vietnamese were selecting sympathetic people who could speak Vietnamese to be their delegates. Father also heard of their plan to educate people in the Vietnamese language. Anyone who did not like that idea would be arrested and sent to work along the border clearing the landmines. This would especially be the case for rebellious teenagers.

It took Father about two weeks to gather the information he needed for Chandy and me to depart on our mission. He told us that we still had a chance to move, and he would quietly look for

ZUCCHINI & ROSEMARY MEATBALLS

COOK 30 MINS · MAKES 15 MEATBALLS

ZUCCHINI & ROSEMARY MEATBALLS

PREP 15 MINS • COOK 30 MINS • MAKES 15 MEATBALLS

INGREDIENTS

500g organic beef or lamb mince

1 cup grated zucchini

2-3 tsp Meadow & Marrow Natural Bone Broth Concentrate

2 tbsp fresh rosemary, chopped

3 cloves of garlic, crushed

Coconut oil for cooking

ONION & BONE BROTH GRAVY INGREDIENTS

5 brown onions, sliced

4 tbsp butter or ghee

4-6 cloves of garlic, crushed

1 tbsp Meadow & Marrow Natural Bone Broth Concentrate

1 cup water or homemade liquid bone broth

MEATBALL METHOD

Heat a frying pan on medium heat and add some coconut oil.

Add all the meatball ingredients into a bowl and use your hands to mix and combine everything evenly.

Roll the mixture into balls and place into the heated frying pan in batches. Don't overcrowd the pan.

Cook the meatballs on all sides until golden brown and cooked through.

Transfer the **cooked** meatballs to a plate and continue cooking **more** meatballs until all the mix has been used up.

When they're ready serve as is or with our Onion & Bone Broth Gravy

ONION & BONE BROTH GRAVY METHOD

MAKES ROUGHLY 1.5 CUPS OF GRAVY • COOK • 40-50 MINS

Best made in advance to save time, then simply reheat and serve with your chosen meal

Heat a large frying pan on medium heat. Add 2 tbsp of butter and allow it to melt all over.

Add the onions and sautée the onions until golden brown, stir through every few minutes. This will take roughly 20 minutes.

Add the remaining butter along with the garlic and continue cooking for another 5 minutes.

Now add the broth and water or liquid bone broth and stir through.

Add the gravy mixture into a food processor or a blender and blitz until completely smooth and creamy.

Now add the gravy back into the frying pan and continue to simmer until the natural sweetness from the onions is gone and you get to your preferred gravy thickness.

Serve the gravy with our Zucchini & Rosemary Meatballs, on top of roasted chicken, beef or lamb, with cauliflower puree or potato mash or with a delicious homemade GF pie.

Will last for 10 days in the fridge.

FOR MORE RECIPE INSPIRATION FOLLOW US
@MEADOWMARROWBONEBROTH

RECIPE BY JORDAN PIE,
NUTRITIONIST & G.A.P.S PRACTITIONER
MEADOWANDMARROW.COM.AU

a truck to take us in the direction of the border. But we had to wait. Father told us to be ready to leave as soon as he found the right truck.

Chapter 22
The Border

BY DECEMBER 1979, there were a great number of boats and ships travelling along the Mekong River, and many trucks used the roads during the day, but the nights were quiet because there was a curfew. There was no more music. People who criticised the Vietnamese were arrested. Those who sought the border were arrested. There were checkpoints to intercept people trying to flee to the refugee camp in Thailand. The borders were dangerous. The Vietnamese were not the only danger; the mines laid down by the Khmer Rouge were a death trap.

Father's plan was that Chandy and I should go with Uncle Chheang, Auntie Imlay's husband. But Uncle Chheang was recovering from an illness and was very weak. He couldn't walk well. This wasn't unusual among those of us who had been in captivity for years.

Father had found a truck that would take us all the way back to Sisophon district. From there, we would escape to the Thai border. For about twenty milligrams of gold, approximately thirty US dollars, we bought a bicycle that would carry my uncle.

'Good luck,' Father said early the next morning. 'Chandy, no matter what happens during the escape, you must not leave your uncle alone.' He turned to me and said, 'Nora! You must listen to your brother and your uncle.' He touched my shoulder and gave me the backpack with rice and food as well as jewellery and gold.

Chandy and I saluted Father and the rest of the family, then Auntie Imlay approached us and begged us tearfully, 'Please take good care of my husband. He is not as strong as you two.'

Father took us quietly to a truck that was leaving, and the three of us hid inside. I wondered what would happen to us. What problems would we have? Would it really be possible for us to escape? We travelled for a whole day, and I slept for a while. I was woken by my uncle.

'We have arrived at Sisophon,' he whispered.

It was about six o'clock. We left the truck and walked around, finding an old house to stay in on the main street not far from the market. Then Chandy hurried off to find a guide. When he came back, he spoke anxiously to us on the porch.

'Uncle, are you OK?' he asked. 'Will you be able to make it tonight, or do you want to rest for a night or so first? How do you feel?'

'I am all right,' said Uncle Chheang. 'Except my butt is a bit numb and sore from the holes the truck drove through. I'm fine. Really, I'm fine.'

'Good! Because I have found a guide, but we must be ready to go at eight o'clock tonight.'

The guide demanded his fee in advance. He would not take us alone, but he had promised to guide us to where one of the refugee camps was.

I went quickly with Chandy and paid our money to the guide. It was already getting dark. With Uncle Chheang's approval, I found bamboo sticks and some wire around the side of the house and tied them to the bicycle to make it stronger and make a comfortable seat at the back for Uncle Chheang to sit on. It was not easy to convert the bike to a cart, but we also made a handle on each side so that Chandy and I would be able to push the bike or lift it where necessary.

We ate our dinner, then it was nearly eight. We put Uncle Chheang on the bike and pushed him toward the large tree near the market. At eight o'clock, people began coming from everywhere. There were a couple of families with children, but most of them were smugglers. The smugglers wore long pants and long-sleeved shirts with a cap and scarf around their necks. Some came with their bicycles.

'Look, there are so many,' Chandy said.

About forty or fifty people came, including five or six of the guide's helpers.

'Follow us closely,' the guide explained. 'You don't want to get lost. If anything happens tonight, stay with your small group. Follow your designated leader. We may be attacked in the forest, or we might meet a Vietnamese patrol. There may be bandits, or even some Khmer Rouge looking for recruits.'

Our leader was large and strong, but he had a friendly face and spoke in a pleasant voice. He wore a kroma around his neck and had a torch strapped to his waist.

'Before we reach the border, we will have to run through a thick forest,' he said. 'We will have to split and go different ways so we will not all be captured, because if we're captured, women will be raped and men will be robbed, tortured or killed, depending on their mood. So far we have been very lucky. My groups have not yet had such an experience.'

'We must stick with the head guide,' I muttered to Chandy and Uncle as we started our journey.

Chandy rode the bike with my uncle sitting on the back, while I pushed from behind. We walked quietly in the dark. Before we realised it, we were on a path through the forest. It was a forest of rubber trees, but not a plantation. It wasn't an easy journey as we followed the leader's torch, helped our uncle and hurried to remain close to our leader. From time to time, he turned around and flashed his torch at us.

The path narrowed and became rough. Chandy jumped down from the bike and we wheeled it while Uncle stayed sitting. We had been walking for two hours. The canopy of trees was thick and when there was space to see the sky, the clouds began to cover the moon. It became more difficult to travel on the narrow track, and we decided to give up on the bike.

'Can we stop for a minute?' I asked our leader.

We left the bike and made a chair from some of the sticks to carry Uncle Chheang, who was very light from his illness. Our group became separated from the others, but we were with the main guide. It was very quiet. The only sounds were our own footsteps and the rustling of the twigs when we stepped on them.

Then we saw flashlights through the trees, and suddenly there was gunfire. We lay down behind logs and bushes and listened to the shooting and screaming. It was hard to tell where it came from because of the trees, but it must have been a couple of hundred metres away. The forest, which was silent minutes before, now echoed the sounds of people all around us.

All we could do was wait. The sound of gunfire sometimes came close. After a while, we sat up. I was still shaking when we heard footsteps. Thoughts of being executed, or being caught by the Khmer Rouge, flashed through my mind.

'Hold it. Stop. Stop. I will shoot,' someone shouted.

We kept quiet and stayed absolutely still. I lifted my head and tried to look around. I could not see anyone, only the moonlight through the canopy of the trees. The moon cast shadows in the darkness: it was not easy to see anyone if they were hiding in the bushes.

We heard more gunfire and waited some more.

'We must go on now,' our leader suddenly called.

We progressed deeper and deeper into the forest, staying away from any paths, and then we heard more shooting. It was close. We lay down quietly again, hidden in the bush. I didn't know who was shooting. Was it Vietnamese? Khmer Rouge? Bandits?

I had to admire our leader. He understood our situation with Uncle not being well, but now he was tense. 'Run,' he called.

Everyone ran. All his people from all around us escaped the area, except for us. We could not pick up Uncle quickly enough before gunfire started again. Our leader whispered, 'You'd better throw away your carrier.'

We crawled quietly through the bushes following him. He knew where the fighting was, and he knew how to lead us away from the danger. After we stopped crawling, we had to carry Uncle Chheang, and we joined up with another group. Now there were about ten of us.

We moved on slowly, away from the area that was being patrolled. We walked, stopped, walked some more and then stopped again. I don't know how warm it was, but I was constantly sweating. Chandy kept quiet, and I knew he was worried. Uncle was struggling, but he was determined. We took turns carrying him and he seemed to get heavier as we did. We were so exhausted. Finally our leader said to stop.

'We are OK now. We are not far from the camp, but it is very dangerous if we walk through their territory without signalling. If they don't know us, we will be shot.'

We saw some lights and heard the sounds of chickens and other animals.

'Is that the camp?' Chandy asked.

'No, that is a Khmer Rouge camp. The torchlight is at one of their posts.'

He led us away from there. Soon we were walking in the grass beside a dirt road. We continued to struggle along the perimeter of the thick bushes and tall grass at the edge of a field. We could hear chickens squawking again, but we could not see any houses.

'We should rest here,' the leader said. He looked at his watch. 'Now it is four. Rest a bit. Wait until daylight comes. There is no point going further now. The sentries at the outposts will shoot at us.'

We stayed close in our group. Uncle lay on the ground. There was a little rain, but we weren't cold. Chandy and I rested by leaning against a tree, and soon we fell asleep.

'Wake, wake now.'

It was Uncle Chheang. I looked around, and everybody else had gone – there were only the three of us. Uncle wasn't well. We started to carry him, but I was exhausted.

'That's where they went,' Uncle said. There were footprints on the sandy road, and we followed them.

I thought about what had happened. In our group were others like us, but there were also smugglers. They wanted to find the refugee camp for trade. They would buy goods, then bring them back to Cambodia to sell for a profit. They couldn't be trusted.

We continued to walk beside the field. I looked around behind us and to the side; the forest grew freely on one side of the road.

Tall trees and hills were everywhere, except for a small rice field beside us. It stood out in this jungle area near the border.

'Look, there's a soldier,' Chandy called.

He was on us before we could do anything, his gun pointed at us from his hip. But he was not dressed like a Khmer Rouge soldier.

'You just arrive?' he said.

'Yes,' I answered. 'Have you seen anyone passing through here?'

'Are you with the others?'

'Yes,' said Chandy.

The soldier walked past without saying any more. He wasn't surprised to see us.

We walked on, now in the middle of a narrow road, which curved into a thick forest. We passed a patrol of soldiers who smiled at us but otherwise ignored us, and then we saw a Red Cross flag.

'What is that?' Chandy said.

Uncle pushed away from our arms. Suddenly he was strong and full of energy.

'It's the camp,' he said, 'and there, there is the Red Cross headquarters.'

The Red Cross flag stood out above the trees on the hillside in the distance. Beside it was a United Nations flag mounted on a post. It was still far away, and I couldn't even see the camp. But it was there, and we had made it.

Chapter 23
Across the Minefield

WE HURRIED TOWARD the Red Cross flag. After a while, the road grew straighter. We were on the edge of a treed plain that stretched out off one side of the road. I could see many small clearings, and there were tents, huts and vehicles.

'I will go and talk to the Red Cross,' Uncle said, his voice full of hope.

We went to one of the wooden offices, which was the headquarters of the Red Cross, and Uncle went inside and spoke to a foreigner. We waited outside and enjoyed watching the people. Children were playing on the ground, people were carrying water from the Red Cross water tank, bicycles were coming into the camp, and groups of riders were leaving with goods piled high on their bicycles.

The door swung open. A man wearing a Red Cross T-shirt was standing beside Uncle, who hobbled over to us. 'Chandy! You and Nora go with him,' he explained with his big smile, 'and he will lead you to a place to stay. I will be staying here to work.'

'Really! Have you got a job already? Wow!' Chandy said.

'I will try to make some contacts to find your sister and your uncle,' Uncle Chheang whispered.

He went back inside the office. He was very capable, I thought. He spoke good French as well as English, and he had an excellent understanding in many areas, including medicine. They definitely needed him, which was why he was sent with us.

The man with the Red Cross shirt told us to come with him. He took us to the edge of the camp, where we saw row upon row of empty box-shaped huts with hay roofs among the trees.

Each hut was about three metres wide and two metres high.

'Here, this is where you will be staying,' the Red Cross man said. 'When we get the green light from the UN headquarters, we will help the refugees to move. This camp is not a safe place, and you can't cross the border from here.'

The man left. 'I'm off to the market,' Chandy announced. 'You prepare lunch.'

He was excited. I was too, as I anticipated finding out how to get from here to the refugee camp across the border. We could hardly believe we had made it this far, but we had to go further to get to Thailand and the official refugee camp. It wouldn't be easy.

I started to unpack and cooked some rice, waiting for Chandy to return with other food. After a while, I could wait no longer. I locked our hut and went to look for him.

There were many hundreds of people in this camp, mostly keeping to themselves with their own business, their own stories. I thought of my family. I thought of Mother. I was sure she had protected me and helped me to get this far. I thanked her as I walked and searched in the hilly forest.

At the market, I traded for some meat and dried fish. Chandy came back for his lunch, then told me that tomorrow he would be up early. He would be leaving with other people to cross the Thai border, collect some goods and bring them to sell here.

Uncle came back in the evening and said that he had been able to send letters to my sister, and to my uncle in the USA. Chandy told him he would be smuggling goods over the Thai border and would ask me to sell them at the market.

Morning came. At 4 a.m., Chandy left the hut. He returned three hours later with sarongs and cigarettes. Uncle had already had breakfast and left for work at the Red Cross, and Chandy asked me to sell the goods he'd smuggled. He was tired, so I took them.

The next morning, he left early again, but he hadn't returned by evening. Uncle came and asked me what happened.

'I did not see him,' I said. 'He left and he never came back.'

We rested, waiting for Chandy, but he didn't come.

Uncle explained where we were. 'This is just a transition camp where people are gathering because they don't want to join the Khmer Rouge. We are far from the next camp, which is the KPNLF camp.'

'What is that?' I asked.

Uncle told me the initials stood for the Khmer People's National Liberation Front, which was headed by Mr Soeung San, an old man who used to be the adviser to King Norodom Sihanouk. His camp was close to the Thai border and had access to the Red Cross.

'This is where people cross the border,' Uncle said. 'The Red Cross come and assist people to cross the border.'

I tapped my knuckles against my head. 'We were briefed by the Red Cross worker on the first day,' I replied. 'He said something about this.'

Uncle looked down.

'It is a dangerous area,' he said. 'Mr Soeung's camp is the best place to cross the border from, because it's closest to the Thai refugee camp.'

He looked up again and I met his eyes.

'The KR have laid down a lot of mines in this area, especially in the direction of the Thai border,' he said. 'They do not want people to escape. They don't want anyone to flee across the Thai border to the refugee camp.'

Chandy came back late the next morning.

'What's happening?' Uncle scolded. He was upset, but Chandy was cheerful.

'I made money yesterday. Would you like to hear what happened?'

Uncle refused to listen, so Chandy and I went outside.

'I want to know what happened,' I said, 'but how do you get to the border? Uncle said there are mines.'

'There are mines, but if you are by yourself there are paths, safe paths. Don't worry, little brother.' He put a hand on my shoulder. 'People cross to the border every day.'

He told me what happened. 'We sneaked across to Thai soil again to buy goods, and I ran into Po-em,' he said. 'He's now a smuggler too.'

'Wow!'

'Then the Thai black soldiers came. They chased us, and we could not cross back. We had to hide, and ended up at the house of the Thai guy who sold goods to us. He could speak some Khmer and let us hide there. I knew Uncle would be worried, but I can look after myself.'

The next morning, Chandy went off with Po-em again. Uncle cooled down and agreed that we could keep doing what we did. He continued his work in the Red Cross office. He had so much work to do that he did not come home for lunch. Chandy also had lunch away most of the time. He would go to the border and exchange goods, or he and his friends would cross the border into Thailand and chase the goods that people in Cambodia needed, then bring them back to sell for a profit. Sometimes he would even miss dinner, depending on the Thai patrol along the border. If the patrol was strong and thorough, he had to stay either just on the Cambodian side of the border, or in the Thai village where he bought the goods.

It was an uncertain time, but at least we were able to stay at the camp while the Red Cross waited for the right time to take us across the border. We were happy to wait. Uncle had written to Vanny, and we were anxious for a reply. He had also sent a letter to his brother-in-law in the USA, giving the Red Cross as the return address. We just had to wait.

One morning at the market, I met some members of a family who used to live near us in Sahakor Seven. The man's name was Ek Sunchan, and he was Father's godson from the time they worked together ploughing at Sahakor Seven. He was tall with a large build, and he had just arrived at the camp with his nephew, who was nine, while his brother went to find information about the official refugee camp.

After we talked for a while, he asked me to look after his nephew for a minute. He said, 'I want to find his father and get some food supplies from the Red Cross.' I agreed. The nephew would stay by my side at the market while I continued to sell my goods: sarongs, cigarettes, household appliances, pumps, tyres and spare parts for bicycles.

Mr Ek went off on his business, and my selling went well. It was another fine day that would become very hot later. Then, just before midday, we heard guns. They were shooting from the other side of the camp, just a shot or two at first.

We all stopped what we were doing and looked in the direction of the gunfire. It stopped, and we continued with our dealings. Then there was more gunfire, much more, and the sound of a bomb fired from a rocket launcher. It hit the trees, which cracked and fell apart, but some caught on fire. We were in the forest, surrounded by trees, and we were trapped. The rocket launcher was fired again and again. The rockets hit the trees near the market. The fire was meant for the market, and we all knew our lives were in danger.

Everyone panicked. Some started to pack, and others ran screaming into the forest. I had just sold all my goods and grabbed my bag, thinking only of going back to my hut to get my valuable belongings.

'Come with me,' I said to the boy. 'I have to go back to my hut to grab things.'

I ran from the market with the boy holding my hand. He held it very tight as we ran toward my hut – but that was where the attack was coming from. The closer I came to my hut, the louder and faster the firing became. We hid behind trees, then ran from one tree to another as the bombs from the rocket launchers became more frequent – 'Weeeeee, bang! Weeeeee, bang! Weeeeee, bang!'

We jumped down behind a log and covered our ears. I had the boy squeezed tight in front of me, and I dared not lift my head. The noise was terrible and my mind went numb. The attack went on and on. Rockets and gunfire from all sides flew over our heads.

I didn't know what to do, but I knew we couldn't stay where we were. I pulled the boy up. He was sobbing loudly and wouldn't open his eyes.

'Come, we must go now,' I said.

I ran in a zigzag fashion from house to house and tree to tree, dragging the boy along, trying to avoid the bullets and rockets. I noticed he seemed a little more determined. We saw some families hiding in their huts as we passed. 'You'd better get out from your hut and head for the trees,' I called.

I kept running, the boy still holding my hand very tight. I frantically kept running to my hut to get my belongings. They were all I had, and I couldn't afford to lose them.

I knew the huts would burn easily, because they were made from the husks of rice, bamboo, and other parts of trees. Some were burning already, and others had black smoke billowing up around them.

'You must get out,' I called again as we passed another hut. Then bang! A bomb hit that hut and destroyed it. I looked back. Arms, hands and heads were thrown into the air. I kept running, dragging the boy along behind me.

There was my hut at last. I raced in, grabbed my bag and ran back away from the gunfire. As I passed other huts, I saw through open doorways that people were still hiding.

'You must get out!' I kept yelling. 'Bombs will fall here again any moment. The shooting is getting closer. You cannot hide here.'

The boy was scared, but he ran fast, holding my hand tight. Some of the families came out and ran with us. Others stayed. I saw many young children with their mothers and realised that they couldn't run.

The heavy gunfire came closer and closer. Some huts had already burnt to almost nothing. I ran past the market area, and then further way from the guns to a clearing where others had gathered.

We were all shocked. Away from the camp, we just stood feeling stunned, sometimes gazing behind, but mostly looking forward, because ahead of us was where the landmines were supposed to be. Not many believed the rumours about the landmines, but no-one wanted to take the chance.

We were on the edge of some old paddy fields. The only way we could go was across the fields, because the forest everywhere else was too thick to push through. There were hundreds of us standing in the heat, wiping sweat and blood from our faces.

People were hesitant, but behind us we could hear more screaming. I looked back to where the Red Cross post had been, but saw only black smoke and tall flames. I was worried about my uncle, but right now I only had room in my head to think about my own life. What could I do now?

'Don't run,' people called. 'Lie down, calm down and stay where you are.'

I heard people talking. Some of us were at the edge of the paddy fields, and others had stepped over.

'It's the Khmer Rouge attacking,' someone said. 'They are coming to collect us from this place.'

They had probably been watching the camp for months, waiting until there were enough people. They knew our camp was a place for smuggling, and they knew it was a place for people getting ready to flee the country. They didn't like us fleeing instead of fighting on their side. They had no chance of persuading us to go with them peacefully, so they used violence. They aimed to capture the few of us who were left and force us to join them.

We were being attacked from three sides. The sounds of gunfire and explosions grew louder as each moment passed. Everyone was frightened, and no-one could think clearly. More and more people were arriving at the clearing, and as the pressure built up, people began to cross the field.

With the guns coming closer behind us, we spilt over like a wave. Suddenly people were running everywhere across the fields, and the whole area was blowing up. Maybe ten, maybe twenty mines blew up around me. I didn't know what to do. I just ran, not knowing where I was going but still holding the boy's hand.

As we ran, the mines kept exploding. People screamed and

cried for help, but those who could run kept going. Many were seriously injured, dying or already dead, but the guns kept firing and the wave of people running into the fields increased. I saw smoke, and people being thrown into the air by explosions. We had no way back, so we had to keep running. I was among the last, but I didn't stop. I didn't slow. I just kept going, watching people before me step on the mines and be blown to pieces in the air.

Finally a shell hit me. I don't know if I stepped on a mine or if I was a victim of someone else's misfortune, but I felt something hit my leg. But I did not look to see what had happened. I thought only of getting out of there as fast as I could.

I grabbed the boy and kept running. We had started as a crowd of about a thousand people, but the crowd got smaller the further we ran. Eventually, we reached the other side and the shelter of some trees. We had made it, but I was in pain. Not many people had believed the paddy fields were full of landmines, and most of them were now dead.

I had been hit by a shell near my foot, but I couldn't check it. I just had to get away from the Khmer Rouge. I kept running and running with the boy. Along the path through the forest I ran, without realising what was happening to my body.

There were people ahead and behind me. Some carried injured friends or relatives. I was just scared and intent on getting away. I kept running and hobbling and running until I couldn't hear any more shooting or gunfire or rocket launchers, any more screaming or bombs.

Finally, we stopped running and began to walk. I'd let go of the boy, and he was walking behind me. My leg hurt and was bleeding heavily. When I saw it, I started to feel dizzy and weak. I hadn't felt anything while I was running, only an inner strength that said to keep going, but now weakness was overcoming me. The pain increased every second I thought about it, and my mind began to spin.

I stopped and leaned against a tree on the edge of the trail. The boy noticed how I was feeling. He must have seen the blood too. He came up and held me and started to cry. He was worried

I wouldn't make it. We were away from the mines now, but we still weren't safe. We had to keep up with the crowds. There was still distant screaming and shouting as people looked for their families.

'How are you doing, Uncle? You OK?' the boy asked. Then he started to sob.

'I'm fine,' I told him. 'Just sit under the tree a moment. I have to fix my leg.'

He kept crying. I braced myself.

'How are you doing?' I asked. 'Do you have any cuts?'

I held him and felt around his body to be sure he wasn't hurt, but he was fine.

I asked him to do me a favour.

'What?' he sobbed.

I told him to stop crying and I asked him again, 'Do you want to help me to get better?'

'Yes! But I don't know what to do!'

'I want you to piss on my wound. Can you do that?'

He didn't dare, and he looked shocked at the thought.

I didn't know what to say any more, because the pain was getting worse and the blood continued to flow. The cut went through a large vein in my foot.

Then I knew what to say. 'I will not be able to live if you do not help me,' I told him.

'What? If you need it that much, I will do it,' he answered.

'OK, come.'

I grabbed him by the hand. I sat down, ripped away a piece of clothing from the bottom of my shirt, and tied it around my leg above the wound.

'Now, here, on the top of my wound.'

He did not dare look at his own penis, but he tried to pee on my foot. It took a while for anything to come out, and then the flow wobbled from side to side.

'It's OK,' I said. 'Hold it still and make sure it falls on my wound. Keep up.'

The urine cleaned out the dirt and the blood and I saw how deep the cut was. I tried to tie my shirt tighter around my leg, but the blood wouldn't clot; it continued to flow and I wondered how much I would have left.

I looked around for a tobacco leaf, but I couldn't find any. Then I saw a man running with his family.

'Get up,' he said. 'You must get going quickly. They said there are buses waiting for us up front, about a kilometre away.'

'Do you have any tobacco?' I shouted back.

Nobody had any cigarettes at that time, but they usually had some tobacco that they wrapped in leaves. He gave me some tobacco. I chewed it and placed it on top of the wound. I got up, and the boy held on to me.

'Get me a stick,' I asked.

It was about four o'clock now, and I knew the buses would be leaving soon. The boy found a low-hanging branch on a tree, broke it off and gave it to me. We started to walk again. The more I walked, the more I bled. I was uncomfortable and sore and weak and hot, and my leg was numb because I had tied the bandage too tight. I fiddled with it, but then it came loose and the tobacco fell off.

People were still running past us. We stopped, and I patched up my leg again. Everyone was running in one direction. They were running to something, but there were too many trees and it was too far away for me to see. After nearly a kilometre of walking and running, I saw what they were running to – Red Cross trucks, and they were waiting for us.

We ran again. From a few hundred metres away, I could see crowds jamming onto the trucks. People were shouting and pushing. This was another camp; it must be the KPNLF camp. As we approached, I heard talking and yelling. The Red Cross knew about the attack at our camp and had received permission from the Thai authorities to help us.

Suddenly there were loud announcements from a speaker.

'Please don't go. You have to stay and fight for your country.' It was the KPNLF people and it was coming from the forest. 'Cambodian people, please don't go. Please don't go. Save your country. You have to fight back for your country. If you leave now, your country will be doomed. Don't go. You think another country can provide you with a future, but you are Cambodian people, and your country needs you.'

There were people everywhere and the trucks were filling quickly. There was crying and yelling. Many needed help for friends and family who had been injured in the minefields. Others just wailed for those they had lost. Still the voice over the speaker went on.

'If you care for your country, you should stay. We will fight together to get our country back. We should not let the communists take over the country. We must liberate our country from the Vietnamese-installed government. We must not let them control our country.'

I saw some of the KPNLF soldiers now, but they were not physically doing anything to stop us. They were standing near a truck with their guns on the edge of the field.

Then I realised others were among the crowds – men and women without guns – trying to convince us of the wisdom of what we had heard through the loudspeakers. We could see they were sincere, and some stayed back to join them.

I had lost focus now. I hardly heard what was being said. All I wanted was to get up onto a truck with the boy.

'Come on! Hurry up, hurry up! We are going to leave in a minute,' the Red Cross people called from the trucks.

Still some families hesitated. I kept pushing myself forward, slowly inching closer to the trucks. Some of the trucks drove off, and new ones came. I was hopping on one leg now and reached a truck, but I could hardly move. The heat of the sun didn't help. Neither did the bodies pressing all around me.

Everything felt dark for me. I heard the words of the KPNLF, but I couldn't analyse what was being said. I just held on to what I was here for: we needed to be rescued, to get away from here, to be safe and to find my family.

One of the Red Cross people helped to push me up onto the truck. The boy followed. I sat down as the Red Cross closed up the back of the truck and started to drive off.

The KPNLF were still speaking out, begging us to stay. They played their national music. As the music kept playing, the truck kept driving. Soon I heard other music. It was the radio from the cabin of the truck, and it seemed to fill my ears and my mind – it was playing 'Without You', a song that seemed to capture just how I felt at leaving my country. Then darkness fell over me.

I had no idea how many days had passed when I opened my eyes again and looked up into sunshine. I saw something white, and squinted: it was a cloud. I thought of my mother, and remembered thinking of being dead and floating somewhere in the heavens, and now I knew it was only a dream. As I lay there, the wind blew and the cloud dispersed. It wasn't a cloud at all. I was in a tent, a Red Cross tent, and the wind blew open the flap at the entrance. I turned. It was a large tent with other patients and nurses inside.

A nurse came to look at me.

'Are you OK?'

I didn't answer.

'Open your eyes wider.'

I did as she said, and I saw I was on a drip. I looked again and saw blood going into one arm, a clear fluid going into the other.

'Where am I?' I asked. I smiled at the nurse. 'What happened to me? Am I dead?'

She smiled back and spoke, but I couldn't hear her.

'How long have I been here?' I asked.

I still couldn't hear her clearly, but she put two fingers up.

'Two days?' I asked.

She nodded.

'Where am I?' I asked again.

'Kow I Dang Camp,' I read on her lips.

'Oh, OK.'

'Are you hungry?' she asked.

I nodded. She said something else and then left. I looked around. It was morning, some time in January 1980. I wondered where the boy was. And where could I find my brother and my uncle?

I sat up, and the nurse soon returned with food.

'Did you see the boy?' I asked. 'The boy who came with me?'

'Yes.'

'So where is he?'

As her mouth opened to answer, the boy ran into the tent. He ran up to the side of my bed. His father followed, and his brother.

'Thank you,' his father said, 'for bringing him along safely.'

I nodded and mumbled, 'That's OK.' Then the boy said goodbye.

After they left, I ate. Then I lay down and fell asleep to dreams of Mother and others I knew who had passed.

Around noon I woke.

'Do you know my uncle?' I asked the nurse.

'Yes, I know your uncle. He has been here just now but you were asleep. He said he would be back later.'

Half an hour later, the nurse returned.

'I'll take this from you.' She began to disconnect the two tubes. 'You're fine now. Your wounds are healing.'

As she and another nurse took the tubes from my arms, my uncle returned.

He wore a big smile and looked healthy and strong, not like before.

'I have just sent a message to your brother. He has been looking for you in the camp.'

I was so pleased to see Uncle and hear of Chandy.

'He should be here to see you tomorrow, I would think,' Uncle added. 'You had better just rest. Tomorrow, we've got to find a place to stay.'

Uncle brought me some fruit and snacks. A little while later, I rose from my bed and hobbled around the tent, and then went outside in the sun. I was in a huge camp with many white Red Cross tents. It sat at the foot of a mountain, and I couldn't help but stare up at the mountain slopes.

I was alive. I was well. But I didn't know anything about this place.

Uncle came back and told me that the mountain was called Khao-I-Dang.

My hopes were higher than they had ever been. It was a beautiful sunny day, and everyone was excited and happy. I walked past the tents and saw people building their own huts, then I returned to my tent and my bed.

I stayed there one more night. Uncle came in the morning to get me. Just as we were about to leave, Chandy arrived, looking healthy and strong. I felt tears form in my eyes when I saw him.

'Brother, it's time to go,' he said.

We collected rice and other goods that had been allocated to us – pots and pans and cans of fish. Uncle had been given a hut, and we headed there.

There was no tension now, just thoughts of contacting Father. 'But you will have to contact someone at the border,' Uncle said to Chandy. 'The people you worked with on the smuggling. I don't want you going back yourself. Just send a message. Tell our family we are safe and we've heard from Vanny but not Uncle Lieu. Tell them we made it.'

Chapter 24
A New Beginning

DURING JANUARY 1980, in the beautiful sunshine on the mountain slopes of Thailand, I recovered slowly while Uncle wrote his letters. He made good use of new contacts in Thailand and within the Red Cross. Chandy passed some of the messages on to smugglers who did business across the border. I wanted to help, but my leg was still healing. I hobbled around on crutches among the cabins and the white tents, looking for things to do. Life was different now. It was relaxed and friendly. It reminded me of home in Phnom Penh with Mother when I was young.

We had to wait at the camp to see if we could find family or other contacts who could help us. It was a slow process, but letters came back from some of our relatives.

Vanny had written from Australia to say she was well and pleased for us and would be writing again soon.

We wrote again to Father, telling him we would send someone to bring them to the border camp, and that someone else would bring them across the border to meet us in the Thai refugee camp.

Two weeks later, Uncle sent Chandy for Father. Soon afterwards, a letter came with very good news – Uncle had heard from our Uncle Lieu, Father's younger brother.

Chandy was gone for four days, and we began to worry. But on the fifth day, at about three in the afternoon, someone called out to me while I was going to the registration office and told me my brother was back.

I raced to the hut. Everyone was there. Father looked good. Stepmother was tired but smiling. Puthea ran and hugged me, and I saw Sophea's smiling face.

'Are you OK?' she asked.

'I am fine,' I answered. She must have seen my tears. I was weeping with delight. I said, 'I'm just happy we are all here!'

Stepmother was pregnant. She had been unwell and didn't think she would be up to the journey, but now she was relieved, and everyone was fussing over her. Their journey to us had been full of adventure and near-disaster like mine, but now it was over.

Father told us that we would go and live in another country, a country much better than Cambodia. It felt right. We had struggled so hard to get to the refugee camp that I don't think any of us considered ever returning to Cambodia.

But in the refugee camp, new challenges faced us. We needed to be sponsored to move to freedom in another country.

As the weeks and months passed in the camp, we became more and more anxious. What lay ahead of us? We couldn't stay here forever. When I walked around the camp, I began to notice things I hadn't seen before. Many people were worried. There was happiness, but there was also fear.

One development was particularly alarming. Refugees at another camp had been taken away in trucks and told they would be resettled in another country. Months later, some of them returned and reported that the trucks had taken them to the Cambodian-Thai border. A few of the refugees had got away, but the others were sent on a forced march back into Cambodia, where thousands of landmines lay ahead of them. We later discovered that more than half of them had died. We heard about what had happened when the people who escaped turned up at Khao-I-Dang. The thought of being pushed back to the country we had just escaped cast a shadow over everyone.

At times, it seemed that we would never be able to leave the camp either. But then we received good news from Vanny. She wrote to say that she would give us time to unite our families – Father's and Uncle's – then we would be sponsored to come to Australia.

Vanny had received a lot of help from her foster family. A number of countries had become open to accepting refugees from Cambodia, and she knew Australia was one of them. She had launched an application with the support of her foster family and their friends in the Rotary Club of South Melbourne, the organisation that had sponsored her.

The Australian government had stringent guidelines, and many requirements had to be met. In six months at the Khao-I-Dang camp, we seemed to be making little progress. Then we were told we were moving to a transition camp called Phanat Nikhom, which was in Chonburi province in southern Thailand, much further away from the Cambodian border. The authorities also said that we were progressing in the queue to be resettled.

It was a long wait at Phanat Nikhom camp. We were there for five months. Those months were difficult, but they were good too. I think of them now as the best months of my life. At last we were sure that we had escaped the killing fields of Cambodia.

There was a medical centre next door to my hut, and every day many people came to get medicines and see doctors for treatments for their illnesses. I spent days and nights devising a strategy to get some work at that centre.

A tall, skinny man of Chinese origin called Huor registered people in the clinic as they arrived in the camp. He took their names and other details, then recorded medical measurements such as blood pressure, temperature and pulse. I spent about a week watching and talking to him, then I offered to work for him on a voluntary basis.

'Go away. Come back when I'm not too busy,' he said. But he was a friendly person, a bit older than me. He could speak some English because he had already been in the camp for six months, but when I asked him again, he tried to ignore me.

The clinic was operated by Catholic Relief Services (CRS), and I kept my eyes on the people in charge. They were two very tall American ladies with stethoscopes around their necks. Their names were Margaret and Catherine. Everyone seemed to report to them and listen to their instructions, and I thought they were doctors.

Margaret seemed older, so I guessed she must be in charge of the clinic. I approached her and spoke some English I had heard from Huor. With words and gestures, I tried to tell her that I wanted to help Mr Huor when the patients came for registration. She just smiled, then asked her assistant to come and translate for her what I was trying to say. He did, and she told him to let me help Mr Huor. I was so happy.

From the next morning on, I got up very early. I worked well, and soon I was sleeping where I worked. But it was voluntary work. I knew it was only a stepping-stone, because what I really wanted was work that I would be paid for.

I had no money for English classes, but I needed to speak English to get paid work. Private English classes were provided for the refugees in the camp, but they were not free. I felt trapped, as though I was running around in circles like a mouse on a wheel.

But after I had done two weeks of voluntary work, the CRS decided to pay me. It wasn't much, but it was enough for me to save for English classes. Then, when I had enough money, I found the classes were full. Everyone wanted to learn English for work, or to speak in the country they were hoping to migrate to.

I didn't give up. I stood outside and looked through the open window. I could easily hear and see what was written on the blackboard, and I saved my weekly salary for other purposes. And I made friends.

I met Lim Suor in June 1980 at the clinic after getting my job with the CRS. Mr Lim had been working as a supplementary doctor – someone who was knowledgeable with medical terms and medicines – helping the Khmer people. When Phnom Penh was taken, he had been a pharmacy student, so they used him to assist the CRS's doctor.

He was very kind. He helped many Khmer refugees and treated all the staff at the CRS clinic well. He was also placed in charge of the clinic when the staff left the camp at night.

I enjoyed my work with CRS. Every month a new team would come, usually from the Philippines. We had fun – there was a lot of fooling around and joking – but we worked to save people as well. When there was an emergency, I took patients to the Panath Nikhom Hospital at Chonburi, riding in the ambulance. The wind was cool through the open window, and I saw streetlights on every corner in the city. It was exhilarating, as if I was back home before 1975.

Admitting patients to the Thai hospital was not easy, though. Documents had to be signed and approved, and the hospital only admitted very serious patients – usually those needing life-saving operations. The job was very tiring, but I loved every second of it, even when I had to sleep on a bench in the park or on the floor of the hospital hallway while we waited for a patient to be released.

I made friends with the nurses at the hospital, and we sent letters to each other when we couldn't meet. They sent us some of their photos, and we sent them our photos from the refugee camp. They were never allowed to visit us at the camp, but we were able to keep our friendships alive.

These friendships couldn't last long, though. There was a lot of movement through the refugee camp as different ones among us were given refugee status by other countries.

I was always anxious to know what other countries were like. I imagined them as heavenly places, even though I did not know about heaven. The books we used for the English lessons had taught me a little. I had a picture of countries with many cars, a great number of tall buildings with a lot of lights and many people dressing well for work. All these things made me eager to go to any other country. But we had to wait, and a grey cloud hovered over us as the months passed.

One day about mid-afternoon, Uncle sent for us from the camp office. It was beginning to rain, and Father and some of the others hurried across with newspapers over their heads. I followed behind the others. It was as if they were dancing across the fields. I wondered if they knew something.

'You've got it! You've got it!' cried Uncle. 'You have your names on the list to go to Australia.' We had been granted refugee status in Australia at last.

The most wonderful feeling overcame me. It was as if angels had picked me up and set me down in paradise, surrounded by their soft wings. Everything felt magical during the following days as we prepared to leave for Australia. I did feel sad to leave my workplace and my friends at the camp and the hospital, but I was bursting with excitement too.

We were leaving my uncle behind in the camp, because his brother-in-law in America had sponsored him to go there. For a long time, my uncle had dreamed of going to America. When he studied English, all the books he read were about the USA and England, so he knew much more about those countries than he did about Australia. A couple of months later, he and my auntie's family were accepted to live in the USA.

When our departure time came closer, we were moved to a transition camp at Suan Plu in Bangkok city. It was a three-storey building, very cramped and with no outside space. We spent our last ten days in Thailand there before we were allowed to leave for Australia.

Finally, we were put on a bus to Bangkok Airport with other refugees. Everything at the airport seemed new. The whole place was brightly lit, and there were escalators and lifts, which we had never seen before. I could tell that things would be very different where we were going. I would have to adapt – we all would. But as I got on the plane, my mind was full of a wonderful future.

Epilogue

WE ARRIVED IN Australia on 30 November 1980, and everything was like a dream. I felt as if I had stepped out of one world into another: no more forests, but no more struggle and no more poverty. No more dusty roads and broken cities, broken people, destroyed hopes. No more need to travel constantly in search of somewhere better.

So why am I now back in Cambodia, the country I fled? The main reason was the nightmares that haunted me. They started when I was at school in Melbourne, where I had to strive hard to overcome a double set of obstacles. I had been taken out of school at a critical time and missed out on five years of education during the killing fields, and I had virtually no English language to assist my studies.

Though Cambodia seemed far away and long ago, there were memories that I could not get rid of. I became unsettled, but there was nothing I could do. I simply tried to ignore the bad dreams. My nightmares were always accompanied by the soundtrack of 'Without You', which seemed to sum up how I felt about leaving Cambodia.

The years passed quickly in Australia, and I adjusted to new ways of doing things, but my dreams continued to take me back to Year Zero. By the time I was at university, I was sure that something strange was happening inside me. I longed to be back in Cambodia as it used to be. I felt pain at all the suffering we had endured, and I had a million questions about why it had happened, none of which could be answered. The only reason I could figure out for what took place in Cambodia was that uneducated people had been easily manipulated into taking part in the atrocities.

After finishing my bachelor's degree in applied physics, I decided to become a teacher so I could share with my own people what I had learnt through being educated in a developed country. If more Cambodians were educated, I hoped that the country would not return to Year Zero.

But the nightmares kept coming. Eventually, I was having bad dreams every night. Sometimes I woke covered in sweat, shaking and trembling. I sought assistance from the university and from other professionals, but nothing could cure me of those recurring nightmares.

Then, out of nowhere, I was told about a possible solution. I was riding my bike one Anzac Day and went to Melbourne's Fitzroy Gardens, where I sat on a bank to take a break. Opposite me was an old man, and after a while he asked me what was wrong. I must have looked pretty miserable.

He explained that he was a war veteran and was taking a break from the long Anzac Day march. He told me he had spent years in prison during World War Two, and afterwards he had experienced personal problems like mine. I could cure myself, he said, by returning to Cambodia and revisiting the places of torture and execution and death. Only then would my nightmares cease and my curse be lifted.

From that day on, I started looking for an opportunity to return. I also wanted to look for Sivanchan, my eldest brother, or at least find out what had happened to him. From Australia, we had tracked down Mealea, my mother's youngest daughter, who was still alive and living with her foster parents in Kampong Speu province. My father asked my uncle in America to help her, and he arranged for her to escape into Thailand along with a cousin and his family. Eventually, my uncle was able to sponsor her to come to the USA.

But we heard nothing of Sivanchan, no matter how hard we looked. For a couple of years after he joined the elite teenage forces in 1977, there was occasional news about him, but it was only rumours. Then the news stopped coming at all.

We searched for him while we were in Thailand, and then later from Australia. We asked many people if they had seen him, and we sent messages to every contact we had. While we were in the Thai refugee camp, someone said they had seen him in a KR camp, but when we paid a man to look, Sivanchan could not be found. Others said he was executed under the KR regime while he was in the elite forces. We assume that he died during the time of the killing fields.

In 1992, I booked a flight to Cambodia, just for a visit. Then a friend told me that Australian Volunteers Abroad were looking for people to work in Cambodia for six months. I applied, thinking I would have a better chance of being cured if I stayed longer; afterwards, I expected to return to Melbourne and continue my work as a teacher at Oakleigh High School.

One night, I was watching the TV news and saw Gareth Evans, the Australian foreign minister, announce that the UN had been invited to intervene in Cambodia under the Paris peace accords. A UN Transitional Authority in Cambodia (UNTAC) had been established and was mobilising staff to help it conduct a general election. UN peacekeeping forces would also be sent to establish peace after decades of civil war. This sparked my interest in working with UNTAC, and I wrote to Senator Evans asking him to assist me in applying for a position there so that I could help the country of my birth.

Three weeks later, I received a phone call from United Nations headquarters in New York at four o'clock in the morning. It was a phone interview, and they asked me to join their electoral operations. I would be leaving for Cambodia in two weeks. I applied for leave of absence from teaching and went to Cambodia in July 1992.

As soon as I stepped down from the UN plane onto my birth country's soil, my nightmares disappeared without a trace. From that day on, the bad dreams were wiped from my mind, and I still wonder why. Had there been a curse on me that had now been resolved?

I've mostly lived in Cambodia since then. After completing my contract with UNTAC, I worked in various positions with the Royal Government of Cambodia, starting from a diplomatic position as a second secretary to the Cambodian Embassy, then as an assistant to the Secretary General of the National Assembly before I accepted a job in the Ministry of the Environment, earning about $200 a month as the Deputy Inspector General. I am also involved in independent consultancy with international donors who carry out projects in Cambodia.

For people who have a choice, living in Cambodia may not be easy, but for me it is a must, even though so much was destroyed – not just the people but the land as well. I would like to return to Australia to be with the rest of my family and many of my friends. But not yet. Now the Khmer Rouge war crimes trials are taking place, and they are of critical importance for the Cambodian people.

The steps Cambodia takes over the next few years are all-important for the country's future. Cambodia is still in a mess. There is confusion, poverty, greed, corruption, and no identity. How can we steer a population that has lost its most educated and responsible people? The Khmer Rouge regime is more than thirty years in the past, but there still has not been enough time to regrow a society where millions of people have been killed. As I see it, Cambodia needs an antidote to the grudges and vengefulness that have motivated its leaders. It requires a carrot not a stick if the country is to live in harmony and peace.

To honour those who died, we must rebuild our once mighty nation. I remember the school I went to as a child, and the one I attended as a teenager. I remember being torn away and pushed into the countryside, only to return five years later to a world that had changed beyond recognition. The memories fade, but they do remain, and so do the hurts. My life since surviving the KR regime has been spent trying to understand what happened, what has to happen now, and how I can live in the face of what I have experienced.

I solemnly pray for Cambodia, for its people and the land. I would give anything for it to become what it once was, or even better. We have suffered for many decades. We have endured this suffering in poverty and in an atmosphere of fear and tyranny. Now this must all end.

Appendix: The Universal Declaration of Human Rights

THE DECLARATION OF Human Rights was proclaimed for all people and all nations as a guide to understanding our fundamental rights. This book is a story about a man, a family and a nation where these basic human rights were disregarded.

The Universal Declaration of Human Rights states that:

We are all entitled to rights and freedoms regardless of race, language, religion or political viewpoints (Article 2).

No one should be a slave: all slavery should be prohibited (Article 4).

No one should be tortured or treated cruelly or inhumanely (Article 5).

No one shall be subjected to arbitrary arrest, detention or exile (Article 9).

We all have the right to freedom of movement and residence (Article 13).

We all have the right to own property and should not be arbitrarily deprived of it (Article 17).

We all have the right to express our opinion 'without interference' (Article 19).

We all have the right to work in 'just and favourable conditions' (Article 23).

We all have the right to have time for leisure and recreation (Article 24).

We all have the right to a reasonable standard of living (Article 25).

We all have a right to education (Article 26).

No one has the right to destroy any of the rights and freedoms outlined in this Declaration (Article 30).

In Cambodia, millions were tortured and killed, and a nation was devastated. Now, years later, we as a society and species have not learnt our lesson. Genocide, abuse, persecution and intolerance occur every day, and the rights of perhaps most of us on this planet are constantly abused.

This story is a story for our times. It is such an important story that many of us on this planet devote our lives to revealing such stories, and the lessons we should be learning from them. And what do those of us who *can* do about all this?

Greg Hill

Acknowledgements

FOR HELPING ME through the events that have made this book, I would like especially to thank my father, my brothers and sisters, my uncles and other relatives, and all my friends. You were there. You shared your lives with me, experienced death with me, and saved my life. It is you who have made this book possible.

Since my teenage years and my move to Australia, then back to Cambodia, my family has grown. I would like to acknowledge the love and support of my two grown-up daughters Bonita Kallida Sovannora and Anitha Rachannar Ieng, my sons John Ieng and Sondhos Sovannora, and my wife Khiev Nak, for her trust and her constant love and support. Last but not least, my family and I jointly thank my oldest sister Vanny for her relentless efforts, once she knew we were still alive, to bring us to Australia.

I would like to acknowledge the support given to me from Malcolm McKenzie, whom I regarded as my godfather. When I moved to Australia as a teenager and was living in a hostel with elderly people while completing my Year 11 and 12 studies, he believed in me and was totally supportive.

I would like to thank Mr Suor Lim, also known as Richard Lim, my old friend from the refugee camp when we worked together in the CRS clinic. He currently owns Lim's Pharmacy in Springvale, Victoria, which was given the award of Pharmacy of the Year in 2013. Thanks also to Mr Loong Kwong Cheong, also known as Allen, who was my classmate and a constant friend from the time we met at Taylor's College. And thanks to Mr Robert Hisshion for believing in my story from the moment I told it to him, and for suggesting it was a story that had to be shared with the world.

The genuine support and encouragement from these four men has been crucial.

Finally I would particularly like to thank Greg, my co-author, whose assistance, patience and advice over the years has been invaluable.

Sovannora

MANY EVENTS AND happenings have mixed together to make the publication of this book possible. Peter McMahon was the catalyst who brought Sovannora and me together to discuss his story. Antoni Jach, the co-ordinator of the writing courses at RMIT University in Melbourne, liked what he saw of the first few chapters and sent them out to several publishers. If not for Antoni's encouragement and support at this time, and throughout the following years, this book would never have been finished.

Brian Cook, the director of The Authors' Agent, has been a great agent to work with. He had recently returned from a holiday in Cambodia when I first rang him one afternoon. He liked what he read, and soon found interest at The Five Mile Press. The rest is history, or soon will be.

Many thanks are due to Kay Scarlett, the publisher at The Five Mile Press, for being so keen to take the book on; Julia Taylor, the senior commissioning editor, who has organised us efficiently every step of the way; Luke Causby for his great cover; Shaun Jury for internal design and typesetting; Samantha Forge for proofreading; and Zoe Burdack for production. We would particularly like to thank our editor, Jenny Lee, for her indefatigable work and midnight skyping with Sovannora. You have been wonderful, Jenny.

Most importantly, I would like to acknowledge the patient and professional support from my wife Lilette. Without your tireless love and support, Lilette, I don't know where I would be.

Greg